Prepublication praise for
HOW GERMANS NEGOTIATE

D1400158

"This groundbreaking book analyzes and interprets German negotiating behavior, offering a refreshingly unconventional explanation of its historical origins and an excellent as well as thorough study of the post–World War II conduct of negotiations typical for Germany's diplomacy and business."

—KARL KAISER
Otto-Wolff-Director, German Council on Foreign Relations, Berlin

"This book is meant to take the surprise out of negotiations with German diplomats and managers for Americans who might otherwise become confused and frustrated by the importance of the Gesamtkonzept (the philosophical basis for the German position). It could also prove to be very useful for Germans who want to understand how their American counterparts think and act. Given the ever closer political and economic interdependence in the world, with increasing possibilities for conflicts of interest, the book might well help to 'keep the peace.'"

—HERBERT WINKLER
Washington Bureau Chief, Deutsche Presse-Agentur

"W. R. Smyser adeptly explores the divergence between American and German approaches to negotiating, which has been obscured by fifty years of close cooperation. While Americans negotiate from a consensus-oriented modus operandi, Germans negotiate from a comprehensive concept, Gesamtkonzept, resisting determinedly and tenaciously incremental changes of consensus-building style. Understanding this incongruity is a critical component for reaching agreement. Invariably, as Smyser points out, careful intellectual and substantive preparation has remained the hallmark of German negotiating style. The book is a must read for Americans and others looking for winning strategies in negotiations with Germans."

—J. D. BINDENAGEL
former U.S. Special Envoy for Holocaust Issues

How Germans Negotiate
Logical Goals, Practical Solutions

W. R. Smyser

UNITED STATES INSTITUTE OF PEACE PRESS
Washington, D.C.

The views expressed in this book are those of the author alone. They do not necessarily reflect views of the United States Institute of Peace.

UNITED STATES INSTITUTE OF PEACE
1200 17th Street NW, Suite 200
Washington, DC 20036-3011

First published 2003

Printed in the United States of America

The paper used in this publication meets the minimum requirements of American National Standards for Information Science—Permanence of Paper for Printed Library Materials, ANSI Z39.48-1984.

Library of Congress Cataloging-in-Publication Data
Smyser, W. R., 1931–
    How Germans negotiate : logical goals, practical solutions / W. R. Smyser.
      p. cm.
    Includes bibliographical references (p.) and index.
    ISBN 1-929223-41-2 (cloth : alk. paper) — ISBN 1-929223-40-4 (paper : alk. paper)
    1. Negotiation. 2. National characteristics, German. I. Title.

BF637.N4 S59 2003
302.3'0943—dc21
                             2002032855

For Cameron

Contents

Foreword

THIS BOOK IS THE FOURTH IN A SERIES of volumes published by the United States Institute of Peace about the negotiating styles of different countries. Previous volumes have explored Chinese, Russian, and North Korean negotiating behavior; studies of Japan and France will soon follow. Each of those books has been based on the premise that a nation's negotiating behavior is shaped not only by circumstantial factors (such as the personalities of individual negotiators) and structural factors (such as a country's political system and institutions) but also by a nation's cultural traditions. Furthermore, each of those volumes has been written and published in the belief that diplomatic and business encounters are more likely to yield positive outcomes if we better understand our counterparts across the negotiating table.

The need to improve such understanding seems self-evident in the case of countries such as North Korea, famous for its secretiveness even before the advent of communist rule, and China, whose collectivistic and Confucian traditions remain unfamiliar to many in the West. But what of Germany and the Germans? Do we really need to know more about a people whose intellectual and cultural achievements (by such diverse geniuses as Gutenberg, Hegel, Goethe, Beethoven, and Mann) have enriched all of the West, and whose scientific and economic endeavors (for instance, Bessamer's steel and Benz's automobiles) have helped fuel Western industrialization? German's role in the world may have been distorted and disfigured in the past by Prussian militarism and Nazi fascism, but today Germany is an important ally and a pillar of the global economy, a key member of NATO, the European Union, and the G-8. Are we really in danger of seriously misunderstanding such an important strategic and economic partner?

The answer, says William Richard Smyser, a former U.S. and UN policymaker and a noted scholar of German politics and economics, is "yes." "On the surface," he notes in the introduction to this incisive study, "German diplomats and business leaders seem to resemble Americans. They also seem to resemble other Europeans. . . . But Germans are neither like Americans nor like other Europeans. They have a dramatically different history. They reside in different geographic surroundings. They read different philosophers. They see a different world across their borders. They confront different problems and see them from a different perspective. Germans may use the same words as Americans or others, but the words do not mean the same thing and they are not spoken in the same cultural context."

In the following chapters, Smyser describes, explains, and elaborates on these differences and analyzes their impact at the negotiating table both while the Berlin Wall was still standing and, especially, since its destruction. Throughout, he paints a fascinating political portrait—fascinating not least because it so often surprises us by confounding our stereotypes and upsetting our preconceptions. *How Germans Negotiate* begins, for example, by attesting to the crucial importance of history in shaping the German worldview. But the history that counts the most, Smyser argues, is not the fading nightmare of the Nazi years, nor even the sixty-odd years when Germany was united under Prussian domination, but rather the preceding thousand years when Germany was a patchwork of small duchies, principalities, archdioceses, and city-states within the expansive Holy Roman Empire. Among other things, this experience taught the Germans the value of diplomacy, for the danger of war with one's numerous neighbors was ever-present and put a premium on the creation and maintenance of defensive alliances. The lessons of the past have not lost their relevance: today, Germany has more neighbors on its immediate borders than does any other country in Europe, and diplomacy remains critical to Germany's peace and prosperity.

Germans often refer to their country as *das Land der Mitte* (the land in the middle), a description that is true both literally—for Germany lies in the heart of Europe—and metaphorically—for Germany often, though not always, takes a middle path in its approach to contentious issues on the agenda of such bodies as the European Union, NATO, and the G-8. "No matter what Germany tries to achieve," observes the author, "it cannot avoid having to deal with others in order to achieve it. This gives German negotiating behavior a much more central importance for German security than U.S. negotiating behavior has for U.S. security." It also, we might add, underscores the importance to Germany's diplomatic and business partners of understanding how Germans negotiate.

Smyser identifies seven points that guide German negotiators. In a provocative and novel analysis, he outlines how those seven points determine German objectives and negotiating tactics, whether in diplomatic or business matters. I will leave it to the reader to discover what this book says about the origins, influence, and interplay of these seven points. But I will note here that Smyser's analysis is much like his subject matter: historically rooted; argued with logic and brilliance; richly illustrated; down to earth; and formidable.

I should also emphasize that Smyser's analysis encompasses economic as well as political and security issues. Given that Germany has the world's third-largest economy, such attention is well merited. The author offers an unusually penetrating economic assessment, drawing on his experience as a consultant to American and European companies to dissect the tacks and tactics adopted both by German businesspeople and by German officials involved in negotiations over mergers, monetary policy, and other financial and corporate concerns. Among other insights, this book distinguishes between two types of German business negotiators: adherents of the "old" style, which resembles the behavior of German diplomats and stresses thorough preparation, persistence, and fidelity to an overarching rationale (the *Gesamtkonzept*); and exponents of a "new" style, which is more aggressive and incisive, prepared to tolerate substantial risk for the chance of rich and swift reward. The latter are fewer in number but higher in profile, featuring within their ranks men such as Jürgen Schempp, who orchestrated the brash takeover of Chrysler by Daimler-Benz. Americans and Europeans from other companies targeted by German firms—or from firms merely looking to do business with German partners—will find this volume indispensable for its crisp analysis and practicable advice.

In the amount of attention it gives to economic issues, *How Germans Negotiate* differs from the preceding volumes in this series of books that spring from United States Institute of Peace's cross-cultural negotiation project. In other respects, however, this volume continues and complements the achievements of that project. All too often, international negotiations have stumbled on cultural misunderstandings and then collapsed amid mutual recriminations. For instance, a Western negotiator may have failed to read subtle, nonverbal cues from a counterpart whose national culture puts great weight on unspoken signs. By the same token, the Westerner's direct manner and eagerness to press ahead with discussions may have been misinterpreted as unseemly and insulting. The aim of the cross-cultural negotiation project is to reduce the chances of such misunderstandings and thus enhance the prospects of diplomats from different cultures finding peaceful solutions to contentious issues—and of businesspeople reaching mutually rewarding deals. Culture is not of course the only determinant of negotiating behavior; indeed, its influence may often be overshadowed by other factors. But cultural differences do play a part—sometimes a very large part—in international negotiation. The Institute's series of studies of national negotiating styles seeks to ensure that culture is neither excluded from nor exaggerated in the equation that determines negotiating styles.

Even among close allies, differences and misunderstandings, whether rooted in cultural or political soil, can quickly grow, blossoming into resentments and antipathies that obscure the similarities and sympathies —again, both cultural and political—that have always nurtured the relationship. Indeed, in the space of just a few weeks in September 2002, the government of Chancellor Gerhard Schröder and the administration of President George W. Bush suddenly found themselves trading verbal blows and diplomatic insults while commentators warned gravely of the consequences for the two countries' long-standing alliance. Insofar as such arguments reflect policy differences, their course will be determined by policy decisions. But to the extent that such disagreements grow out of, or are magnified by, cultural dissimilarities, then their impact will rest in part on how well we understand one another. At a time when there is an unusually high degree of strain in the German-American political relationship, Smyser's analysis holds even more relevant and valuable insights for those in government and the commercial world who would restore this critical relationship.

How Germans Negotiate is sure to enhance our understanding of our German allies. Moreover, whereas policies and personalities come and go, the behavioral patterns and stylistic traits that this book so ably identifies are almost certain to endure.

Richard H. Solomon, President
United States Institute of Peace

Preface

WRITING A BOOK ABOUT GERMAN negotiating behavior presents many hurdles, especially if the book is intended to be part of a series on the cultural foundations of diplomacy. For German negotiating behavior reflects a combination of many diverse and sometimes contradictory influences.

An author must look at geography, for Germany has more neighbors than any other European state. He or she must also look far back into history, for the Germans existed as a nation in the center of Europe for more than a thousand years before they formed the last of Europe's major states. And the long history of the German nation has left a far deeper imprint on German culture than the short and often tragic history of the German state. Finally, German negotiating behavior reflects the nation's distinctive philosophical and logical outlook as well as its economic background.

To forge a coherent thesis out of these diverse influences, I began by consulting written sources on Germany itself and on its history and philosophy since the empire of Charlemagne in the ninth century. I then looked at the German economy and at its role in the European Union and other multilateral organizations. I tried to distill the essentials to give readers a practical guide.

To bring the material to life and to learn what Germans thought about themselves, I interviewed many Germans about their culture and diplomacy.

Finally, and most important, I interviewed American, British, French, Russian, and other diplomats and scholars to learn what they experienced when they negotiated with Germans.

Because most of my interviewees were Germans or people who expect to deal with Germans in the future, I have had to honor their requests to protect their identities. I will not cite them by name except when they have chosen to speak for the public record. I will thus follow the same practice as have the earlier authors in this series, identifying interviewees mostly by their functions and the dates of the interviews.

I have drawn on my own recollections and impressions as well as on other sources. I have seen and experienced Germany over six decades, first as a Nazi dictatorship, then as an occupied land and divided country, and finally as a sovereign and united democracy. I negotiated and consulted with countless Germans during that time and wrote about German history, politics, and economics.

One of my books, *From Yalta to Berlin: The Cold War Struggle over Germany,* reviews the history of German diplomacy since 1949 and goes over much of the material presented here. It is sometimes cited here as a source because it offers a summary of most of the events described in this book and a listing of other sources.

Germans do not negotiate identically on economic and political matters. To help businesspeople, the book therefore contains two separate chapters on German business negotiations and German government negotiating behavior regarding a range of economic issues. The chapters analyze some mergers and acquisitions, such as the Daimler-Chrysler talks. They also describe German negotiations about monetary policy and the European Central Bank as well as within the International Monetary Fund.

I have drawn to some extent on an earlier book of mine, *The German Economy: Colossus at the Crossroads,* to offer relevant background for the economic chapters, but most of the information comes from interviews and recent financial news sources.

Although the United States Institute of Peace series on negotiating styles is intended primarily to serve American diplomats and business leaders, this book should serve readers of other nationalities as well. My interviews have shown that Germans behave remarkably alike no matter who sits across the table, although they do sometimes show special deference to their larger negotiating partners.

Because West Germany was the larger and more independent of the two German states between 1949 and 1990, Bonn's diplomacy during that period was often called "German" instead of "West German." I have also often used the term "German" when I meant "West German." The meaning should be obvious from the context in each case. Moreover, from

1949 to 1990 West German negotiating behavior was, in effect, German behavior. West Germany pursued some parts of the German diplomatic tradition, whereas East Germany tried to break with it. East German behavior was often dictated by Moscow. I ask readers to bear with this anomaly and not to expect a specific reference to *West* German diplomacy each time I refer to the western part of divided Germany.

I want to thank the United States Institute of Peace, and especially its president, Ambassador Richard H. Solomon, for encouraging me to write this study and for supporting it. I also want to thank those who read the manuscript at various stages: Ambassador J. D. Bindenagel, Professor Carl Cerny, Professor Curt Gasteyger, Professor Hope Harrison, Professor Stanley Hoffmann, Dr. Jackson Janes, Professor Karl Kaiser, Dr. Robert Gerald Livingston, Jeremiah Murphy, Ambassador George Ward, and others who preferred to remain anonymous. They offered helpful suggestions. They deserve credit for any merit this work may have. I accept full responsibility for any shortcomings.

I would also like to thank Daniel Snodderly, Judy Barsalou, April Hall, Patrick Cronin, and Nigel Quinney at the United States Institute of Peace. They patiently offered a great deal of help and very useful advice on how to organize my thoughts in the process of editing and preparing the manuscript for publication.

How Germans Negotiate

Introduction
The Context

A BOOK ON GERMAN DIPLOMACY, and particularly on the cultural foundations of German negotiating behavior, may strike at least some potential readers as odd.

After all, such a concept as "German negotiating behavior," like the broader term "German diplomacy," seemed like an oxymoron for half of the twentieth century. The slash of the German war machine across Europe, the silent glide of the U-boats under the world's oceans, and Adolf Hitler's high-pitched rantings left the chilling impression that Germans preferred to attack and brutalize others rather than to deal diplomatically with them. For many years, Germany used war instead of diplomacy to promote its interests.

It must seem even stranger to offer a text on the cultural foundations of German negotiating behavior. After all, Germany's culture seemed to consist of bombs and bombast, hardly the stuff of calm and productive discourse.

Yet German negotiating behavior produced remarkable results for West Germany from 1949 to 1990, although Germany was divided and could not support its diplomacy by military force like many other states. And it has continued to produce results for Germany as a whole since unification. West Germany and now Germany have pursued a pattern of successful diplomacy based on cultural foundations that most

Americans and others did not and still do not know. The Germans have used a unique style that deserves a close look.

During the Cold War, West German diplomacy brought the Federal Republic of Germany into the center of several important Western organizations, such as the North Atlantic Treaty Organization and the European Community, which has since become the European Union. But it also opened contacts to others, including the Soviet Union.

Since the end of the Cold War and since German unification in 1990, Berlin's diplomacy has surrounded the united German state with a circle of relationships that have given German citizens genuine security for the first time in a millennium. Germany regained the full attributes of sovereignty in long negotiations with its former occupiers.

Germany now lies at the center of the wider Europe, of the entire transatlantic community, and even of Eurasia. When a U.S. president wants something to happen in Western Europe, Kosovo, or Afghanistan, he often turns to a German chancellor to support the process. And he mostly gets a positive reply, as do European states that turn to Germany for help.

The German economy has also done its share. German business and labor have helped turn Europe into a prosperous continent. Germany conducts financial as well as political diplomacy, not only within the European Union but across a much wider spectrum. Germany helped to institutionalize international financial consultation, now reflected in the Group of Eight. German firms from Daimler-Benz to Deutsche Telekom have conducted mergers and acquisitions all over Europe and in the United States. And German business has developed a negotiating style of its own.

Germans see diplomacy differently than Americans or, for that matter, than other Europeans. They need diplomacy more than any other state. They cannot use force. Nor can they retreat into "splendid isolation," as London once did, or into pure "isolationism," as Washington often did. Diplomacy offers the only route to German survival and success.

This is, therefore, a good time to review how the German government conducts its diplomacy and what we should expect in German business negotiating behavior. American diplomats and business leaders need to pay attention to differences in negotiating styles, even among allies.

Germany is not a world power, but it is the linchpin of the European landmass. Any organization that plans to function in that area needs to think about how Germans approach and make a deal.

❐   ❐   ❐

The notion that there is such a thing as a culture of diplomacy and that different countries have identifiably different negotiating styles remains very real to diplomats and business leaders who have served—or who must serve—in negotiating situations. They know from experience, from many talks and many meetings, that they can expect different kinds of behavior from negotiators of different nationalities. They also know that they must speak differently with such negotiators.

A number of scholars have also written about these differences. Clyde Kluckhohn concluded, and Raymond Cohen agreed, that "historically derived and selected . . . ideas and especially their attached values" become part of the "programming of the human system," of the "software" that generates action.[1] Professors Richard Porter and Larry Samovar have stressed the importance of culture as "the deposit of knowledge [and] experiences . . . acquired by a large group of people in the course of generations through individual and group striving."[2] Others, including Professors Kevin Avruch, Hans Binnendijk, and Jeswald Salacuse, have written books and articles to illustrate how different countries negotiate differently.[3]

Books that the United States Institute of Peace has already published on Russian, North Korean, and Chinese negotiating behavior show that each of the three states has its own distinct negotiating style.[4] And American business leaders are beginning to recognize that an understanding of cultural differences can make the difference between success and failure in a negotiation.[5] The author has come to similar conclusions from his own experience of negotiating with persons from many different countries and cultures.

Appreciation of different negotiating cultures represents only a first step, especially with respect to Germany, for Germany has taken the most jagged course of any modern state. Any author who tries to write on German culture runs many risks, the greatest of which is that the very concept of

German culture can still provoke bitter arguments even within Germany. It is a controversial enterprise, but all the more important because there is as much of a culturally derived element to German diplomatic behavior as there is to any other state's. Diplomats and business leaders must recognize that if they are to deal successfully with Germans.

German history, the single most important influence on the culture of German diplomacy, presents a particular challenge. The "burden of German history" has become a codeword for the effects of the Nazi era from 1933 to 1945, and particularly for Adolf Hitler's murder of millions of Jews and others as well as for the destruction that the Nazis wreaked upon a continent and upon Germany itself. Most Americans know more about the dozen years of Hitler than they know about any other part of two thousand years of European history. But although the Nazi years remain an important part of the German legacy, especially as a negative example, they actually do not have as deep an influence on the culture of German diplomacy as some earlier and longer periods. This book will explore and explain that.

German diplomacy itself has an uneven record. Germany has had some distinguished diplomats, such as Prince Otto von Bismarck, the "Iron Chancellor" who crafted the first united Germany in 1871 and whose massive figure dominates the painting on the jacket of Henry Kissinger's *Diplomacy*. Despite Bismarck's mistakes, students of diplomatic history admire his achievements even as they might admire those of Prince Talleyrand, Lord Palmerston, Thomas Jefferson, or Dean Acheson. And his years form part of German culture and must be understood by Americans dealing with German diplomats of today. But Bismarck does not represent the full sweep of German diplomacy, for either good or bad, and he will not play a determining role in what is to follow.

To complicate matters further, German foreign policy is still in a process of transition. Historically, Germany has not yet settled into any stable mode. It is a young democracy and even a relatively young nation-state. It is still trying to find its way, with some of its recent and current policies representing tentative initial steps.

Yet although Germany may still be formulating the specific elements of a foreign policy, it has already shown a remarkably consistent diplomatic style. There is a distinctly German pattern of negotiating behavior that has developed over the centuries and has been clearly manifest in the actions of German diplomats. By the same token, German business and economic negotiations also follow strikingly similar patterns. This book will describe all those patterns and suggest how best to respond to them.

◻   ◻   ◻

To put all this into context and offer guidance for those who will negotiate with Germans, the book will deal with different aspects of German diplomatic behavior in separate chapters.

◻ Chapter 1 will dwell mainly on German history because that history plays such a pivotal role in the evolution of German diplomatic culture. But the chapter will also review the crucial impact of geography, philosophy, and economics in that evolution.

◻ Chapters 2 and 3 will go into more detail about the actual process of a negotiation with Germany. They will show what an American or other negotiator may expect from the beginning to the end of a negotiation, first analyzing various phases and then describing specific German tactical behavior patterns. The two chapters will use examples drawn from West German and united German diplomacy since West Germany's founding in 1949. Chapter 3 will discuss, among other things, German negotiating behavior on European Union political matters. The chapters rely extensively on interviews with persons who have negotiated with Germans and who will describe procedures in detail.

◻ Chapters 4 and 5 will describe German negotiating behavior in economic matters. Chapter 4 will describe German business negotiating behavior, and chapter 5 will describe how official German institutions conduct economic negotiations. The latter will also discuss, among other topics, German negotiating behavior on European Union economic matters. The negotiating style of German managers and bankers resembles that of German politicians and diplomats in some ways but not in others. The German economy has its own history and culture, justifying separate study.

◻ Chapter 6 will look into the future, showing how German diplomacy is likely to evolve.

❐ Chapter 7 will offer advice for those who expect to negotiate with Germans. It will suggest steps to take before and during any such negotiations, whether on political or economic matters.

❐   ❐   ❐

Readers should understand that this book, although it concentrates on formal negotiations, is intended to be useful to anybody planning to consult or deal with Germans in any way. Normally, Germans behave in a very structured way when they are engaged in a formal negotiation. In such a negotiation, which might deal with highly important matters such as a new treaty, a new relationship, or a new business arrangement, they are very precise and they proceed in a very painstaking manner. Much of chapters 2 and 3 will reflect that, as will the chapters on business and economic negotiations.

But the principles that govern German behavior in a negotiation also apply in consultations and other forms of contact. When Germans are engaged in less formal contacts, they can move much more quickly. Americans and others who have been involved in consultations with Germans have found the experience much easier than formal negotiations. But Germans still follow the same principles, albeit if in a more relaxed manner.

The guidance offered in chapter 7 focuses on how to prepare specifically for negotiations with Germans. But even those people who do not expect formal negotiations should read chapter 7 with care, for many of the practices that Germans show in negotiations reappear in their consultations and other contacts. One should be ready to handle either process if one wishes to be successful.

❐   ❐   ❐

As indicated in the preface, this book is intended not only for Americans but for anybody who expects to negotiate with Germans. Nonetheless, Americans should still give the observations in the book particular attention. Germans are, in many ways, closer to Americans than they are to citizens of other nations. There are more Americans of German descent than of English, Scandinavian, French, Irish, Italian, Spanish, or Mexican descent.

Germany and the United States have been allies for five decades, with millions of American soldiers having served in Germany during that time span. Many aspects of German culture fit with American culture. German music dominates the programs of American orchestras. American music dominates the airwaves in Germany.

On the surface, therefore, German diplomats and business leaders seem to resemble Americans. They also seem to resemble other Europeans. Many speak excellent English as well as continental European languages. They eat similar food and drink similar wines and beers. They wear the same clothing styles. One might assume that they think like Americans or like other Europeans.

But Germans are neither like Americans nor like other Europeans. They have a dramatically different history. They reside in different geographic surroundings. They read different philosophers. They see a different world across their borders. They confront different problems and see them from a different perspective. Germans may use the same words as Americans or others, but the words do not mean the same thing and they are not spoken in the same cultural context.

Americans and Europeans also need to divorce their thinking from individual personalities. Although this book on occasion describes the foreign policies of several West German and German chancellors since 1949 to focus attention on particular aspects of German diplomacy, those specific chancellors and those policies did not and do not themselves determine German negotiating behavior.

German negotiating behavior arises out of German geography, history, philosophy, and economics. It does not change from chancellor to chancellor, from foreign minister to foreign minister, or from business manager to business manager.

Each German chancellor, foreign minister, and business executive will, of course, have his or her own ideas and approaches, and each will use different colors on the palette of international negotiating behavior. But the German style will not change materially from one government to another or even over decades and perhaps generations yet to come.

The validity of this book does not, therefore, depend on any particular personality or set of personalities. Each may bring his or her own predilections to foreign policy and diplomacy. But the broad course of German negotiating behavior rolls on, impelled by forces that go beyond any single individual.

Negotiating with Germans can be a trying and costly experience for those who have not thought about it well in advance. One can easily make the kinds of mistakes from which it can be very hard to recover. But such negotiations contain no unfathomable mysteries. A clear understanding of what to expect can usually lead to good results.

1

The Foundation

Geography, History, Philosophy, and Economics

BETWEEN MAY 7 AND MAY 9, 1945, Germany imploded into what Germans have named *die Stunde Null,* "the zero hour," as German forces capituled to the victorious Allies of World War II.

The term marked both an end and a beginning. It meant the total collapse of Adolf Hitler's Third Reich and, with it, the end of the German state. Germany ceased to be a fully sovereign national entity and did not become one again until forty-five years later, on October 3, 1990.

But "the zero hour" also meant a new beginning. It meant that the clock started running again and that a new German state could one day arise, like the mythical phoenix, reborn and renewed.

That kind of pure rebirth and renewal may happen in mythology, but it does not happen in life. The new Germany bore the consciousness of its past as well as the wish for something new. It could not wipe out its collective memory. It could not change its location or its history. It could not change its culture. It could not change the attitudes of others. It could not wipe the slate completely clean. Thus it could not conduct its diplomacy as if nothing had happened.

Germany could, however, take two important steps. First, to look back, to understand what had gone wrong. Second, to look realistically at what remained. On the basis of those two steps, Germany could proceed forward. The roots it found and fostered, as well as its subconscious memory, would breed the German style of diplomacy, a style grounded in geography, history, philosophy, and economics.

Geography: At the Center of Europe

Germany's location frames German diplomacy. The German peoples have occupied the heart of Europe for almost two thousand years, ever since the days of the Germanic tribes and the Teutonic knights. Throughout their history, they have fought off the Romans, the Huns, the Mongols, the French, the Swedes, the Russians, and others. They have more neighbors on their immediate borders than do the people of any other European state.

Germany has only one easily defensible land frontier, the Alps, as part of its southern border. Every other frontier offers convenient avenues for a land or sea attack in both directions. Germans are surrounded on almost all sides by nations with which they have at times fought long and brutal conflicts. Germany is literally, as Germans often call it, *das Land der Mitte* —the land in the middle.

The size of the German population and the width of its geographic surface have always placed Germany in an ambiguous position. Geography condemns the Germans to be either too strong or too weak. They have been too strong to feel that they needed to defer to all their neighbors, but they have been too weak to hold off and defeat a combination of those neighbors. The German state is too large to lose itself easily in the crowd of Central European states, yet it is not large enough to dominate those states. It does not draw protection from the great oceans, like Great Britain or the United States; neither does it have natural boundaries on three sides, like France; nor is it protected by the vastness of its spaces, like Russia.

Geography compels Germans to look constantly in at least two directions, east and west, seeing dangers and opportunities in both. And it condemns them not only to think of their neighbors but to try to imagine how their neighbors see them.

German geography thus constrains the German state and the German nation. Germans cannot escape from the center of Europe to a less exposed periphery. They must make constant adjustments toward their neighbors.

They have had to do it throughout their history. The new "Berlin Republic" of 1990 cannot change that reality.

German geography compels Germany toward diplomacy and toward negotiations. Germany must have relations with many states having myriad —and often conflicting—interests and policies. It must, therefore, consider its neighbors' interests, for good or ill. And neither the Germans nor their neighbors can now try to resolve differences by the use of force, as they often did in the past. In the modern age and in the future, Germany must pursue diplomacy as its main instrument of foreign policy. It must find a way to work together with its many neighbors. It must try to shape systems and join them.

Negotiations thus form an essential part of German security and stability. No matter what Germany tries to achieve, it cannot avoid having to deal with others in order to achieve it. This gives German negotiating behavior a much more central importance for German security than U.S. negotiating behavior has for U.S. security. Realistically, there can no longer be any German unilateralism.

History: The Late State

Although geography may pose some particular dilemmas for German diplomacy, German history has shaped the culture of German diplomatic policy and behavior more than any other single factor. In Germany, the past is ever part of the present. And Germans, consciously or unconsciously, always reflect on elements of their past as they conduct diplomacy.

But German history complicates rather than clarifies German diplomatic behavior, for that history offers no easily identifiable record that can be used to guide or justify any single pattern of policy or behavior. It sends confused and confusing messages, both positive and negative. It offers little comfort to Germans or others. And yet, upon careful examination and reexamination, it does offer some clues on what a foreigner can expect in the way of German diplomacy.

The German people have been a nation at the center of Europe for more than a thousand years, but they did not form a nation-state until 1871— or ninety-five years after the United States was formed. Before then, they remained under various forms of outside rule and suffered from divisions within their own nation. They lived under the dominion of the Holy Roman Empire for centuries. They suffered terrible losses during the Thirty Years' War (1618–48), the invasions of Louis XIV later in the seventeenth century, and the Napoleonic invasions between 1800 and 1814. Germany was then united under Prussia's Hohenzollern dynasty and Prince Otto von Bismarck in 1871, only to suffer through World War I and then to endure total collapse and disgrace during and immediately after the Hitler years.

Germany was the last major European nation to form a united and independent government. It became a nation-state about six hundred years after England, four hundred years after France and Spain, and even a few years after Italy.[1] Germans in the late nineteenth century often called themselves *die verspätete Nation* (the delayed nation) to stress that they had arrived later than others and that, by implication, they needed to be in more of a hurry.

The Origins of Germany: The Holy Roman Empire

During most of the Middle Ages and well into the modern era, the German nation formed the most important part of the Holy Roman Empire, which was established under Emperor Otto I in 962 A.D. and which stretched around the year 1000 approximately from Hamburg in the north to Rome in the south and from Aachen in the west to Prague in the east. The Holy Roman Empire remained the dominant political realm in central Europe until Napoleon put an end to it at the beginning of the nineteenth century. Its precise borders shifted from time to time, as when the Hapsburg emperors laid claim to Spain and the Netherlands or when Louis XIV and Napoleon seized major portions of the imperial lands for France. It also lost its papal connection under Emperor Maximilian I during the fifteenth century, becoming less holy and less Roman.[2]

Although the northern part of the Holy Roman Empire might often be called by a name that identified it as German, such as "The Kingdom of Germany," and although the entire empire was sometimes titled "The Holy Roman Empire of the German Nation" after it had lost its Italian possessions, the empire had no distinctly German political or sovereign authority. Some early emperors, such as the Hohenstaufens, were German. The later emperors, the Hapsburgs, had originated in Germany, but they thought in terms of the interests of the entire empire and not only of Germany. The Holy Roman emperor might be king of Germany, but he had possessions not only in Germany but also at times in what are now Italy, Spain, the Netherlands, Central and Eastern Europe, and the Balkans. The emperor claimed, and served, the universal realm of Christendom, not a national state, and certainly not a German one.

During the reign of Charles V in the seventeenth century, the empire extended across much of Europe. Charles did not make imperial policy to suit German needs. He and other emperors would often draw on their German possessions for help in fighting wars that did not represent a national German interest. Charles, like other emperors before and after him, even suppressed repeated German efforts to build national structures because he did not want German separatism within what he regarded as his universal reach. The papacy, which had a powerful voice within the empire until the fifteenth century, also fought any separatist tendencies because it wanted to use the resources of Germany for its own purposes.

The area that is now known as Germany consisted of a jigsaw puzzle of aristocratic and ecclesiastical holdings, often changing in precise number but always running well into the hundreds. Some major entities—such as the duchies of Bavaria, Franconia, Lorraine, Saxony, and Swabia, or the archdiocese of Mainz, Trier, and Cologne—were larger than others. But all authority was minutely divided and rights carefully assigned or assumed. Each prince, aristocrat, or other ruler had obligations toward others, even toward citizens, while they had obligations toward him. Above all of them arched the wide dome of the empire.

The Golden Bull of 1356 fixed the existence of Germany and the Holy Roman Empire on a federal basis with seven "electors" having a primitive form of semisovereignty as well as the authority to choose the emperor. Four of those electors were princes; three were bishops. And hundreds of minor princes and aristocrats retained their separate realms even if they were not electors.

The German princes, dukes, or bishops who ruled separate entities had many realms of independent authority and often used that authority against the emperor. But none of the princes governed an area that could be termed "Germany." For "Germany" represented a geographic and ethnic expression but not a state or a separate government.

When Martin Luther in 1517 published his Ninety-five Theses criticizing the Catholic Church and the papacy, sparking the Protestant Reformation, strong German national sentiment and perhaps even a nation-state might have emerged in opposition to the Catholic Holy Roman Empire. But the Protestant Reformation did not spread over all of Germany; about one-third of Germans remained Catholic and fought against the Protestants in the Counter Reformation. Lutheranism still retains a specifically German appeal, although its meaning for German culture and national identity remains a subject of expert as well as political debate to this day. Some later rulers of Germany tried to use it to justify their authority. But it did not spark a German nation-state in its own day.[3]

Because of the emperor's Olympian perspective and continental interests ranging well beyond Germany itself, the Germanic states and various princes within the Holy Roman Empire often had to take care of themselves. They could not count on imperial power to defend them or their interests. They needed to make sure that they could protect their own particular territories against potential enemies on all sides. They engaged in continuous diplomatic activity to keep themselves and their people safe.

The German people lived under constant threat of war except for brief intervals. They even experienced more of it than others did, as many foreign states fought each other in or over German lands as if Germany were a conveniently located central chessboard on which they might improve their European position. Germans found themselves continually involved in local or international conflicts owing to petty quarrels between local lords, European ecclesiastical wars during the Reformation and Counter Reformation in the 1500s, or the invasions of Germanic lands by already consolidated nation-states such as France and Sweden.

Princes, dukes, bishops, and cities negotiated and plotted with and against one another. They cemented alliances through marriages or other arrangements. They practiced a diplomacy of maneuver, operating within the structure of the empire—including the Reichstag (imperial diet)—while taking care of their own particular interests. Alliances represented transient and often fleeting interests. But those and other tactical devices worked sufficiently well that many states could protect their lands much of the time by a combination of wide-ranging diplomatic contacts, intrigue, military displays, or force where necessary. They could never break diplomatic contacts because they all lived as neighbors. Nobody could withdraw because they had no other place to go and no room to escape. And they had to make their views known clearly in order to avoid misunderstandings and to come to their agreements without unnecessary delay.

The German states thus found some security through diplomacy, especially after the Treaty of Westphalia, which ended the Thirty Years' War in 1648. That security might have been far from perfect, but it had something to offer in a Darwinian world. They practiced a kind of diplomatic immersion, a routine of dialogue with those that mattered. Constant contact became a guiding principle. The states that wanted to thrive had to have many contacts in all directions. They had to use those contacts purposefully to promote their own political and economic interests. Isolation meant extinction, as did ineffective diplomacy.

The borders between the separate German states could and did shift because of wars, alliances, treaties, or marriages. Occasionally, as in the Treaty of Westphalia, many borders shifted simultaneously and the German state system as a whole was rearranged. But the basic form of the empire did not change until 1806, during the Napoleonic Wars, when the French emperor during one of his periodic invasions drastically reduced the number of separate aristocratic and ecclesiastical holdings in Germany and abolished the structure of the Holy Roman Empire itself.

During the existence of the Holy Roman Empire, Germans functioned within a multiplicity of associations, whether between larger states and smaller states or ecclesiastical realms or whether between farmers, tradesmen, merchants, silversmiths, and beyond. Every trade, every profession, and every form of activity had its association. And those associations, whether small or large, weak or powerful, had bonds with others. Most Germans lived within a compendium of associations. The associations served the needs of their members, establishing or cementing bonds and offering some protection against others.

Each of the various associations to which a German belonged had its own sphere of membership, action, and responsibility. And each in turn might belong to other forms of association, and each of those in turn might have a sphere of its own. Within the shelter and through the opportunities offered by those associations, an aristocrat, a merchant, a family, or a small group might find the equivalent of personal autonomy. Germans accepted the duties that they had toward others, just as others in turn might have duties toward them. Although formal structures existed within the Holy Roman Empire, most of the system functioned by unwritten consensus more than through decisions reached in such formal structures. And the search for consensus and social peace permitted agreement even among widely differing nationalities and faiths. It became an important element of German culture.[4]

Persons fitted into communities that in turn fitted into other communities. The autonomy of individuals and the autonomy of various different entities merged into a continuum of mutually understood obligations, loyalties, and rights, recognized and respected by the immediate participants but almost incomprehensible and undefinable for those who stood outside. The structures resembled modern federalism in many ways, although few relations or functions were formally defined and delineated.[5]

Germans appreciated those multiple forms of association within and between political, economic, or other entities. They understood how to cooperate with others against common enemies even as they might compete within the community itself. They believed in the sanctity of any pledge within that community. They could be devoted friends, faithful to the point of self-sacrifice toward those with whom they felt they shared a communal bond. And they found a measure of security and freedom within the framework of these bonds.[6]

Germans also became acutely aware of hierarchy. Each fitted into a certain space, either as an individual or through an organization. Each knew where he or she belonged. Germans could find comfort and a certain level of reassurance in that knowledge. They understood who might be above and who might be below them, and they maintained a certain distance from both. They addressed each other formally, linking names with titles, to reassure themselves and others where they stood and where others might stand. Within the complex structures of the empire and its many components, little would change quickly and few saw reason to rush it.

The German peoples thus lived in a jumble of contradictions. They had their personal, communal, and hierarchical relations and associations. They had their moments of peace and stability. But they also found themselves caught up in the internal and external struggles of the Holy Roman Empire and the surrounding states whether they wanted to or not.

Germans became tough. They did not surrender quickly, either in war or in diplomacy. They had reputations as hardy fighters and tenacious negotiators. They could be, and often were, purposeful, determined, assertive, haughty, and unbending. They believed with good reason in the survival of the fittest, in politics, war, and economics.

◻   ◻   ◻

Germans also developed intellectual, cultural, and religious traditions. German princes, towns, and bishoprics founded many of Europe's principal universities and libraries and earliest publishing houses. They built some of the most important early churches in Europe, especially in the larger ecclesiastical states and cities. Many towns and princely states supported musical institutions from chamber music ensembles to full orchestras. In times of peace, they hired composers and musicians.

In order to continue and justify their existence, German states and towns had to offer services to their citizens and manage their lands and finances reliably and efficiently. For that, they developed pervasive bureaucratic systems and, in the process, a firm tradition of bureaucratic management and service. The noblest of aristocrats and the smallest ecclesiastical states as well as all towns and cities learned that they had to provide cohesive and effective administration in order to hold the loyalty of their citizens and to distinguish themselves from their neighbors.

The German states and cities therefore founded important bureaucratic institutions, especially toward the end of the seventeenth century and during the eighteenth. Public service attracted some distinguished personalities, such as Johann Wolfgang von Goethe and several German philosophers, but for the most part bureaucracies put their stress on anonymous performance. They established a long record of a relatively honest, dedicated, and incorruptible civil service holding together whatever area any single state or town might seek or need to administer. With that, they also developed a tradition of bureaucratic rules and regulations governing many aspects of civic life. Germans came to accept these systems of rules.

The smaller German states began fostering their own political and diplomatic traditions within the empire. The Rhineland states nurtured a Roman Catholic cultural tradition closely linked to the empire and the papacy but were independent minded in their politics. The southwestern German states favored political liberalism. Saxony and Bavaria pursued diplomatic interests of their own, concentrating respectively toward the east and the south of the Holy Roman Empire. Many princes had their own nascent diplomatic services separate from the emperor's.

But Germany lacked a crucial element of the modernizing state. Even as Germans could build local institutions and lead in economics and philosophy, they could not, and did not, develop a sense or a practice of national policy. The contending aristocrats, including even those who were powerful enough to become one of the seven electors, operated largely in limited terms and for limited purposes. Their circumscribed responsibilities confined them to erudite bargaining maneuvers that might advance only very narrow local interests.

❑   ❑   ❑

The consciousness of a German nation could only manifest itself slowly under the surface of the Holy Roman Empire and the crazy-quilt multiplicity of competing entities. The emperors, who at first perceived—or at least described—themselves as the guardians of a universal domain, would not tolerate any kind of nationalism. They consistently quashed any nascent pan-German political sentiment anywhere within their reach. Although such sentiment did arise on several occasions over the centuries, it only became a political factor in European history when the empire itself collapsed.

Some German national sentiment emerged through the rise of German literature, although that literature had more of a cosmopolitan than a national theme. The use of German language, the printing of German texts, and the slowly rising awareness of a common German culture played a unifying role even within the splintered polity. It could not and did not lead to a German nation-state, for it did not directly stimulate a sense of political cohesion. But it flourished nonetheless within the confines of the empire.

While the kings of England, France, Spain, or Sweden were building national governments and functioning on the basis of an ever-widening and ever-deepening national consciousness, German kings, dukes, and others were largely playing regional and local games. They concentrated most of their political and diplomatic energy within the Holy Roman Empire itself. For them, intra-German and intra-imperial politics became the stuff of foreign policy and of diplomacy.

In such an atmosphere, German national policy took its time in coming. Even into the nineteenth century, German leaders were still busier with one another than with the outside world, although some of them sent envoys or missions abroad. They embarked on only limited ventures into any kind of European-wide foreign policy. England had by then already set forth the founding concepts for a national foreign policy, including its balance-of-power doctrine toward Europe. France had already developed its principles of national *gloire* and conquest in the days of Louis XIV. London, Paris, Madrid, and Lisbon had begun conquering vast global empires.

Germans had neither a national polity nor a national policy. Even in the young American republic, President George Washington had outlined principles for the conduct of foreign affairs in his Farewell Address before Germans could dream of conducting diplomacy on a national basis. England had William Pitt, Lord Castlereagh, George Canning, and Lord Palmerston, and France had Cardinal Richelieu and Prince Talleyrand, long before Germany had a single national statesman.

German Philosophy

Just as German political structures differed from those of other western European nations, German political philosophy went its own way. German philosophers did not join the debates about the prerogatives of states and citizens that seethed in English and French political theory from the seventeenth century forward, largely because they faced different issues. German philosophers lacked the immediate political purpose and impact of such English political theorists as Thomas Hobbes (1588–1679) and John Locke (1632–1714).

Hobbes in *Leviathan* had perceived the state and the individual as polar opposites. He had argued that people had to accept even a dictatorial government because any form of government was better than the "brutish" state of nature. Locke had written that the state had to serve as a liberating, not a confining, force, and that people had the right to oppose a dictatorial regime.

Because Germany did not have a nation-state, German philosophy did not wrestle in the same way with the relationship between the individual and that nation-state. German political debate did not focus on Louis XIV's dictum *"l'état, c'est moi,"* as French and English discussion directly or indirectly did. Germany did not have the equivalent of Louis XIV. If anything, the Germans might have thought *"l'état, c'est nous,"* for in the complex web of relationships under the Holy Roman Empire and its successors each person and each group had its own sphere. German philosophy also lacked the economic analysis and impact of the English theorists Adam Smith (1723–90) and John Stuart Mill (1806–73). It had no national economy to analyze.

One German political philosopher, Samuel Pufendorf, looking at the German situation in the early 1700s, perceived the vital importance of individual rights. But he linked those rights to a self-limiting sovereignty, a theory that fitted the German model better than others.

Germans did not seek liberty in the struggle against a single dominant national state but in the multiplicity of smaller states and associations.[7] They might have heeded Hobbes's advice to form a state to escape their "brutish" situation, but they did not do so because they lived in spheres far removed from Hobbes's state of nature. Germans saw themselves as members of communities that might sometimes be restrictive but that also provided safety against rapacious German and especially foreign neighbors.

Lacking political focus, German philosophy concentrated on the internal processes of the mind, on the logical rationalism that Gottfried Wilhelm Leibniz (1646–1715) stressed. The best-known German philosopher, Immanuel Kant (1724–1804), addressed problems of philosophical logic far removed from the practical world of politics. He stressed the importance of abstract thought and pure conceptual reasoning, of what he termed "transcendental idealism." He bequeathed a cosmopolitan reverence for logic without advocating precise political or economic systems, although he favored democratic institutions without prescribing particular forms. When he dwelt on politics, he engaged in wide-ranging universalist reflection on moral issues and perpetual peace.

Kant did not try to deal in the same terms as Hobbes or Locke with the issue of individual freedom. Some readers of Kant thought that he had offered a moral basis for political obedience and some thought that he had offered a moral basis for political liberty.[8]

Johann Gottlieb Fichte (1762–1814) echoed some of Kant's themes, asserting that the idea was more important than the thing and that subjective thought could lead to truth better than objective observation. He advocated German democratic nationalism in reaction to Napoleon, but he concentrated his main efforts on issues of consciousness and reason. Kant and Fichte laid the foundations for the powerful German faith in abstract logic as the path to truth.

Georg W. F. Hegel (1770–1831) became the German philosopher who most directly and consistently addressed the philosophy of history and of the state. Writing and teaching during and after the Napoleonic Wars and the post-Napoleonic reconstruction of Europe, he tried to devise a system that linked what he termed the Spirit *(Geist)* to the broad development of humanity. Numbingly obscure at times, he linked the Spirit to God, to the state, to the very process of evolution of history itself.[9]

Hegel saw the movement of the Spirit and the whole progression of history as an advance dominated by the dialectic, the notion that every idea—or thesis—contains within itself the seeds of its own contradiction —or antithesis. That contradiction between thesis and antithesis, he argued, would be reconciled and transcended at a higher level—or synthesis. This kind of logic defies linear progression or argument but moves in phases over time to ever loftier forms of consciousness and reality. It provides the engine of history as well as of philosophy.

Hegel argued that "the real is the rational." Some critics have denounced this notion, asserting that it could be used to justify any existing system or any ruler, be it Napoleon, Wilhelm II, or even Hitler and Stalin. They have linked Hegel's concepts to many forms of political extremism, including Nazism, fascism, and communism. Karl Marx, in fact, based his dialectic materialism directly on Hegel's dialectic. Hegel's supporters have defended him, arguing that Hegel himself defined democracy as the ultimate mission of humankind and that his concepts were intended to guide humanity to new and wider visions of freedom based on the inevitable and imperative ascent of the Spirit to ever higher forms. Systems that fall short of the ideal mark way stations, not ultimate goals.

Hegel's doctrines had a populist element, despite his abstract and obscure form of expression. They inspired revolutionary movements like the American and European radicalism of the 1960s. Wherever they have gone, they have spawned the conviction that logic and abstract thought form the true basis of reality.

Like the Spirit itself, Hegelian philosophy in general and the dialectic in particular have pervaded German thought ever since the middle of the nineteenth century. They have also had a powerful influence on global political philosophy, for they can help to explain the force of cyclical events as well as the apparently self-contradictory evolution of history and politics. But their greatest effect has been felt in German philosophy and in general German attitudes.

Hegel actually made a greater contribution to German culture through his dialectic method than through any single political conclusion that he reached or was alleged to have reached. That dialectic method remains at the unconscious core of German philosophy and culture. German philosophy thus differs from British, American, and French philosophy in two fundamental ways. First, it stresses dialectic, not linear, logic. Second, it places deductive reasoning on a higher plane than inductive reasoning.

The dialectic makes it possible to perceive any thought or concept not as an entity in itself but as part of a process toward the reconciliation of apparent opposites at a higher level. This reinforces its logic and, Hegel believed, legitimizes it at that higher level. Applied to politics and diplomacy, Hegelian thought opens the door to a deeper range of analysis than direct (and thus, in Hegel's terms, simplistic) logic. In particular, Hegel made it possible to see opposites not as contradicting but as complementing each other.

In the process, Hegel has also left a mark on German diplomatic behavior. Under Hegel's influence, as well as under the influence of other German philosophers, German negotiating style has developed a profound attachment to logical method. Nothing can be real without a concept to make it real and make it pertinent. Germans do not argue in immediate and specific terms, seizing principally on the details of any particular issue or any particular solution. Instead, they insist that any proposal must have a thorough foundation in logic and abstract reason. Any solution to any kind of diplomatic problem must pass the test of deep analysis from the first step to the last.

Hegel also makes it possible for German diplomats and political leaders to accept what others may regard as opposites. They can, for example, reconcile potential contradictions between the interests of separate states and a community of states; in the Holy Roman Empire or the later German Confederation, for example, one could reconcile separate political entities coexisting with pervasive associations. Nationalism could become internationalism, and vice versa, to a degree that could be difficult for other large states to emulate or even to assimilate. Diplomatic solutions grounded in the logic of the dialectic could escape facile categorization and could serve multiple and seemingly irreconcilable purposes.

Hegelian philosophy thus reinforced the federalist thrust of the German experience in the Holy Roman Empire and in the German Confederation that followed. In Hegelian philosophy, as in the empire, all things were both related and opposite. People could have their links within groups, which could in turn have their links within associations, which might in turn have their links to a town or a small principality, and those could in turn have their links in an empire or a confederation. And all could remain distinct and separate individuals while being part of a common political logic that sanctioned distinctiveness and community alike. Thus the nine hundred years of German existence within the Holy Roman Empire and the legacy of dialectic logic reinforced each other, sinking deeply into the German unconscious and the culture of German diplomacy and negotiating behavior.

Whereas Hobbes had perceived a contradiction between freedom and security, suggesting—if one puts it in current European terms—that persons would have to choose between freedom or a European Union "superstate," a German steeped in dialectic logic could legitimately recognize the value of a community in the search for individual freedom and expression. One could, as the German historian Friedrich Meinecke later wrote, have cosmopolitan and national feelings at one and the same time.[10] Under Hegel's dialectic synthesis, an international community could serve a national purpose even if the nation surrendered part of its authority. This kind of logic has helped to place Germany more than any other major state at the core of the historically unprecedented level of integration that the European Union and other international structures have been able to implement.

The cosmopolitan style of German history and philosophy influenced the main thrust of German literature until and through the Napoleonic era. Germany's best-known authors, Johann Wolfgang von Goethe and Friedrich Schiller, wrote more on universal themes than on German political matters, although Schiller wrote with great yearning of a freedom that clearly did not exist within the empire. Neither Goethe nor Schiller trumpeted the unabashed nationalist appeal of Shakespeare's historical plays. And Ludwig van Beethoven's paeans to liberty, the opera *Fidelio* and the final chorus of the Ninth Symphony, also had universal rather than national settings and themes.

The Economic Setting of German Culture

Despite its problems and multiple internal boundaries, Germany did not remain an economic backwater. The German portions of the Holy Roman Empire prospered during sporadic times of peace. They became important centers of production as the European economy expanded throughout much of the Middle Ages and the Renaissance, and especially at the beginning of the modern era. German towns and states nurtured small crafts as well as early industrial development. They encouraged and fostered a standard of high manufacturing quality that remains a hallmark of German output to this day. Over time, towns became more prosperous than aristocratic holdings because they began promoting industry and commerce, whereas the aristocratic holdings remained agricultural.

German cities and industrial entities lay at the center of many European commercial nets. They traded with each other and with countless other areas throughout Europe. Germany anchored the western end of the Hanseatic League, which joined the cities of the North Sea and the Baltic from Hamburg and Bremen to northern Finland during the fourteenth century. German towns and other entities harbored strong mercantilist leanings, always trying to export more than they imported in order to make their trade profitable.

Through all these modernizing activities, Germany added industry, agriculture, and commerce to its earlier traditions of learning and culture. It also continued to expand its strong bureaucratic institutions, for many towns and states justified and consolidated their existence by establishing as effective and honest a local administration as possible within an unstable environment. The rulers and the bureaucracy supported economic development, especially trade and especially exports, in order to boost the well-being of their realms no matter how small they might be.

Austria and Prussia

Only two entities, Austria and Prussia, formed exceptions to the empire's pattern of small states. And Austria, although its people regarded themselves as Germanic and although it had the seat of the empire in its capital, Vienna, increasingly saw most of its immediate interests to its east and south rather than in Germany itself. By the eighteenth century, Austria had developed a separate existence and a separate mind-set from the other Germanic states, thinking of itself not only as German but as European and as having a European-wide area of immediate interest.

Prussia moved in two directions, toward Germany and away from it. It remained a strongly Germanic state while also controlling large lands outside the Holy Roman Empire itself. It began in what became known as East Prussia, but its center lay in Berlin and Brandenburg from the seventeenth century on. It also came increasingly into possession of territories along the Rhine River and in Poland. Like the Hapsburg emperors of Austria, the Hohenzollern kings of Prussia began to think in European terms during the 1700s. They saw important interests outside the empire and especially toward the east, where they could maneuver more freely and could exercise greater dominance than within the confines of the imperial state system. They divided Poland with Austria and Russia. They also recruited and deployed an efficient army. Prussia's King Friedrich Wilhelm I in the early eighteenth century became known as the "soldier king." Unlike the Hapsburgs, the Hohenzollerns still saw themselves primarily as Germans and they wanted to increase their influence within Germany as well as in eastern Europe. But they also had wider ambitions.

Prussia developed a different style from that of the other German lands. It controlled areas inside and outside the empire and had to think differently for each. It had developed an effective army as early as the eighteenth century. It could, therefore, act more forcefully than the smaller German states. It did not need to think in limited terms, functioning within long-established associations and relationships, for it could stand apart. It did not need intra-German alliances as others did and did not assimilate federalist principles.

Friedrich II ("Frederick the Great") of Prussia attacked Austria in 1740 and seized the Austrian province of Silesia. He also established a strongly centralized Prussian government and modernized the Prussian bureaucracy and the Prussian state. Berlin could then increasingly play continental politics on an almost equal basis with Paris, Vienna, or St. Petersburg, at least as long as its military could outplan, outmaneuver, and outfight all opponents.

Prussia became a German Sparta, strong and unflinching, under its own rigorous codes of conduct. It established the Prussian Military Commission —later to become the Prussian and the German General Staff—in 1806, thus over time building by far the strongest military force within the German nation. The General Staff was to be part of a broad reform of the Prussian system, moving away from absolute monarchy toward constitutional monarchy and toward a more widely recruited officer corps that would promote on merit rather than aristocratic rank. It had been created to fight Napoleon, and it remained to become the central element of Prussian power.[11]

France and the Rise of German National Sentiment

The French Revolution of 1789 and the rise of Napoleon Bonaparte forced German politics and diplomacy out of their tracks. They pushed Germany into a pressure cooker of modernization.

The destruction of the French monarchy, followed initially by the installation of a revolutionary government, compelled Germans like others to look at the world anew. Many Germans hoped that they too could break free from the encrusted system under which they lived. They yearned for popular government and saw France as the leader of a new world.

But German attitudes changed when French revolutionary armies and Napoleon's legions in quick succession began attacking German lands. Napoleon's conquest of Germany, his seizure of the Rhineland, and the plunderous marches of the Grande Armée back and forth across German territory between 1800 and 1814 aroused a German patriotic fervor to match the upsurge in democratic sentiment. When Napoleon abolished the Holy Roman Empire and established the puppet Confederation of the Rhine in 1806, he fueled a national consciousness that it should have been in his interest to leave quiescent. And the new methods of war that he introduced, especially the use of massed contingents and high mobility, changed the context of international politics forever. They particularly shocked Germany, Napoleon's closest neighbor and the one that he tried most to reshape.

After Napoleon's retreat from Russia and his subsequent defeat at Waterloo, the Congress of Vienna of 1814–15 favored restoration of former royal and imperial regimes. It tried to reestablish European stability on the basis of the old monarchical system. To do so, the congress nurtured a carefully calculated balance of power that would neither humiliate France nor give predominance to any other continental European state. It forbade the states of the German Confederation, which had succeeded the Holy Roman Empire and Napoleon's Confederation of the Rhine, to combine to fight a war of aggression.[12] And those states, freed from the structures of the empire, found themselves in another, even looser, form of federalism.[13]

But German opinion had been too deeply shaken by the French Revolution and the Napoleonic aftermath. Even after the Congress of Vienna, Germans realized that their old system could not continue in the new world. Many Germans, especially intellectuals, students, and political activists, would not accept continued German dismemberment on the altar of the ancient monarchic system. They wanted a national and democratic German polity. Many wanted to give Prussia a leading role because it had been the first German state to challenge Napoleon both before and after the retreat from Moscow. Prussian field marshal Gebhard von Blücher became a national hero after the battle of Waterloo, although he had played only a peripheral role in Napoleon's defeat there. Germans also admired Prussia's movement to modernize and reform its government, including the General Staff.

German national sentiment continued to grow and spread even as it remained frustrated. Between 1832 and 1834, German states established a common tariff area, the Zollverein (Customs Union), to link their economies more closely. Freed from the hierarchical structures of the empire, German states and associations took up ever more direct contact with one another.

Many Germans wanted to link unity and democracy. At the Frankfurt Assembly of 1848–49, several hundred leading German political and intellectual personalities tried to establish a national German state on a democratic basis. They wrote a constitution and a bill of rights. They wanted a constitutional monarch on the English model. But the assembly failed, in part because of the impractical idealism of many of its members but mainly because of the firm opposition of the Hapsburgs and the Hohenzollerns. The king of Prussia would not deign to accept a German crown offered by a popular assembly.

Although no German nation-state emerged in 1848–49, the longing for it had caught hold. For the first time, one could speak of the beginnings of a clearly articulated German popular wish to form a nation-state that would match France or England. Many Germans wanted such a state mainly to prevent another attack by France, but others wanted to have a state as a sign of identity. They wanted to be able to hold their own in the European arena. They wanted a common foreign policy. And they wanted a democracy to shape that policy and to govern that new Germany.[14]

The wish for a German nation-state had a highly romantic element. It thrived on German myths such as the Siegfried saga, the legend of Beowulf, and the tales of the Nibelungs. Organizations such as the *Turnvereine* (gymnastic clubs) and the *Burschenschaften* (youth groups) hiked through the dark German forests and along the winding rivers, singing patriotic songs. They recalled the legend that Barbarossa, the heroic twelfth-century Hohenstaufen emperor, had not really died but had promised to return from his cave in the Kyffhäuser Mountains to save the German people in their hour of greatest need. A huge memorial was built for Arminius, the Germanic prince who had defeated three Roman legions in the Teutoberger Forest in 9 A.D. to save the original Germanic tribes of that era from Caesar's domination.

Richard Wagner's operas, with their powerful evocations of such ancient legends as Lohengrin or the Ring and such distinctive German institutions as the master craftsmen of Nuremberg, stoked the new emotions. Many of those emotions sought to split Germany from the broad Western tradition, insisting that Germany had its own character, its own history, and its own road.[15]

The German poet Heinrich Heine wrote that France and Russia controlled the land and England the seas, but that Germans owned "the realm of dreams."[16]

❏   ❏   ❏

The Holy Roman Empire left a lasting cultural legacy despite its turbulent history and its estrangement from some of the more dramatic movements and events sweeping Europe. It left a sense of structure and order as well as a faith that diverse institutions could find ways of working together. Long before federalism had become a formal concept, the empire laid the foundations for the kinds of layered authority that would later come to be called federal. It also left most Germans with the lingering realization that safety lay not in solitary power but in constant cooperation with others and in an accurate understanding of what might or might not be possible. The fittest would survive, but so would those who appreciated the essence of what we would now call multilateral diplomacy. Out of diverse philosophies, the German tradition in the empire also left a devoted attachment to logic.

Unification under Prussia

A new and striking figure, the Prussian chancellor Prince Otto von Bismarck, stepped to the center of the German scene around the middle of the nineteenth century as all these notions swirled about in Prussia and the German Confederation. He opposed the liberal democratic national leanings of the Frankfurt Assembly, looking to other, more conservative, German national solutions. He observed romantic German nationalism with the skepticism of a born cynic, but he was enough of a power politician to recognize how to use it.

Alternately stimulating and exploiting German national fervor for his own and Prussian purposes, Bismarck instigated successive wars against Denmark (1864), Austria (1866), and France (1870–71). He concluded the last war with a formal peace treaty ceremony in the Hall of Mirrors of the Palace at Versailles at which he launched the united German Reich under a new emperor, Wilhelm I, the Hohenzollern monarch of Prussia. In that treaty, however, he made the fatal mistake of annexing the French provinces of Alsace and Lorraine. Although this annexation might have been justifiable because France under Louis XIV had itself taken Alsace-Lorraine from the Holy Roman Empire, it made France an irreconcilable foe. It thus restricted Bismarck's room for diplomatic maneuver, limiting him to Austria and Russia as principal continental allies.

The Frankfurt Assembly had tried to institute a democratic united Germany under a parliamentary system. It had tried to link liberalism and nationalism. But Bismarck and Prussia had blocked that. Instead, Prussia's victories and the new German Empire captured German national sentiment for Prussia, which was—under Bismarck's direction—increasingly governed by its most reactionary elements.

The German conservatives, not the liberals, had delivered unity. In a fateful moment, German nationalism and German liberalism diverged, not to be united again for generations.

Bismarck achieved his main purpose of giving Prussia effective control over all of Germany through the new German Empire. With Prussians dominating the cabinet and the legislature, the new Germany followed Prussian dictates. Although the other German states could and often did try to resist specific Prussian ideas, Berlin controlled the new Germany and could determine its course.[17] The Prussian elite concentrated its energies on military and diplomatic policy. The Prussian General Staff, its prestige raised to the sky by its lightning victories over three opponents, became the German General Staff. It set strategic policy in ever more ambitious directions. The top Foreign Office staff, made up of the Prussian aristocracy, directed diplomacy under Bismarck's tight supervision. When he did not trust them to do it right, which was often, he took over himself.[18]

Bismarck's merger of Germany and Prussia—or, more properly, his merging of the smaller German states into the new Prussian-dominated German Empire—brought under one roof two different diplomatic traditions and divergent ways of thinking:

❏ On the one hand, Prussia's tradition of domineering influence and sometimes direct rule over many of its neighboring states and peoples. This brought to German foreign policy the attitudes and domestic politics of a state that occupied foreign territory and that had colonial possessions and ambitions, in Prussia's case toward Poland and the east.

Following their recent successes, Prussian politicians and generals saw no reason to change their ways. They tied the entire German nation to their colonial possessions, their support of Austria in the Balkans, and Bismarck's humiliation of France.

❐ On the other hand, the tradition of other German states—mainly in the Rhineland and other non-Prussian portions of the Holy Roman Empire—of living for centuries in a heavily populated environment in which they had learned to adjust, compromise, and cooperate with one another. They, too, could be purposeful and direct, but they remembered that they still had to work together with those they might have bested in war or diplomacy. The older and smaller members of the German Confederation, however tough they might have sometimes been in their dealings, still practiced a more flexible and accommodationist style than did Prussia. They also shared a less authoritarian tradition, despite their own monarchies and aristocracies, for in their many mutually interlinked and mutually reinforcing institutions they had found a measure of political space. Some had joined the new empire only with the greatest reluctance.

Because Bismarck and Prussia made the foreign policy of the new empire, the two styles did not mingle. Prussians simply brought to German diplomacy and strategy the same attitudes and techniques that they had applied in their own immediate neighborhood. Bismarck and Wilhelm's military advisors applied to France in 1871 the kinds of policies that had often been effective in Poland, eastern Europe, and the Balkans. They did not realize that France would not react as those others had.

The contradiction between the two German styles remained unresolved. The methods of the old Holy Roman Empire sank into disuse if not into oblivion. Power shifted toward the Prussians, who had suddenly acquired a heady authority over Europe's largest population, strongest economy, and most powerful army. Berlin, the brash new German capital, did not even perceive the tension that it had inherited.

For most of Germany, and especially for parts of the Rhineland and for the south German states, Prussian dominance meant a turn away from old traditions and old ways of thinking. Germany found itself united under a form of domination that was German but also foreign. Society, like diplomacy, became conservative, turning away from the liberal hopes of the Frankfurt Assembly and the democratic leanings of the West.[19] Germans bowed to the service of something they could not fully understand. They welcomed it in the enthusiasm of unification and in their happiness that they had finally founded a nation-state of their own, but they did not grasp all its implications, including the centralized administration that replaced the loose federal structures they knew.

The multiple contradictions of Bismarck's regime did not appear to present a problem at first. With the creation of the German Empire, Bismarck himself shifted German foreign policy from annexation to accommodation. As chancellor and foreign minister, he wanted to preserve German gains and to establish a system that would protect Germany against French revisionist ambitions. He believed that Europe needed time to adjust to the new Germany. He also saw that some burgeoning problems, like the impending collapse of the Ottoman Empire in the Balkans, warranted a common European approach.

Bismarck did not change his style, which remained direct, purposeful, and often confrontational. But he tried to keep the new Germany on good terms with all the major powers of Europe except France, whose thirst for revision left no hope for accommodation. Knowing that Paris would try hard to find allies, he wanted to build systems that would isolate France.

Bismarck, however, like a sorcerer's apprentice, risked losing control. Having firmly opposed the liberal and moderate forces within the empire, he found himself having to contend almost alone with the newly inflamed emotions aroused by German and especially Prussian expansionary enthusiasm. Some of that might have been considered normal. After all, new nation-states had usually burst their seams in the first waves of enthusiasm after their creation. England had tried to seize control over major French territories after it had first become a nation-state; France in its turn had annexed parts of the Holy Roman Empire; Spain and Portugal had seized vast possessions in what was to become Latin America; the United States had expanded to the west; Italy had seized parts of Austria. One German historian spoke of the *"Versuchung des Unendlichen"* (the temptation of the infinite).[20] But Germany, surrounded by a host of other states, had no empty spaces around to conquer.

Bismarck fought for control of German diplomacy. He devised a labyrinthine system of treaties and understandings to keep the new Germany on good terms with both Russia and Austria-Hungary, although those two states opposed each other directly in the Balkans. He kept some of his agreements with them secret, including especially the 1887 Reinsurance Treaty, in which he assured St. Petersburg that under certain circumstances Germany would not support Austria in a war against Russia.

Calling himself an "honest broker," Bismarck crafted several Balkan agreements that preserved the peace of Europe even if they left his friends in both Vienna and St. Petersburg bruised and resentful of the compromises he had forced on them. He avoided offending England. His work through that period has been generally hailed as a model of sagacious, if byzantine, diplomacy.

But Bismarck did not try to mold domestic understanding for his maneuverings. He had no faith in democracy and paid it nothing but the most sarcastic deference. He did not believe that he needed to craft widespread appreciation and support for Germany's efforts to maintain a European balance and a global peace. Instead, he operated largely under the surface, building a network of secret contacts out of his own office. He systematically excluded the political figures of the German parliament from foreign affairs. He also often excluded his own emperor and certainly the German people. *Realpolitik,* the name he chose for his policies (presumably drawn from Richelieu's *raison d'état*), reeked with a deception that defeated its often sensible purposes.

Bismarck met the swirling controversies about his personal direction of the new nation's diplomacy with derision instead of explanation, winning by the massive force of his personality instead of using his prestige to build a consensus for the diplomatic needs of a powerful new state in the center of a crowded continent. He thus failed to construct understanding and support for the cautious diplomacy that a united Germany had to practice to avoid provoking a hostile system of alliances. He could operate brilliantly, but he could not lay the foundations for a stable system.

Bismarck's failure was to come back to haunt Germany and Europe. Wilhelm II, who became the emperor of Germany in 1888, dismissed Bismarck in 1890. He wanted a more important role for himself in directing the affairs of the Reich. Moreover, Wilhelm found Bismarck increasingly irascible and prone to plotting directed not only against popular government but also against the emperor's policies.

Having dismissed Bismarck, Wilhelm decided as one of his first acts in foreign affairs to reject a Russian request to renew the Reinsurance Treaty. This destroyed Bismarck's careful construct of alliances by compelling St. Petersburg to turn toward a welcoming France. It fundamentally altered the strategic balance in Europe, becoming the first step toward the doom of Wilhelm's Reich. As time went on, he continued to exercise amateurish, if intermittent, control over German foreign affairs, often issuing thoughtless pronouncements that alienated even those who wanted to be friends with Germany.

Wilhelm and the new generation of Prussian political, diplomatic, and military leaders saw the outside world in simpler terms than the older German states had seen it. Impelled by the new wave of nationalism, they overrode the warnings from some of the smaller German states. They sought adventure. But they did so in a hideously dangerous environment. Germany, the core state of Europe, had fallen into the hands of reckless incompetents.

Suffering from the *verspätete Nation* syndrome, German foreign policy and diplomacy under Wilhelm's erratic guidance tried to make up for lost time by reaching for military power and colonies. Wilhelm was not alone in imperialist ambitions: Britain expanded across the world; France invaded North Africa; the United States seized the Philippine Islands. Almost all the major powers were seizing whatever they could of China. But Germany was the new player on the block and generated greater frictions than the others.

German forces appeared on continents where they had not appeared before. Wilhelm II claimed a "place in the sun" and created a sizable German oceangoing navy despite urgent warnings from London. German diplomats tried to explain Berlin's vainglorious and sometimes belligerent posturing to world leaders, but they had little success.

German policy and Wilhelm II's behavior contributed significantly to the arrival of World War I and to Germany's growing diplomatic isolation as the war drew near. As the lines were being drawn ever tighter across Europe, and after the Serb nationalist Gavrilo Princip assassinated the Austrian crown prince in Sarajevo on June 28, 1914, Wilhelm II gave

Austria what was often described as a "blank check" to punish and humiliate Serbia. When Russia objected and mobilized some of its forces, the demands of its own mobilization schedule forced the German General Staff to attack. Neither Wilhelm nor anybody else could arrest the fatal plunge to war.

Germany on the Road to Ruin: World War I

Wilhelm II still hoped that Britain would not join the front against Germany. But the General Staff's decision to conduct a lightning invasion of France across formally neutral Belgium made British entry inevitable. And Wilhelm's support for German submarine warfare, conducted despite ever more frantic warnings from his ambassador in Washington, made certain that the United States would in 1917 join the alliance against Germany.

The German people entered World War I confused and without genuine understanding of what had happened or was happening. No German expected a long war. Neither did anyone else. Crowds in the major German cities cheered the troops going off to the front, as other crowds did in Paris and London. German war plans included prospects for major territorial expansion, especially in the east, and projected early victory. But more sober voices warned of disaster.

After four years of exhausting warfare, with millions of dead on both sides, Germany's military campaigns had reached different results on the eastern and western frontiers. German forces had won the war in the east by 1917 as the tsarist regime collapsed and was to be succeeded by a revolutionary popular government and then by the communist dictatorship of Vladimir Lenin (whom the German General Staff had transported to St. Petersburg in a sealed railway car). With Lenin determined to pull Russia out of the war, Berlin imposed the Treaty of Brest-Litovsk, which forced Russia back from Europe. But by then the German nation had been exhausted by the war and an Allied blockade. At the insistence of the General Staff, Germany had to accept an armistice. Wilhelm II fled Germany for exile in the Netherlands. And the armistice led to the Treaty of Versailles of 1919, in which the Western Allies made Germany accept war guilt and ruinous reparations. The treaty also forced Germany to surrender a number of traditionally German-populated lands, including Danzig, parts of Silesia, and the German parts of what became Czechoslovakia. It saddled Germany with total defeat and total responsibility.

The Versailles Treaty staggered Germany. Most Germans had not even realized that the war had become unwinnable. The reports they had received from the front had not told the true story. The people had been glad that the German government had accepted a cease-fire with the Western Allies, but they had not understood its full implications. They had thought that the cease-fire and the peace treaty would be negotiated on the terms proclaimed by President Woodrow Wilson's Fourteen Points and that a stable peace of accommodation would follow the war. They had not perceived the deep-seated hatred that others felt toward "the Huns."

The terms that the principal Western Allies, France, Great Britain, Italy, and the United States, negotiated among themselves and then imposed on Germany and Austria-Hungary thus came as a shock. The Germans could accept, if unhappily, that some territories (such as Prussian conquests in Poland) would be lost because those were non-German lands. But they could not understand why Germany also lost large central European territories with German majorities. Nor did they believe that they should be forced to accept sole responsibility for the war. Germans also resented that France was to occupy portions of the northern Rhineland and that other parts would be demilitarized, reestablishing the strategic boundaries of Louis XIV and Napoleon.[21]

Prussia's and Bismarck's Legacy

Forty-three years of Reich diplomacy, under Bismarck, Wilhelm II, and the Prussian aristocracy and General Staff, left a mixed legacy etched into Germany's consciousness and diplomatic culture—a few positives but many more negatives.

Many Germans, especially in Prussia, tended to forget Bismarck's mistakes, such as his humiliation of France and his disdain for a democratic system. They also failed to perceive how the Prussian-dominated structure that he had built played a major role in the disaster that followed. Instead, they remembered him as a magisterial figure who united Germany and then tried to maintain the European peace and to protect Germany from isolation on two fronts. He became a kind of cult diplomatist, admired in many places for his adroit skills. But many other Germans did not share this admiration. For them, Prussia's seizure of the reins of German power still rankled, and Bismarck's misdeeds and mistakes loomed more important than his apparent triumphs. They would have preferred to go back to older regimes and older institutions.

Germans did agree, however, on Wilhelm II's legacy. Except for a few royalists and loyalists, Wilhelm's capricious and often improvised diplomacy, like Wilhelm himself, became objects of ridicule and textbook examples of how not to conduct and articulate foreign policy. His main legacy, and a negative one, was the lesson that Germany should never again pursue a diplomatic strategy that would lead to isolation.

But German popular and even intellectual debate after the war did not address the central question of Germany's role in the world after Versailles. In the heyday of German romantic nationalism under Wilhelm II, German strategists and even many other Germans had believed that Germany should be on a par with Great Britain as one of the major world powers. World War I proved that Germany could not aspire so high.

But neither did the victorious Allies have a concept of their own for a future German role. They did not understand that they were exacerbating rather than resolving the tensions within the German system and between that system and its presence in the heart of Europe. They had humiliated the Reich, not granting Germany even a minor role in Europe or a membership in the new League of Nations. They made Germany virtually an outcast from the European and the world stage. Many Germans felt that this was too steep a fall and too harsh a verdict.

The statesmen at Versailles failed to build the kind of lasting structure that the statesmen at Vienna had built a century earlier. And Germany for its part could not contribute. Bismarck had left no guidance and no persuasive example. Fifty years after German unification, neither the Germans themselves nor their neighbors had reached a consensus on Germany's place in the world.

The Weimar Republic

In Germany itself, a new popular government came to power after the war. It became known as the Weimar Republic because its constitution

had been written and agreed to in the small central German city of
Weimar. When the General Staff had said that the German military could
not continue the war, the fledgling German democracy accepted the terms
of Versailles and thus took the blame for Germany's defeat. This burden of
responsibility ultimately doomed the Weimar Republic while leaving the
Prussian conservative class and its military caste largely free of blame for
causing and losing the war. It further deepened the abyss between German
nationalism and German liberalism and left the articulation of German
patriotic sentiment in the hands of reactionaries.[22]

The mantra for German diplomacy after World War I became revisionism and sullen resistance. Even those Germans who had opposed the war
resented the terms of Versailles for isolating, humiliating, and impover-
ishing the new democratic German government. As the British economist
John Maynard Keynes had predicted, the cost of reparations wrecked the
German economy and currency, leading to a ruinous inflation and destroying much of the German middle class. German resentment grew further
when the Allied governments—especially France—imposed additional
burdens to enforce the treaties, and especially when French forces occupied the Ruhr in 1923. German extremist parties multiplied on the Left
and the Right. The communists dominated the extreme left wing, while
various nationalist parties, including the new National Socialist Party
under Adolf Hitler, dominated the extreme Right. German democrats
and liberals found their political credibility at home constantly under-
mined by the hostile attitude that the two great European democracies,
England and France, showed toward Weimar. Lacking any potential friends
in the West, they turned their diplomacy toward the East and especially
toward Russia.[23]

Germany wanted desperately to break out of its isolation. It reopened
its diplomatic options in 1922, signing the Rapallo Treaty with the even
more ostracized communist regime of the Soviet Union. The General Staff
conducted its own policies, making secret agreements for military cooperation with Moscow. Fear of German-Soviet cooperation and the world-
wide impact of the collapse of the German economy led some Western
statesmen to realize that they could not ignore Germany in the long run
and that they were running the risk of having the communists take over
the center of Europe. They began to rethink the arrangements they had
made at Versailles.

The U.S. government finally took the lead in forging new relationships. It negotiated revised reparations arrangements (the so-called Dawes and Young Plans) that enabled Germany to pay at a more realistic pace. And a new German foreign minister, Gustav Stresemann, bent on trying to reach some reconciliation with France, decided that Germany would stop challenging the terms of Versailles overtly, although he remained committed to changing them by negotiations—especially in eastern Europe and for the German-speaking territories that had been taken over by Poland and Czechoslovakia.

The Western states welcomed the new German policies, although not without some reservations from France. In 1925 they signed a series of agreements, known as the Locarno Treaties, with the Weimar Republic. Under the terms of those treaties the Allies withdrew occupation forces, rescheduled German reparations obligations, and gave Germany a permanent seat in the League of Nations. Stresemann also signed the Berlin Treaty with the Soviet Union to reassure Moscow that Germany would not join in any Western capitalist coalition under British leadership that would try to overturn the Soviet regime. That treaty, like Bismarck's Reinsurance Treaty, completed Stresemann's diplomatic architecture toward West and East. It brought Germany back into the international community.

Stresemann sought stability and largely achieved it. Under his steady hand, Germany drew some advantages from having openings toward the Soviet Union as well as toward the Western powers. He wanted to help construct a stable and peaceful European system that would permit Germany to rebuild her shattered economy and take a place among the major states of Europe.

Stresemann also wanted to strengthen democratic forces at home. He hoped that the success of his policies would prevent the extremist parties from taking over the government. By 1928 those policies appeared to triumph. The international situation stabilized and the German economy grew strongly between 1925 and 1929. The extremist parties, and especially the National Socialists, fell to their lowest vote levels since the collapse of the German currency in 1923.

Stresemann and the Weimar Republic left a short but important legacy of reconciliation for Germany's diplomatic culture. The reconciliation did not include all of Germany's neighbors, but it could perhaps have been made to work. Germany had found a community and a place for itself.

The Hitler Years and World War II

Stresemann's legacy as foreign minister did not last. He found no support in France for what he was trying to do. And, like Bismarck, he left no successor who could manage his system after he died, in 1929, of exhaustion and ill health. The Great Depression, which had a deeper and more lasting effect in Germany than in any other major country, undercut the democratic roots of the Weimar Republic.

By 1933 the National Socialists had become the largest single party in Germany. Hitler forged a link between German nationalism and the most extreme forms of German conservatism, blaming Germany's economic and political problems on Jews and foreigners while exploiting German resentment against Versailles. Although he never received a majority of the popular vote, Hitler won many supporters among unemployed German workers and among the dispossessed middle classes. In 1933, through a series of political maneuvers, the nationalist parties persuaded the senescent German president, Field Marshal Paul von Hindenburg, to designate Hitler as chancellor.

Under extreme pressure from Hitler and from violent Nazi-led mobs coursing through the streets, the Reichstag passed enabling acts that vitiated the Weimar constitution and gave Hitler effective control over all aspects of German life and policy. Many Prussian aristocrats and German industrialists who had disliked the Weimar constitution and Stresemann's policies welcomed Hitler at first because they thought he would restore German strength, influence, and self-respect.

Hitler exuded revisionism, aiming directly and purposefully at the Versailles settlement. Unlike Stresemann, Hitler would not hesitate to use the military. He wanted especially to reestablish German dominance over eastern Europe and use that dominance as the springboard for a policy that would make Germany the strongest state on earth. He wanted *Lebensraum* (living space) for the German people and wanted to use Russian and eastern European resources for the Third Reich.[24]

Hitler understood the reluctance of the Western powers to go to war again. He succeeded in sending a series of mixed messages that enabled him to begin his chancellorship without provoking an immediate Allied reaction, although he also took steps (such as leaving the League of Nations and beginning German rearmament) that defied the Versailles regime. He appeared very reasonable at some moments and totally belligerent at others. He began by denouncing and violating the provisions of the Versailles Treaty that limited German rearmament. Two years later, in March 1936, he sent German troops back into those parts of the Rhineland that the Versailles Treaty had demilitarized.

The German diplomatic service and General Staff opposed Hitler's early actions. They, like many among Hitler's conservative supporters, warned that his moves would provoke an Allied reaction.[25] But no reaction came. Hitler thereupon decided that he understood the West better than others and that he really did not need to negotiate with the Western states except on his own terms. In February 1937 he boasted to the old guard of the Nazi Party in Munich, "Today we are once more a world power."[26]

Hitler envisaged a *Stufenplan,* a step-by-step plan including a series of diplomatic and military strokes that would initially revise the results of World War I and then go far beyond them. Knowing of British opposition to communism, he hoped to win British agreement for an attack on Soviet Russia. He then wanted to use the new lands Germany would win in the east to strengthen Germany for attacks on France and on Britain itself in the 1940s. He planned for war against the United States after that, perhaps by 1945–48.[27] As a first major move, he took over Austria in March 1938, making it part of Germany.

To Hitler's frustration, the British government chose not to make agreements against communism. But Hitler was able to press the British prime minister, Neville Chamberlain, to agree that the German ethnic areas in Czechoslovakia should be transferred to Germany. Their agreement at Munich in September 1938 represented the major negotiated change to the territorial arrangements concluded at Versailles.

Hitler did not actually want Chamberlain to accept the Munich agreement. He would have preferred to invade Czechoslovakia in order to show open defiance of Versailles. But a series of diplomatic maneuvers orchestrated by Hitler's ally, the Italian *duce,* Benito Mussolini, and by officials in the German Foreign Office, forced Hitler to accept a diplomatic triumph when he would have preferred a military one. Furious over his own success, he compensated six months later when he invaded and occupied the remainder of Czechoslovakia.[28]

The Munich agreement again dumbfounded those German officials and generals who had counseled caution and a small group of generals who had even talked of a coup d'état against Hitler. It also convinced Hitler that he could win any test of wills against the Western powers. He entered the realm of pure megalomania, thinking that the West had lost its courage and would not dare to stop him.

Although Chamberlain had negotiated the Munich agreement, Hitler's invasion of Czechoslovakia forced Britain to review its policies. London decided to block further German expansion to the east by offering a guarantee to Hitler's obvious next intended victim, Poland.

Frustrated by Britain and eager to open other routes to the east, Hitler negotiated a nonaggression pact with Joseph Stalin in August 1939. Under the secret provisions of that pact, Hitler attacked Poland from the west in September 1939, while Stalin attacked from the east. In response, Britain and France declared war on Germany. This surprised Hitler, for he had not expected them to act on their commitments in eastern Europe.

At that point, Hitler abandoned his earlier plans and moved fully to a war footing. When Count August Ciano, Mussolini's foreign minister, in September 1939 asked Joachim Ribbentrop, Hitler's newly appointed foreign minister, what Germany really wanted, Ribbentrop answered, "We want war!"[29]

And so, indeed, it was to be. Hitler attacked France in May 1940. He then launched an air campaign against Great Britain. He attacked the Soviet Union in June 1941. On December 11, 1941, he declared war on the United States, four days after the Japanese attack on Pearl Harbor. He appeared to make this decision, which was met with consternation by almost all of his advisors, for psychological reasons.[30] Having put Germany at war with much of the world, Hitler assumed direct control over German military forces, going into field command stations and largely turning his back on Berlin until the closing phases of the war. Then, he returned to the Chancellery bunker, where he committed suicide on April 30, 1945.

To poison his legacy and Germany's, Hitler added a policy of genocide against Jews in Germany and the occupied territories as well as against Gypsies, homosexuals, and mentally ill and handicapped people. Beginning with the Nuremberg Decrees of September 1935, depriving German Jews of their rights, Hitler conducted the Holocaust, killing six million Jews in the most barbaric manner. He not only cost Germany a war but also its reputation as a civilized nation.

Hitler's legacy does not form a part of the legacy of German diplomacy. It had no diplomatic content or purpose except, in its early years, as a preparation for war. Hitler left no mark on the record of German negotiating style. He fired most German professional diplomats. Such contacts as he had with foreign states increasingly bypassed the professionals in the German Foreign Office and went directly either from the Chancellery or through Ribbentrop's immediate staff in the Foreign Office.

Hitler left a slogan for German diplomacy: "Never, never, again." No German diplomat would ever want to emulate Hitler. He also left German foreign policy with a particular handicap. German diplomacy could no longer count on working in conjunction with military power, as diplomacy has traditionally worked—and continues to work—elsewhere. Germans could not ever fight independently again. They could not carry a big stick or even any stick at all. Hitler had mortgaged German diplomacy and forced it into a new mode.

Hitler also wrote an end to Prussian control over German policy. Many in the Prussian elite had supported him from the beginning and had remained loyal, although some Prussian officers formed the core of several failed assassination attempts against him. After the *Stunde Null,* the four victors of World War II turned over much of Prussia's former territory to Polish administration and formally abolished the General Staff and Prussia itself. Whatever Germany might arise after World War II was definitely to have a different diplomacy.

The Legacy of German Unity

The seventy-four years of German unity from 1871 to 1945 left a bitter memory for Germany. During all those years, despite vast military and economic power, Germans had never been really secure. They had often been isolated. They had worried constantly about others uniting against them. They had been forced to accumulate huge stocks of weapons and recruit enormous armies. They had lost two generations of their young. When the Germans looked back on those three quarters of a century, they could conclude only that they had shared in a disaster of unparalleled proportions. And so, of course, had all too many others.

The four victors of World War II, France, Great Britain, the Soviet Union, and the United States, also concluded that German unity had been a calamity. They decided to divide Germany into five parts: four occupation zones and the city of Berlin, which they in turn divided into four sectors. Germany would be split again, as it had been before 1871, although along different lines. Several of the victors had neither expected nor wanted the division of Germany to become permanent, but it was to last for almost half a century. German history had come full circle in seventy-four misbegotten years, and inept German diplomacy had to bear much of the blame.

But with the legacy came the old question all over again: What was to be Germany's place in the world? Bismarck had failed to define it successfully. So had the victors at Versailles. So had Hitler. So had two wars and countless dead. Neither Germans nor others seemed able to find the answer, and yet the answer had to come. Germany could not be left in some distant void. It sat in the center of Europe. Somebody had to decide what to do with it. Either the Germans, if they could be trusted to come up with an acceptable answer, or some other state or combination of states. Or perhaps all of them together.

Die Stunde Null

As it turned out, the World War II victors could not agree. They might have even regarded it as an absurdly abstract question. As far as they were concerned, Germany had reached the end of its road as a united state for a long time and perhaps forever.

Germans would, therefore, need to find their own road, build their own new existence, and seek their own place in Europe and the world. They would have to put together a combination of policies that would serve their needs and be acceptable to a highly skeptical world. And they would need to do it under brutally difficult circumstances.

The Soviets had planned for their part of Germany better than the Western occupiers had planned for theirs. They had their teams set to move in. They installed a communist regime and forced the East German socialists to merge with the Communist Party to form the Sozialistische Einheitspartei Deutschlands (Socialist Unity Party of Germany [SED]). The SED leaders knew where Germany should fit, and that was in the newly established communist world. They proclaimed a total break with the Hitler regime and with its antecedents, rejecting any responsibility for the past and calling themselves the first German state of workers and farmers.

The SED pursued a communist model for domestic policy while following Soviet direction on foreign policy. SED leader Walter Ulbricht sometimes pursued Soviet policies in his own particularly callous manner, but the system functioned with no doubts about the rules to be followed.

The Western occupiers faced a harder problem in their three zones. They wanted a democratic model, never as quick or as easy to implant or manage as a totalitarian one. They had no leadership teams set to take over but had to find political and economic leaders in Germany itself. After several years of occupation, they decided to establish a West German government on a democratic basis. They wanted it to be legitimate and to function effectively within a carefully circumscribed sphere of competence. They decided not to follow the Versailles model: they would not punish the new democratic German government for the sins of the Hitler dictatorship. Over time, this was to offer an opening for a German choice and a return to German diplomacy. It also offered an opening for a link between German democracy and a new form of German patriotism.

After four years of Western Allied occupation and with Allied encouragement, the West Germans in 1949 established the new Federal Republic of Germany. They wrote a constitution that they called the Basic Law to show that it provided only a temporary blueprint until Germany could be united again. The Western Allies promulgated the Occupation Statute, giving the West Germans some limited powers to manage domestic affairs but not at first to conduct diplomacy.

The West German Basic Law followed the same federalist principles that Germany had developed during the Holy Roman Empire. The central authorities had certain powers, but so did the separate states (the *Länder*) and even the towns and localities. The southern and southwestern states of the Federal Republic, regarding themselves as the bearers of the German liberal tradition, insisted on formally designated separate powers. Deeply frustrated that they had ever been dragged into a centralized German state by Bismarck and then by Hitler, they insisted on keeping far more authority than they had possessed during the German Reich.

Members of the constituent assembly saw the Basic Law as the cornerstone of a new German democracy. They wanted a *Rechtstaat,* a state governed by the rule of law. Many members saw the new Basic Law as their crowning achievement.

Konrad Adenauer as Chancellor

Konrad Adenauer became the first West German chancellor on September 15, 1949. Hitler had removed him as mayor of Cologne and had imprisoned both him and his wife. Now Adenauer and his government had to decide what German historical and cultural models to designate as the signposts for the new Federal Republic of Germany.

In diplomacy, Adenauer and West Germany quickly rejected three diplomatic models from the past:

❑ Prussia's arrogance and tendency toward grandiose miscalculation. Although many Germans still admired some aspects of Bismarck's diplomacy, they did not want to return to the Hohenzollern system, including its foreign policies.

❑ Weimar's impotence and yearning for revision. West Germans wanted a functioning democracy. Few wanted to pay the price needed to get back the areas that Hitler had lost.

❑ Hitler's savagery, megalomania, and abuse of diplomacy only as a step to war.

Adenauer and his colleagues would have to find a different design for West German foreign policy, and they would also have to find a different place for Germany in Europe and the world.

❑   ❑   ❑

Konrad Adenauer came from the Rhineland. He saw an older, wider, and deeper flow of German history. He believed that the Prussian hegemony, the Weimar tragedy, and the Nazi legacy of evil constituted a single monstrously flawed seventy-four-year digression from that flow. He detested everything east of the Elbe River, regarding it as un-German and un-European, and he wanted to return Germany to its earlier roots.

Adenauer often spoke to John J. McCloy, the first U.S. high commissioner in the Federal Republic, of the importance that he attached to bringing Germany back to the principles of the Holy Roman Empire. McCloy was amazed and baffled as he realized that Adenauer treated that period as if it had been recent German history.[31] For Adenauer, in fact, it may indeed have been recent history, although an American might not understand that.

Adenauer had to break the link between German democracy and German humiliation. He had to show that a German democracy could serve German interests effectively in domestic and diplomatic policy. He could not openly announce that he would follow the Holy Roman Empire as a model. Neither Adenauer nor any West German chancellor could advocate a return to the weakness and fragmentation from which Germans had suffered during that period.

But Adenauer may well have drawn some important parallels. In 1949, as during the Holy Roman Empire, Germany lay divided. The separate German states had to make their way in a world of watchful neighbors. They had to work with others in multiple avenues of cooperation while trying to find an accepted place in Europe and the world.

Thus Adenauer turned to the Holy Roman Empire as a model without announcing it. He also turned to the notion that Europe could devise structures that could transcend separate states, particularly on the opposite banks of the Rhine. He drew on the ancient German traditions of association for a common end. He drew on the German passion for logic, trying to announce his policies in rational terms. He also tried to revive traditional German economic strength.

Out of those historical roots, Adenauer's West Germany fastened on a broad negotiating strategy modeled on his interpretation of German diplomacy from the kingdoms of Charlemagne and the Hohenstaufens to the middle 1800s. This may have appeared as an improbable model in the modern age, but it evoked a sense of community, of shared existence within a broader realm, and of firm links with the West while open in all directions.

Because Adenauer had himself opposed Hitler, he did not believe that he needed to feel ashamed when he dealt with the Western occupation powers. In one of his early meetings with the Western high commissioners at their offices on the Petersberg high above Bonn, he made a point of standing on the same carpet as the high commissioners, although they had originally expected him and his colleagues to stand in an area off the carpet. For him, such seemingly minute gestures constituted the beginning of German rehabilitation and self-esteem.[32]

But Adenauer still had to remain sensitive to the bitter memories that West Germany's neighbors had of Hitler's invasions and mass killings. He had to keep a low profile. No German could appear at all assertive without reviving memories of the Nazis. And Germans adopted what successive German leaders have called a "special responsibility" toward Israel.

Adenauer could not conceal West German weaknesses: a rump of a nation; a shattered society, infrastructure, and economy; a vulnerability to threat and potential conquest from the Soviet Union; a ruined reputation; and, above all, an immense sense of loss and, for some, futility.

Germany's assets took longer to see, and they resembled those of earlier times: a strategically priceless location that others were ready to claim if they did not have it and to protect if they did; some economic resources below and above ground; and, above all, a sense of history as a process that had come not to an end but only to a turning point.

The German people, strong, intelligent, resilient, and hardworking, also remained an asset. Although defeated and divided, most of them firmly believed they could recover. They stood more than ready to do whatever was necessary to support a democracy in its efforts to rebuild Germany as a free society. They had a sense for what might be possible, in diplomacy as in their own lives. They would be as patient and tenacious as necessary, provided they could see some purpose to what their government was trying to do.[33]

The main point, driven home by bitter experience, was that Germany could not aim for a "place in the sun," especially not by force. But Germany still needed to find a place somewhere. That place could not be at the top of the world. But neither should it be at the bottom. The search would have to continue to be a part of everything that Germany would do, in diplomacy or otherwise.

Finally, Germans saw that there could be no future in old or new dreams. They did not want a return to Bismarck's cynical *Realpolitik,* but neither did they want to be lost in romantic and dangerous ventures.

Germany needed friends. It needed peace and tranquility. It also needed a stable government that the German people could trust, not one that would involve them in ruinous expeditions.

Even if Germany needed friends, however, it could not let them decide everything. Germans might no longer want to attack or conquer others, but they still had to pursue their own interests. If they did not do it, nobody else would do it for them.

Adenauer's diplomacy reflected those national purposes. He linked Germany to the process of West European integration and transatlantic cooperation. In 1951 he signed the treaty for the European Coal and Steel Community, tying the German economy firmly into a West European economic unit whose borders ran remarkably close to those of Charlemagne's empire eleven centuries earlier. In 1954 and 1955 Adenauer brought the Federal Republic into the North Atlantic Treaty Organization (NATO) in exchange for the end of the occupation regime and partial West German sovereignty. Friendships with France and the United States enabled him to turn away from Weimar's early dependence on the Soviet Union. And West German membership in international organizations permitted a return to diplomacy without reviving memories of Hitler and Ribbentrop.

Adenauer hated all forms of dictatorship and especially Stalinism. Although he established relations with the Soviet Union in 1955, he was ready to draw a line across Europe and he even accepted a line through Germany itself in order to block the advance of the communist system across the continent. As part of the price, Adenauer in 1961 had to swallow a bitter pill, the Berlin Wall that East Germany's dictator, Walter Ulbricht, built to stop East Germans from fleeing to the West.[34]

Adenauer fought hard to stop Ulbricht's German Democratic Republic (GDR) from getting international recognition. He announced the Hallstein Doctrine (named for Walter Hallstein, a secretary of state in the German Foreign Office), which held that West Germany would regard it as an "unfriendly act" for any state formally to recognize the GDR. Adenauer sent large West German diplomatic and aid missions to many new African and Asian states during the 1960s to make sure that East Germany could not win support from those states by offering them aid. He made clear that West Germany would react to any such "unfriendly act" by breaking diplomatic relations and stopping aid programs. He did that to Yugoslavia when Marshal Josip Broz Tito recognized the GDR.

Willy Brandt and His Successors

Adenauer's immediate successors, Ludwig Erhard and Kurt Georg Kiesinger, did not react fast enough in the late 1960s when the international mood shifted toward East-West accommodation. West German voters thus elected the Social Democrat Willy Brandt in late 1969 to try a policy of détente—called *Ostpolitik* in Germany—toward Moscow and the East. They specifically hoped that Brandt would make it possible to exchange more family visits across the wall.

Brandt followed a very Hegelian dialectic concept: one could end Germany's division only by accepting it. He succeeded in easing East-West tensions and in permitting greater personal contacts between East and West Germany. He improved West German relations with the Soviet Union and Poland by signing treaties with both states in 1970. But, to make certain that Moscow respected the Western presence in Berlin, he refused to ask the Bundestag to ratify the Moscow Treaty until the Soviets in 1971 signed an agreement assuring Western access to Berlin.

Brandt also signed a treaty with East Germany, although he refused to open diplomatic relations with the GDR. In another careful piece of apparently self-contradictory logic, he accepted the GDR but did not formally recognize it. Soviet leader Leonid Brezhnev, tempted by the prospect of West German economic aid, accepted Brandt's policy. When Walter Ulbricht insisted on full recognition, Brezhnev replaced him with Erich Honecker. In late 1972 West Germany and East Germany established official relations through liaison offices but did not exchange embassies. Within a year, more than two million West Germans had been permitted to travel to East Germany for family visits.

Where Adenauer had cemented ties to the West, Brandt cemented them to the East. By agreeing to accept Germany's division without recognizing the GDR diplomatically, he opened doors for West German diplomacy and for West German citizens. When he had finished, West Germany had ended its isolation and had begun to exercise its diplomatic influence in all directions.

When Brandt had to resign in 1974 because an East German spy was found to have been working in his office, his Social Democratic successor, Helmut Schmidt, continued the same *Ostpolitik*. He helped negotiate the treaty signed in 1975 for the Conference on Security and Cooperation in Europe that had originally been proposed by Leonid Brezhnev. To do that, he overcame the objections of U.S. president Gerald Ford and Secretary of State Henry Kissinger. At the same time, Schmidt expanded German influence in the West, especially in economic matters. Unlike Adenauer and Brandt, who had worked closely with the U.S. government most of the time, Schmidt often disagreed with American presidents from Ford to Ronald Reagan. He gave West Germany a more autonomous and influential position in the councils of the West without, however, abandoning Bonn's strategic anchor in NATO.

Helmut Kohl, who replaced Schmidt in 1983, continued active negotiations in all directions. He deepened Adenauer's links with West European integration, especially supporting European monetary union. He reaffirmed strong ties with the United States and with President Ronald Reagan. He also expanded Bonn's links with the Soviet Union and Eastern Europe, finding a willing partner in Soviet president Mikhail Gorbachev.

When the East German people rebelled against the GDR in November 1989, Kohl negotiated with the Soviet Union and the three Western occupying powers, France, Great Britain, and the United States, for German unification. After intense negotiations with the four occupiers and with a newly elected democratic government in the GDR, Kohl established the new united Germany on October 3, 1990.

Kohl thus re-created the German unity that Bismarck had won in 1871 but that Hitler had forfeited. He also began to permit German forces to venture outside the NATO area, sending them to join peacekeeping missions in states of the former Yugoslavia during the mid-1990s. But he acted only after making sure that Yugoslav public opinion would not perceive the German forces as successors to Hitler's Nazi occupation army in Yugoslavia.

Gerhard Schröder, elected in 1998 to succeed Kohl, concentrated German foreign policy heavily on European integration. He pursued European monetary union, helping to introduce the new European currency, the euro, into Germany and most of the European Union on January 1, 2002. He supported plans for EU expansion into Eastern Europe and offered a proposal for a European federal constitution. He also approved the expansion of NATO into Eastern Europe. He simultaneously established a good personal relationship with the new Russian president, Vladimir Putin, and helped to restructure Russian debt to Germany in order to improve Russo-German relations.

Schröder departed most radically from his predecessors by permitting German troops to venture even farther afield than Europe and NATO. As part of the U.S.-led campaign after September 11, 2001, against international terrorism, Schröder sent German ground forces into Afghanistan as peacekeepers. He sent German naval units to help patrol the waters off Somalia in order to stop any potential flight of al Qaeda terrorists into Somalia from Afghanistan.

The Record

The record of West German and then German foreign policy since the founding of the Federal Republic in 1949 shows a long ascending incline of expanding activity. It also shows a change in German areas of concentration.

During the early years, West Germany concentrated all its negotiating energy on establishing its own identity and on becoming part of an integrating Western Europe and the Atlantic alliance. It also began to open diplomatic links and commercial offices abroad. In those years, German negotiations concentrated on Germany itself and Berlin.

As the Federal Republic began to be widely accepted and supported, and as European integration widened, West Germany focused its diplomacy increasingly on helping to establish a secure and stable Western Europe. It also advanced the economic integration of the European Community.

Later, West Germany became an integrating force across Europe as a whole, trying to open and widen détente with Moscow, Eastern Europe, and East Germany. German political and economic figures also began to concentrate their energies increasingly on international monetary and commercial matters as West Germany became a global player in those realms. Finally, in 1990 the combination of Western and especially German political and economic policies led to German unification.

Since unification, Germany has widened its horizons. It has supported and helped to finance NATO enlargement into Eastern Europe as well as plans for EU enlargement. German forces have gone farther afield, operating in Asia and Africa as well as in Europe. They have functioned under the aegis of the United Nations, NATO, the West European Union (WEU), and the Organization for Security and Cooperation in Europe (OSCE). German military forces have joined UN peacekeeping operations in Central America, Cambodia, Somalia, Rwanda, the Balkans, and Afghanistan. Germany has also contributed funds to other UN peacekeeping efforts.

The Seven Points of German Negotiating Behavior

From the realities of geography and from its historical, philosophical, and economic origins, West Germany and later united Germany have distilled seven points that guide German diplomacy and negotiating style.

Some of those points began to emerge early, even during the first years of West German diplomacy after 1949. Others became discernible over time. All have been reinforced by German practice, especially in extensive negotiations with neighbors and more distant states.

Those points now remain in place as the main guiding principles for German diplomacy and German negotiating behavior.

The first three points are the unspoken but crucial aims of any German negotiating process:

❐ rehabilitation, and an honorable place for Germany,
❐ security and stability, and
❐ reliable associations and a sense of community.

The last four points are the negotiating means by which Germans try to reach those aims:

❐ conceptual logic,
❐ tenacity and persistence,
❐ logically framed compromises, and
❐ the use of economic assets.

The first three points emerge particularly out of Germany's wish to find some kind of stable existence as a united nation-state. The Germans have never experienced that kind of existence for long, having been either divided and dominated by others or united and trying to dominate others. They want to find the combination of democracy, unity, peace, and national pride that some others enjoy. They want to avoid the upheavals of the past two hundred years. They want to find a respected and recognized place, ending the long uncertainty about where Germany belongs.

Above all, Germans want to avoid isolation. They want to be part of a European and a global system and they want to use their diplomacy to that purpose. They strive for multilateralism, associations, and common action. They will enter negotiations to help them reach those goals.

The last four points provide the practical means to reach the first three. But they are not merely tactical, for they reflect German philosophy and German experience in the political, diplomatic, and economic worlds.

Unlike most other major nations, Germans cannot use military force to get what they want. They must use diplomacy. Therefore, they negotiate hard for what they want to get. They also use their economic assets to help their diplomatic position.

❐   ❐   ❐

Reinforcing all these points and attitudes, German negotiating behavior is based on a wish to find and retain friends. And most of all, it is based on the rock of serious purpose.

The next four chapters will illustrate how these points shape German negotiating behavior and any German diplomatic process.

2

The Principal Elements of a Negotiation with Germans

GERMAN NEGOTIATING BEHAVIOR has followed certain clear patterns for more than fifty years, since the founding of the Federal Republic of Germany in 1949. The seven points listed at the end of chapter 1 dominated West German negotiating behavior until 1990 and have since dominated the negotiating behavior of united Germany.

The first three points reflect Germany's strategic needs, including especially the wish for rehabilitation, acceptance, and security and stability in associations on which Germans can rely. German history has conditioned German political and economic leaders to believe that those principles will bring about the best possible results in any negotiation. The examples presented in this chapter will illustrate these points.

The last four points reflect German tactics. The examples in this chapter will show how German negotiators function in certain consistent and predictable ways, whether preparing for negotiations, actually negotiating, or implementing the results. A few examples will show that the German Democratic Republic in its day also drew on these points, helping to confirm the cultural origins of German actions.

This chapter will illustrate how all seven points function within the broad parameters of a negotiating process. The next chapter will discuss German negotiators and some tactics by which they may try to support their main principles.

Preparing for Negotiations

Germany prepares for negotiations very carefully, perhaps more carefully than any other state. But it does so in ways that differ fundamentally from the American model and that reflect the German search for consensus as well as Germany's federal structure.

The German government, like the West German government before it, first looks at the total context of an impending negotiation. The staff of the German Auswärtiges Amt (Foreign Office), or of whatever government ministry is to conduct the negotiation, will begin by listing the views that other governments may have expressed on the topics to be negotiated. It will highlight the views expressed by the other prospective parties to the negotiation itself. It will then study these expressed views carefully to learn what they may mean. It will analyze which other states may support or oppose Germany or German views in the talks. It will also analyze the international and European situation into which the negotiation may fit. Germany wants to position itself within a consensus if at all possible.[1]

After it has studied the views of others and has prepared briefing books summarizing and analyzing those views, the German government will define its own position and the goals that it wants to achieve in the negotiation. At this point, it will look at basic German interests and German objectives in the negotiation. It will then decide its negotiating position, trying to calculate how best to advance German interests in the context of what it expects others to do and say.

This stands in marked contrast to American preparation and to classic doctrine for preparing negotiations. The U.S. State Department or the White House usually begins by defining the U.S. national interest and setting U.S. objectives while also giving formal or informal consideration to American domestic attitudes. On the basis of that combination, the White House, the State Department, or any other pertinent U.S. government office will then define specific U.S. negotiating points. The United States, being a superpower, expects others to adjust their positions to

Washington's views and to U.S. domestic political attitudes. It can also shape the totality of the global environment.

German negotiators do not expect to shape the world. That is a part of the past that they do not want to repeat and could not repeat even if they wished. Instead, they need to work within the existing environment. They try to understand what others will say and how they can best advance their interests within that broad context.

Yet the German curiosity about the views of other states also reflects a German national interest, which is to devise a policy that will draw support. Germans do not want to be talking to themselves. Diplomacy constitutes their main route to establishing the kind of world they want. Unlike the United States, they cannot use force and cannot afford isolation. They want a diplomacy that will work with others.[2]

Sensitive to their country's need for rehabilitation and security, German negotiators generally want to take positions that advance their interests but that also keep them in tune with other parties to a negotiation. They will even recognize some of the needs of those that may oppose them, and they will especially try to understand the sentiment of their neighbors or other members of the European Union. U.S. government officials and business leaders who have negotiated with Germans have often expressed amazement at the degree to which German diplomats or businesspeople have studied the American and other positions. One State Department official said that he felt that the German negotiators knew the U.S. interests better than the Americans themselves did; an American businessman said that the Germans with whom he negotiated appeared to have a better understanding of his company's business and of its prospects than he himself had.[3]

Some senior German officials believe that this kind of caution may be overdone. One said that he felt frustrated that Foreign Office papers for some prospective negotiations did not give him as clear an analysis as he wanted of the German national interest because the German bureaucracy hesitated to articulate it. As a result, he thought that he did not have the best possible view of German priorities and had to define them himself.[4]

But the careful German survey of other views does not mean that a German negotiator accepts those views in advance. Far from it. Instead, the German Foreign Office or the negotiator tries to know and to understand those views in order to find the best way to serve German interests within the context of those views or by changing those views. Nor does it mean that Germans will give up on their interests even before a negotiation. But it does mean that German negotiators will try to find a position that will not foreclose a dialogue.

Germans prepare their positions methodically and thoroughly, often down to the most minute detail. They try to do so on a precise and logical basis, justifying each element of their position intellectually. They analyze carefully what kind of relationship with their negotiating partners they hope to gain through the talks. They also prepare detailed arguments that their negotiators can present in order to justify and advance the German position. This habit emerges from the long-standing German devotion to logical reasoning. As in German philosophy, the idea reigns supreme.

To prepare their logical argument and serve their central idea, Germans usually aim their preparations toward what they call a *Gesamtkonzept,* a comprehensive or governing concept. It expresses the fundamental aim that they wish to achieve in any negotiation. It combines their own national interest and what they perceive to fit with the interests of others. It connects the elements of their position and provides intellectual coherence. It also gives the purpose of the negotiation as a whole—including the views and objectives of others. Detailed negotiating proposals then flow from it and seek to express it.

Nothing in German preparation happens by accident. Like any other government, the German government may miscalculate what it should or can achieve in any particular set of talks, but it will not do so casually.

But no German negotiating team can sit in an ivory tower elaborating its positions. German diplomacy is no longer the province of a few aristocrats but that of many politicians, generals, economists, and diplomats. With rare exceptions, the process of preparing for a negotiation does not include only a few elite experts but instead usually involves what can be a massive bureaucracy of those who may have an interest in the negotiation. They may play different roles at different times and on different topics, and especially when they prepare for negotiations with the United States or with any other major state. Many ministries and many other offices may become involved in that preparation. Like anything else that Germans do, it proceeds in a studied sequencing of players and roles.

The chancellor has the largest single share of German state authority. Germans call this the *Kanzlerprinzip,* the notion that the chancellor directs the government. The chancellor has *Richtlinienkompetenz,* the authority to set the broad lines of his government's policy, and he cannot avoid that responsibility in the conduct of German foreign policy.[5] Article 65 of the German Basic Law expresses this principle. Often, when the chancellor has a particularly powerful personality, Germans speak of *Kanzlerdemokratie,* with the chancellor still bound by the rules of popular government even if he exercises his authority fully.

Like other principles and generalities, this one needs clarification and some modification. The chancellor in Germany now rarely rules through only one political party. And the chancellor is rarely foreign minister as well. Otto von Bismarck often kept the Foreign Office in the hands of a state secretary while he conducted the main lines of diplomacy from the Chancellery. So, briefly, did Gustav Stresemann during the Weimar Republic's financial and political crisis of 1923. Konrad Adenauer chose at first to hold both offices, although he later had a foreign minister. Adenauer also made sure that he himself controlled the most important relationships and negotiations, such as those with the United States, France, and the nascent European movement, whether he had a foreign minister or not. But it is now essential for the Foreign Office to have its own minister.

Throughout the existence of the Federal Republic, whether in its West German or all-German phase, the chancellor has ruled through a coalition government, and the foreign minister has mostly come from a junior coalition party instead of from the chancellor's own party. The chancellors and chancellor-candidates have usually come from one of the three major German political parties: the Christlich-Demokratische Union (Christian Democratic Union [CDU]); its Bavarian sister party, the Christlich-Soziale Union (Christian Social Union [CSU]); and the Sozialdemokratische Partei Deutschlands (German Social Democratic Party [SPD]). Since the late 1960s, German foreign ministers have come either from the Freie Demokratische Partei (Free Democratic Party [FDP]) or, as in Chancellor Gerhard Schröder's cabinet, from Bündnis 90/Die Grünen (usually called the Green Party or the Greens).

Although Article 64 of the Basic Law gives the chancellor the power to appoint his ministers, he must heed the wishes of his coalition partner in picking a foreign minister. The coalition partner has for decades wanted its leader to hold the high-image post of foreign minister and vice chancellor, although there is no constitutional or legislative requirement for that.

In a two-party coalition, the *Kabinettsprinzip* applies, with the entire cabinet and thus the entire coalition bearing broad responsibility for government policies, although the chancellor still has the most direct personal responsibility. Under that cabinet principle, the entire government must present a policy. No single party in the government can reject any part of a government's policy unless it is ready to leave the coalition. This principle has traditionally been strongest in Great Britain, where "cabinet government" began and where it is still practiced to the fullest, but it also functions in Germany.

Under the *Kabinettsprinzip,* each ministry functions in accordance with the *Ressortprinzip,* which holds a minister responsible for the functioning of his or her office. The foreign minister thus bears direct responsibility for foreign policy or at least shares it with the chancellor. When the minister handles things that interest the chancellor, the two must coordinate carefully if they want to avoid embarrassment and perhaps disaster. And it goes without saying that the Foreign Office, in preparing for negotiations, must keep the wishes of the chancellor in mind.[6] Before the coalition government is formed, the member parties reach a *Koalitionsvereinbarung,* a detailed agreement on the policies that the coalition will follow in foreign and domestic affairs.

Hans-Dietrich Genscher, foreign minister of the Federal Republic of Germany from 1974 to 1991, sometimes appeared to operate independently from the chancellor. He functioned within the broad parameters of German foreign and diplomatic policy, but he regarded and treated the Foreign Office as his personal domain. Even so, both Chancellor Helmut Schmidt and Chancellor Helmut Kohl, while giving Genscher broad authority, often stepped directly into the management of foreign affairs themselves. At times they acted without telling Genscher.

Chancellor Schröder and Foreign Minister Joschka Fischer, while occasionally differing on specific issues, worked more closely together than some of their predecessors, but the differences between SPD and Green Party foreign and security policies from time to time tested the coalition. Schröder almost provoked a split within the Greens when he supported the U.S.

bombing of Afghanistan in 2001. Only Fischer's prestige and the party's wish to remain in government held the Greens together in support of Schröder's policy.

The *Kabinettsprinzip* cannot be neglected no matter how the chancellor and the foreign minister may or may not cooperate. It has its roots in German history and culture. Germans believe that a collective body represents an important shield against the excessive accumulation of power by any single individual or party. They do not want to repeat the experiences that Germany had with Wilhelm II and especially with Hitler. Because Germans do not like to give any party a clear majority, they will often vote for minor parties just to keep a single party from becoming too strong. This may weaken the government on occasion, but the voters like it that way.

Most foreign policy coordination is conducted in meetings between the chancellor, the foreign minister, and the defense minister or their subordinates, not with the entire cabinet in session. But the *Kabinettsprinzip* can apply with full force when the German government prepares for an important negotiation or faces a particularly important international issue. Many ministers want to express their views and will insist on being able to.

To make certain that the *Kabinettsprinzip* will hold, the government parties often organize a *Koalitionsrunde,* a coalition meeting. There, German parliamentarians from the ruling parties sitting in the lower house, the Bundestag, gather to discuss the most important items on the foreign (or, at other times, the domestic) agenda. The meeting gives parliamentarians a chance to discuss major issues and develop common positions. Such meetings enable the chancellor and the foreign minister to present their thoughts on any particular negotiation that may have a wide political impact and to get a sense for what the parliament wants and what it may support.

When Germany prepares to negotiate a treaty, which must be approved by the parliament, advance consultations with the Bundestag and the upper house, the Bundesrat, become essential. Such consultations can limit the government's freedom of maneuver. They also risk leaks. Therefore, Chancellor Willy Brandt did not consult the parliament as he prepared for détente talks with the Soviet Union, Poland, and East Germany in 1969. He could not predict how the talks might proceed, and he wanted to be able to adjust his positions or call off the talks if necessary. He also wanted to keep the essence of the talks secret from the press and the opposition.

Nonetheless, Brandt did consult with a few important political and parliamentary figures in his coalition.

Despite the *Kabinettsprinzip,* one or another specific ministry will normally have responsibility for preparing any particular negotiation. The German bureaucracy will describe that ministry as *federführend* (literally, guiding the pen). In the first part of the negotiating process, that ministry will prepare the negotiations and shape the basic German bargaining position. Later, it will coordinate with other ministries and perhaps other offices as necessary to finalize the position. Most of the time, the Foreign Office will fill that role, but in some cases another ministry, such as the Defense, Finance, Trade, or Environment Ministry, will do it.

The *federführend* ministry cannot control everything connected with a negotiation unless the topic is within its exclusive jurisdiction. In some cases, as in arms control talks, the Foreign Office must consult closely with the Defense Ministry as it prepares the basic German position. The two will act almost as a single entity and will usually convene a joint diplomatic-military staff to prepare and conduct the talks. In international financial and monetary negotiations, as in the Group of Eight (G-8), the Finance Ministry will normally take the lead but with the Foreign Office and the German federal bank, the Bundesbank, very much involved.

To prepare for a negotiation, the *federführend* ministry must at some point bring together all the ministries that have a potential or real interest in the negotiation. Each must have a chance to express its views and influence the position. And any minister can go to the chancellor if he or she believes that his or her ministry's needs and responsibilities are not given enough weight by the *federführend* ministry.

The chancellor does not normally play a leading role in preparing a negotiation. He and the Chancellery will not become involved until the point at which definitive decisions on the German negotiating position need to be made or approved. They may, however, want to know where the preparations stand and they have increasingly become involved in the preparations themselves.

When ministers disagree, however, the chancellor or the Chancellery may need to conduct negotiations between them in a manner reminiscent of the U.S. interagency process. This frequently happens in negotiations regarding military and economic matters, such as European Union rules governing foreign and security policy or international financial agreements. The chancellor may need to make some difficult decisions so that the German position reflects the right combination of views.

For example, if an issue requires the chancellor to take a position at an annual G-8 summit, the chancellor may lead the government preparations early on. The German "sherpa" (from the name for a Himalayan mountain guide) who consults with other G-8 "sherpas" to prepare the G-8 summits normally comes from the Chancellery or the Finance Ministry. Chancellor Helmut Schmidt controlled virtually all international financial negotiations, from basic preparation through to the end, no matter who might have been finance minister or "sherpa" at the time. But other chancellors have left the early running or climbing to others.

Because of a chancellor's close interest in foreign affairs as well as ultimate responsibility for German diplomatic negotiations, the chancellors of the Federal Republic usually appoint a special assistant for foreign affairs within the Chancellery itself. That official has most often been a member of the permanent Foreign Office staff such as a senior professional diplomat.

But the chancellor may not want to be advised by a Foreign Office official. Therefore, some chancellors—like most U.S. presidents—have appointed a person of unquestioned personal and political loyalty instead of a career diplomat. Helmut Kohl, for example, named his longtime associate Horst Teltschik to the position, although a career diplomat succeeded after Teltschik resigned. Kohl was often accused of running diplomacy through a "kitchen cabinet" headed by Teltschik instead of through official government structures. Gerhard Schröder initially appointed Michael Steiner, who had a Foreign Office background but was known to be highly independent. After Steiner resigned in late 2001, Schröder selected less controversial senior Foreign Office professionals.

The Chancellery foreign affairs staff usually help the chancellor prepare for any negotiation by reviewing the draft negotiating papers for the chancellor and, if necessary, by chairing a Chancellery-level committee to help coordinate and decide the German position. This can become important in a coalition government because the chancellor may want to put a personal stamp on a negotiation rather than to have it managed by the Foreign Office alone.

With senior government leaders all over the world now traveling everywhere and telephoning one another as much as they do, no German chancellor wants to find himself with nothing to say when another chief of government raises a question regarding some negotiation. Needless to say, the Foreign Office may not see it the same way, wanting the chancellor to say exactly what the foreign minister wishes rather than something that has been worked out mainly or only with the Chancellery staff.

On rare occasions, the chancellor will take upon himself and his office the sole task of preparing a negotiation. The following are two well-known examples:

❐ Willy Brandt's Chancellery prepared the *Ostpolitik* negotiations with the Soviet Union, Poland, and East Germany during 1969–72 virtually by itself. Brandt thought the negotiations so sensitive that he wanted to control them from his own office. He mistrusted the Foreign Office because it had been in CDU hands for almost two decades and because the CDU bitterly opposed his policies. Brandt feared that the Foreign Office would not do what he wanted and might even leak his ideas and proposals to the opposition or the press. Thus Brandt used neither the *Koalitionsrunde* nor the Foreign Office to prepare those talks but instead consulted almost exclusively with his confidants Egon Bahr and Herbert Wehner.

❐ Helmut Kohl's Chancellery acted alone in preparing the 1989–90 unification negotiations with Moscow and others. Kohl had an objective similar to Brandt's, wanting not only to keep the talks under his own control but also to keep them away from the Foreign Office. He did not trust Foreign Minister Genscher, fearing that Genscher would be too accommodating toward Moscow on matters relating to NATO and specifically on having all of united Germany remain in NATO. He also regarded Genscher with some suspicion because of Genscher's position as leader of a rival party. Kohl wanted the preparations to be totally secret. He used only a few aides, and especially Teltschik himself, to prepare the German ten-point position on unification in late 1989. When Kohl edited the draft over a weekend, his wife retyped it. Kohl kept it secret until he announced it in the Bundestag on November 28, 1989, irritating some allies as well as Genscher by not telling them in advance.[7]

The Chancellery must also become increasingly involved in preparing negotiations on matters involving what the Germans call *Europa-Politik*, or policy toward the European Union. The topics governed by the European Union have come to impinge so closely on all aspects of German life that the chancellor and the Chancellery must deal with them directly.

As the German chancellor must increasingly handle European matters and must also speak personally with other heads of government from all over the world, the Chancellery office for foreign affairs has grown from a single state secretary in Adenauer's Chancellery to dozens of people. A large office, labeled Directorate-General Two, deals with foreign policy, security policy, and development policy. It is staffed by career experts from the Foreign Office and the Defense Ministry as well as by development experts and intelligence personnel. Like the U.S. National Security Council staff, it gets increasingly involved in details that had traditionally been handled by diplomatic specialists. The preparation for negotiations has become a part of that larger agenda.

◻︎   ◻︎   ◻︎

The chancellor and the foreign minister must almost always consider other interests than those of the German federal government itself. Because Germany's Basic Law has established a federal structure and because Germany has had a tradition of divided authority during much of its history and especially during the Holy Roman Empire, separate *Länder* (federal states) will insist on having a voice in many German negotiating positions. For example, such German states as Bavaria, Baden-Württemberg, and Rhineland-Palatinate, where the U.S. Army and Air Force had (and still have) major bases, often want more control over U.S. and other foreign troops stationed on their soil than the German federal government may be prepared to demand.[8]

Article 32 of the Basic Law provides that only the German federal government can conduct international negotiations, but Articles 23, 24, and 50 provide a basis for *Länder* participation in any negotiation that may affect their interests. The federal government must consult with the *Länder* if those negotiations might affect the powers or basic interests of the *Länder*. The federal government in 1957 concluded the Lindauer Abkommen

(Lindau Agreement) with the *Länder* to spell out the arrangements for this consultation, and that agreement, like several 1992 amendments to the Basic Law, reinforced *Länder* authority to play a role in any international negotiations that may affect their interests. The *Länder* do not want to let another Bismarck, kaiser, or Hitler represent *Länder* interests. They want to have some control over what a chancellor or foreign minister can say.[9]

The federal states can go so far as to negotiate some matters directly with local and regional authorities in neighboring countries such as France, Luxembourg, or Switzerland. Several *Länder* have their own representation offices in the capitals of neighboring states or the Baltic countries. Some scholars of German foreign policy have even spoken of the *Nebenaussenpolitik* (parallel foreign policy) conducted by several German *Länder,* especially those bordering on other states or having substantial international financial or commercial interests that they want to protect directly.

The *Länder* guard their authority in foreign affairs jealously, reflecting their suspicion of the central government. They have established a Standing Commission for the Assessment and Approval of International Treaties to help protect and enforce their authority. No single *Land* wants some Foreign Office diplomat who may have been born in another part of Germany negotiating its rights and interests away.

The German *Länder* thus become intimately involved in preparing any negotiations that directly affect them. They participated very actively and with great attention to detail in preparing German positions for the Status of Forces Agreement (SOFA) negotiations that the newly united Germany conducted in 1990–93. Those negotiations covered the rules governing the presence of U.S. and other forces stationed in Germany under the NATO treaty arrangement. They often dealt with very local concerns, such as the degree to which allied forces had to obey traffic regulations or pollution controls, and whether any infractions of the rules would be handled by allied or German authorities. The *Länder* insisted strongly on a role in the talks because they wanted allied forces to be subject to their local rules and answerable to their authorities. They helped to make it one of the most complicated German-American negotiations ever.[10]

The *Länder* become even more intensely interested in preparing any negotiations that might affect or involve the European Union, a realm in which the German search for multilateralism and community action particularly manifests itself. As the European Union has increasingly moved toward becoming a single market, EU rules and regulations impinge on such very minute details of life within member countries as labor, education, health, tax, social, cultural, and environmental regulations or conditions. The body of such EU rules and regulations, known as the Acquis Communautaire, now covers almost one hundred thousand tightly printed pages instructing the member states how they are to manage literally tens of thousands of matters that had earlier been handled on a local basis. Because the German federal system gives the *Länder* authority and responsibility in many of these matters, EU rules may directly affect *Land* legislation and regulation.

The European Union also allocates funds, known as the Structural and Cohesion Funds, to less developed areas and communities such as the former East German *Länder* and even to some relatively less developed regions in the former West Germany. The *Länder* want to make sure that those funds are not massively diverted toward the admittedly poorer states or regions that may be joining the European Union after 2004.

The *Länder* often suspect that the German federal government may try to usurp power over *Land* affairs by negotiating with the EU Commission or with other national governments on matters that will directly affect the *Länder*. The German federal government can then tell the *Länder* to follow the rules that it has negotiated with other countries. The *Länder* insist that the federal government cannot negotiate on such issues without their approval and without having them help prepare any negotiation. They also notify their representatives in the Bundesrat of any EU actions and plans.

The German federal government must in some instances even pass the authority for EU negotiations to a representative of the *Länder* designated by the Bundesrat. The federal government and the *Länder* sometimes disagree about whether that authority can be invoked in any particular negotiation, but the *Länder* will not yield it.

Each *Land* has its own office accredited to the German federal government in Berlin. Those offices have large budgets, large staffs, and wide-ranging agendas. Each *Land* also has an office accredited to the European Union in Brussels and a representative in the EU Committee of the

Regions. The *Länder* governments collectively now have more representatives in their various offices at the European Union than the German
federal government has. These offices have the assigned responsibility of
apprising the *Länder* immediately of any impending EU regulations that
may affect *Länder* interests. The *Länder* offices then lobby to make certain
that the Foreign Office as well as the European Commission takes German
Länder interests into account.

Any German government that prepares a negotiation affecting *Land*
matters without prior and ongoing consultation with the *Länder* faces
serious problems in the Bundesrat when the time comes for ratification of
whatever it may have negotiated.[11] The federal government must consult
the *Länder* as it prepares virtually any kind of negotiation with the European
Union, neighboring states, or states that station forces in Germany. Later,
of course, it must consult with the *Länder* as the negotiation proceeds.
Unlike U.S. senators, the members of the Bundesrat vote not on their
own account but as representatives of their *Land,* so the German government must persuade the *Länder* governments if it wants to obtain Bundesrat
approval for anything.

President Charles de Gaulle of France once expressed doubt during a
conversation with Adenauer whether the Federal Republic of Germany
could be considered a state in the classical sense. Accustomed to the highly
centralized French government structure, he thought that the German
federal system had gone too far, as had the authority of the German Constitutional Court to involve itself in political matters. De Gaulle could
perhaps not even understand how that might have been precisely what
Adenauer wanted—the historical pattern of federalism in the Holy Roman
Empire, not the centralism of the French Republic.[12]

The *Länder* are not alone in wanting a voice on *Europa-Politik.* Virtually
every ministry in the German federal government also wants to help prepare
and conduct negotiations in any EU forum. They have come to realize
that the EU regulations in the Acquis Communautaire can determine
what and how German ministries themselves can regulate.

To help coordinate European policy throughout the entire bureaucracy,
the German government has established a special Committee of State
Secretaries for European Affairs (Staatssekretärausschuss für Europafragen)
in the Foreign Office. The committee meets to help prepare negotiations

on EU matters, including the accession of new members. When necessary, the full cabinet will meet for that purpose. When Oskar Lafontaine was finance minister at the beginning of Schröder's chancellorship, he tried to move the European portfolio and the State Secretaries' Committee from the Foreign Office to the Finance Ministry. Foreign Minister Joschka Fischer blocked him in a bitter bureaucratic battle that the chancellor had to decide personally and that helped to convince Lafontaine to resign from the government.

The staggering and bewildering array of functions, interests, and responsibilities within the executive, the legislative, and the *Länder* can sometimes paralyze the decision-making process and place enormous demands on those who try to manage German diplomacy and negotiations. The complexities of the German system exceed even those of the U.S. federal model and go far beyond anything that one could imagine in France or the United Kingdom. Only the chancellor and the Chancellery's corps of foreign affairs specialists can sometimes cut through the bureaucratic tangle.

All these processes take time. If the chancellor demands a quick position, it can perhaps emerge within a week or less. But if Germany has to prepare for a major negotiation that involves the interests of multiple ministries and many or all *Länder,* the Federal Republic may well need more than one to two months to prepare for a negotiation.

Because of the complexity of the German bureaucracy, the Chancellery and the Foreign Office try to handle many urgent questions informally rather than formally, by quick interministerial meetings, telephone calls, or (increasingly) e-mail. These methods often permit quick action without requiring senior officials to take too much time and without producing masses of paper. Nonetheless, under the *Kabinettsprinzip* and the *Ressortprinzip,* the *federführend* ministry must still prepare a formal record and make certain that it is circulated to all concerned with proper descriptions of actions taken and of responsibility.

As the *Kabinettsprinzip* guides German positions, the labyrinth of German intragovernment relationships results in a delicate balancing act that can confuse and sometimes frustrate German's foreign negotiating partners.

The process also exacts a price on the German negotiators themselves. One retired German diplomat said that the work of preparing for a negotiation has become so complicated and so time-consuming that the German

delegation at an international conference or negotiation often arrives in a
state of exhaustion. They hope that their foreign negotiating partners will
be less difficult than their German colleagues.[13]

Opening Phase: Presentation

German negotiators usually regard their opening presentation as the most
important part of their negotiating process. They give it a great deal of
care and attention. The presentation follows a methodical path that moves
coherently and logically from the beginning to the end. It reflects the careful and comprehensive preparation that Germans offices have conducted.
It may take some time to complete.

The first item that Germans normally present is the philosophical basis
for their position, the *Gesamtkonzept* that they have prepared. This can be
quite elaborate, for they want to persuade their negotiating partners that
the position they will present makes sense from a logical standpoint. In
doing so, they reflect the importance of logic in German culture and intellectual history. One American who has negotiated several times with Germany said that he believed the *Gesamtkonzept* represented Hegelianism in
its fullest form.[14]

The *Gesamtkonzept* provides the foundation for a German negotiating
position. It presents the conceptual framework for the detailed points of
the position. It incorporates the essence of Chancellery, Foreign Office,
government, and *Länder* views.

Because German negotiators believe that they have fully studied the views
of others as they have prepared their position, they believe the *Gesamtkonzept* not only expresses their own national interest but also meets the true
needs of their negotiating partners and any others who may have an interest in the outcome of the negotiations.

Many negotiations with Germany in the past fifty years have really been
about Germany itself, no matter what issues the negotiators addressed
directly. Those negotiations have dealt inter alia with Germany's alliances,
sovereignty, troop levels, and relationship toward its occupiers. They have
thus focused, directly or indirectly, on one or more of the three main
objectives that Germany tries to pursue: rehabilitation, security, and community. A *Gesamtkonzept* may, therefore, directly or indirectly, address

Germany's search for an accepted place in the world or the role Germany is to play in various alliance policies. Germans often see the *Gesamtkonzept* as vital to their basic interests and goals.

The *Gesamtkonzept* normally incorporates, directly or indirectly, what the German negotiators, the German government, or a German company regards as the most important issue to be resolved in the talks. It will describe where the German negotiators want the talks to lead. It may reflect German concerns about sovereignty or German wishes for an international architecture. It also undergirds the entire structure of the German negotiating position. Every part of the position should fit into the total concept, and the total concept should in turn illuminate and justify every part of the position.

German negotiators focus a great deal of their attention on gaining acceptance of their *Gesamtkonzept*. They want that concept to be understood and agreed to, for it holds their detailed positions together. And they want others to accept not only their proposals but also the logic behind those proposals.

German negotiators normally present their specific positions after presenting their *Gesamtkonzept*. Those positions grow out of the *Gesamtkonzept* and detail how the concept applies to every aspect of what is to be negotiated. At this point, they may want to justify each element of their position on the basis of the logical outline that preceded the detailed presentation. Subtlety is not a German strong suit.

This detailed and coordinated method of presentation can sometimes leave the other party to the negotiation almost overwhelmed. One American negotiator said that in thirty years of diplomatic experience he found the German presentations to be the most thorough that he had ever encountered, even to the point of being intimidating. Another said that he thought the German delegation had researched every possible topic. He added that the German delegation not only clearly understood its own position but also assumed that it could foresee positions that the Americans and others might take. He added: "They knew the facts of our situation and what we might want better than we did ourselves."[15]

One American who negotiated several times with Germany during the late 1980s and early 1990s, as the Federal Republic was assessing its new international role and position, said: "The Germans come at you like a moving wall. They give you a total and unified presentation that covers everything." He added that the German position seemed almost elegantly comprehensive, with all parts flowing together from a logical foundation to the point of appearing impregnable. It was, he said, also like a "full-court press."[16]

□   □   □

When they present their positions, German negotiators do not normally play shadow games. Nor do they waste time. They state their views openly and plainly. They have no mysteries and do not try to keep their proposals opaque. What you see is what you get. They know what they want and they want their partners to know what they want. They do not try to present one position in order to advance another. They do not normally use devious tactics, such as presenting false issues as a tactical ploy while planning to drop those issues at the first opportunity. They simply outline, sometimes at staggering length and in painstaking detail, what they believe they can legitimately claim on the basis of the concept they have presented.

They also speak very directly, making no effort to conceal. A German lets you know what Germany believes it needs from a negotiation. Germans can sometimes be very blunt and to the point. One observer contrasted this habit with that of some other negotiators, such as Asians or some other Europeans, and concluded that Germans ranked near the top of the "directness scale."[17]

Germans often present their views on the basis of numbered points. The following examples from various German negotiations illustrate this as well as their readiness so speak directly:

□ Chancellor Kohl in November 1989, after the East Berliners had burst through the Berlin Wall, announced a ten-point *Gesamtkonzept* that would move Germany toward unification. He was careful to talk with some restraint because West Germany did not control the situation. He did not want to threaten Germany's neighbors or provoke its allies. He set no deadlines and suggested that the process might take a long time. And he stated that German unity, when it came, was to come within a European framework and within a new "peace order" that would not disrupt what he called "existing arrangements." But Kohl stated his views clearly. He left little doubt about where he wanted to go.

❐ Chancellor Brandt in 1969 had a *Gesamtkonzept* for better relations across the Berlin Wall. He wanted to end the human division of Germany. But he did not want to surrender the hope for ultimate unification, so he insisted that he would not give formal diplomatic recognition to the German Democratic Republic. He made no secret of his views. His concept made clear to the Soviet leaders that Germany would remain firmly within the NATO alliance and would continue to be a reliable partner of the West and especially of the United States, even as he provided for better relations with the Soviet Union and East Germany.

❐ By the same token, when Brandt met with the East German premier Willi Stoph in 1970, he listed twenty points that indicated that the Federal Republic's *Gesamtkonzept* would permit an exchange of representatives between Bonn and East Berlin even if he would not formally recognize the GDR. He knew by then that the Soviet Union would accept such a proposal even if the GDR would not. He did not want or need to make any false pretense.

Much of the time, of course, a German negotiator and the outline of a German position deal not with ten or twenty points but with hundreds and even thousands. The negotiations over the Status of Forces Agreement (SOFA) between 1990 and 1993 serve as an example of the multiplicity of issues that can arise. The negotiations had to cover the enormously wide range of privileges and immunities that members of U.S. and other forces stationed in Germany had enjoyed from the 1950s through the 1980s and that the German national and *Länder* governments wanted to curtail. Those included such matters as dependent visas, customs regulations, income taxes, sales taxes, vehicle registration and inspection, maneuver rights, firing practices at night as well as in daylight, traffic rules near military installations, and many other matters that could affect the rights and duties and even the way of life of different nationalities living and working together in one small area. Those privileges and immunities concerned not only the forces that had been serving in the relatively sovereign West Germany itself, but also those that had been serving in Berlin under occupation rules dating back to the Allied victory in 1945.[18]

Thus, for example, the German negotiators for the U.S. SOFA at first wanted U.S. soldiers to license their private cars through the German vehicle registration system and to have them inspected by German inspectors in accordance with German standards—which on some points differ significantly from the standards under which the cars had been purchased and inspected in the United States. A U.S. or British soldier unaccustomed to German regulations or the German language could not handle all these requirements and still have time to perform military duties.

As a further example of the complications that could arise, German negotiators wanted the American Red Cross (ARC), which handles family emergency travel and other personal crises for U.S. soldiers and their dependents abroad, to pay German taxes. The U.S. delegation could not accept such a demand because the ARC performs an essential nonprofit service for the military and could not afford to pay German taxes.

The SOFA negotiations also brought out a full array of delegates on each side, each with differing views. The U.S. delegation included not only State Department officials but also Defense Department officials and military officers, lawyers, representatives of families and other dependents, voluntary agency staff, and countless others. The German delegation included Foreign Office diplomats and officials from the Defense, Interior, Justice, Transportation, and Environment Ministries as well as *Länder* and local representatives. One American observed that the delegations on both sides were "huge" and that it sometimes seemed as if everybody had a lot to say. He added, however, that all the Germans did appear to be operating under the same *Gesamtkonzept*. Although the division of authority within the German federal system made it necessary for so many authorities to take part in the talks, they had all shared a clear common objective in German sovereignty.[19]

In an equally complex negotiation, the talks regarding compensation for victims of Nazi forced labor and slave labor practices, the German negotiators also came out strongly and clearly in their opening position. Even before the negotiations had begun, Chancellor Schröder had stressed in 1998 that he had become the first German chancellor of the postwar generation and that Germans of his generation did not need to feel personal guilt for the Nazi past, although they could and would never forget it. But German organizations, and especially private German corporations, faced class action suits in U.S. courts for having used foreign slave labor or forced labor during World War II when almost all young German men were in the Wehrmacht or on other duties tied to the war effort. Germany had to turn to the U.S. government to solve the problem posed by American lawyers filing those suits. Schröder might be of a new generation, but he could not escape a past he had not even experienced.

Nonetheless, Schröder insisted from the beginning on his *Gesamtkonzept* —the basic condition that Germany would pay no compensation unless it was assured of subsequent closure, which his negotiators termed "legal peace." From the German standpoint, this meant that the negotiations regarding compensation for slave and forced labor would be the last negotiations in which Germany would be asked to indemnify victims of the Hitler regime. After that, U.S. courts would accept no new lawsuits. To make sure of that, the U.S. government had to agree to intervene against any related claims or any subsequent claims that might be raised in U.S. courts against the German government or German companies.

The German companies involved in the negotiations, which included such major firms as Allianz, Daimler-Benz, Deutsche Bank, Volkswagen, and others, made the same demand. Many of them even refused to pledge any contribution to a potential compensation fund until they were assured that, under the "legal peace" agreement, they could not be sued again. They did not want to admit any responsibility in advance. And Schröder himself regarded the concept of "legal peace" as an important breakthrough. He considered it important enough that he spoke personally to President Bill Clinton on several occasions, and that his office remained in contact with National Security Advisor Sandy Berger throughout the negotiations.[20]

❐   ❐   ❐

German political leaders have continued to outline their positions in terms of a *Gesamtkonzept* and in very plain language during the new millennium. Thus, when the German government wanted to propose a new type of organization for the European Union, Schröder presented a *Gesamtkonzept* for a federal Europe before the European Council on April 6, 2000. A month later, on May 12, 2000, Foreign Minister Fischer outlined a similar *Gesamtkonzept* before the European Parliament. A year later, German president Johannes Rau reiterated the German proposal. They wanted to move the European Union away from an international organization toward a federal system. That concept included major changes in the European Union, increasing the authority of EU offices over individual states, creating a legislature of two houses, and dramatically reducing the authority of separate national governments, including their authority to exercise a national veto over EU decisions. No other major European state offered such a federal concept, with both France and Great Britain staking out positions that preserved significantly more power for the separate sovereign states. London and Paris were skeptical as to whether Schröder was even ready to yield so much power to the European Union. Nonetheless, they found themselves forced to address the far-reaching *Gesamtkonzept* that Schröder and Fischer had outlined.[21]

In all instances, German political leaders and the German negotiators stated their ultimate goals in their opening private or public presentations. They made no secret of either their fundamental intent or its logical basis. Their opening presentations may, indeed, at times have appeared overwhelming and intimidating, but they were not deliberately intended to have that effect.

A German negotiator wants to make German views crystal-clear. Germans at whatever level of government do not like to waste time by being mysterious. The German government wants to make sure that it uses diplomacy as effectively as necessary. It sees nothing to be gained from beating around the bush.

Middle Phase: Re-Presentation

As negotiations proceed, the principal German conceptual objective becomes ever clearer. The negotiators reiterate it as necessary. They hang their strategy on it and let it dictate the pace and direction of their talks. And they do not normally abandon that conceptual objective, although they may be ready to negotiate secondary issues more flexibly in order to win agreement on the basic objective.

German negotiators weigh the importance of various elements in their positions in accordance with the degree to which any particular element may express Germany's logical objective. If, for example, they want to gain respect for what they regard as their sovereign rights as part of the process of rehabilitation, they yield only slowly, and perhaps not at all, on those issues that most fundamentally reflect and protect those sovereign rights. Even if they concede any particular point, they try to do it in ways that protect their concept. Thus, when they made concessions that permitted allied forces to operate flexibly under the new Status of Forces Agreement, they still insisted that the allies seek permission to do whatever they wished to do. This preserved their principle of sovereignty but permitted the kinds of tactical adjustments that the Western forces needed. It helped make a success of the negotiations. It also kept Germany within a community of friends. It therefore satisfied all three principal objectives of German diplomacy.

A great deal may depend on the entire international situation. German negotiators generally want their talks to fit into whatever else may be happening in the world. They handled their détente negotiations in 1969–72 with one eye constantly on other East-West talks. They tried hard to make certain that the other talks proceeded successfully because that would help their own talks to succeed. And they planned their negotiations for a united Germany in 1989–90 to keep them in step with the views of U.S. president George Bush, who had become the strongest foreign supporter of unification. They also kept in step with Bush's negotiations with Soviet president Gorbachev. Chancellor Kohl knew that British prime minister Margaret Thatcher opposed German unification and that French president François Mitterrand had mixed feelings about it. Kohl needed Bush and Gorbachev to keep Thatcher and Mitterrand from opposing unification. He wanted to negotiate fast because he feared that Gorbachev might be deposed by the Soviet military. Kohl had to control not only German negotiating behavior but that of its main allies and main negotiating partners.

The same principle applied during the negotiations on intermediate-range ballistic missiles (commonly known as the INF talks) during the 1980s. Despite considerable pressure, the Soviet negotiators could not force Kohl to forgo deployment of the U.S. missiles. Kohl saw enormous international tension all around him as Washington and Moscow headed toward diplomatic confrontation and as NATO governments faced rioters in the streets. He decided that he had to act on the *Gesamtkonzept* of alliance loyalty. He continued to insist that West Germany would deploy the missiles. Soviet foreign minister Andrei Gromyko did not understand how much Kohl valued that *Gesamtkonzept*. Gromyko thus crafted a major failure for Soviet diplomacy.

As suggested earlier, the pace of any negotiation depends on how the appropriate German *Gesamtkonzept* is advancing. Because Germans absolutely want to achieve their conceptual objective, the negotiators must agree on that objective or must agree to modify it in mutually acceptable ways. That process can be tedious, depending on the importance of the topic.

One former U.S. diplomat who had negotiated many times with West Germany and later with united Germany said that Germans needed to reach what he called "their comfort level," a sense that they had achieved their basic negotiating objective without violating either their *Gesamtkonzept,* any basic principles, or any other commitments. He could not define that "comfort level" or predict when it might be reached, but he believed that he had come to grasp instinctively when he was close to reaching it. He then knew that he was close to a deal; he also knew that he was not close to a deal when he sensed that the required "comfort level" had not been reached.[22]

Detailed discussions can proceed even as negotiators continue to argue about the basic German demand. In fact, one way to solve a disagreement on a German *Gesamtkonzept* may be to agree on specific details in ways that meet the concept even if the entire concept is not accepted. Therefore, talks can and perhaps must continue even when it appears that they are going nowhere.

Thus, negotiations with Germany can proceed in different ways:

❐ In some cases, Germany's negotiating partners meet—or promise to meet—the basic German concept early in a negotiation. When Willy Brandt and Egon Bahr negotiated with the Soviet Union and East Germany between 1969 and 1972, the Soviets privately made clear to Brandt during early and informal discussions that they would not insist on full West German diplomatic recognition of the GDR. This met Brandt's single most important condition and opened the door to the détente negotiations. Soviet leader Leonid Brezhnev later had to remove East German leader Walter Ulbricht, who bitterly opposed any such concession, in order to bring negotiations with West Germany and the Western Allies to a successful conclusion. Brandt in turn had to accept some Soviet terms that he regarded as less important, such as establishing official—if not formal diplomatic—contact with the GDR. Brezhnev designated Erich Honecker, who had accepted Brandt's condition, as Ulbricht's successor, and the talks concluded.

❒ Similarly, the Western Allies decided to express respect for German sovereignty during an early phase of the SOFA negotiations of 1990–93. The allies, and especially the American negotiators, recognized that they would have to do that before they could make real progress on the multitude of secondary issues. By expressing their full recognition of German sovereignty, the allies showed that they would not try to preserve all the rights of the occupation but wanted only to concentrate on the very practical needs of foreign forces. Without early recognition of German sovereignty, the negotiations might have dragged on even longer as each minor point might have had to be negotiated as a test of German sovereignty.[23]

❒ In other cases, the basic German demand may not be met until all the other points have been negotiated. For example, during the negotiations on compensation for slave and forced laborers, Germany's demand for "legal peace" could not be met until June 2000, after the lawyers for slave labor plaintiffs had agreed to drop their cases against German companies. But the principal U.S. negotiator, Stuart Eizenstat, and the principal German negotiator, Count Otto Lambsdorff, needed to negotiate the amount of German compensation and the details of the compensation process before American lawyers agreed to drop ongoing suits. The concept of "legal peace" then still had to be tested in American courts. Under the negotiated terms, the U.S. Department of State could only then file a Statement of Interest, which would inform a judge that claims should be pursued not through American courts but through a foundation to be funded by German contributions. This statement met the demand of the German government and German companies for "legal peace," but it could not come until other points had been settled. In that case, the *Gesamtkonzept* came last, not first.[24]

The record of these and other West German and German negotiations since the founding of the Federal Republic of Germany in 1949 shows that Germany's partners in any negotiation must sooner or later deal with the German *Gesamtkonzept*. They do not need to accept it in its entirety. They can demand—and can expect to receive—concessions on other points. But they cannot evade the *Gesamtkonzept*. It represents a basic German interest and will continue to arise in one form or another throughout a negotiation. When Germans are building something new, or when they believe an important principle is at stake, they want it to come out right.

A *Gesamtkonzept* can pose a problem even for Germany and for German negotiators. It can become a straitjacket that may prevent them from getting an agreement or that may cost them some important opportunities.

For example, German chancellor Ludwig Erhard of the CDU and his foreign minister, Gerhard Schröder (not the later chancellor by the same name), were unable to make progress in East-West relations during the mid-1960s because of their insistence that they would not deal with East Germany at any level and on any topic. Brezhnev would not accept that and Erhard could not make a breakthrough. Germans elected Brandt as chancellor in 1969 because they believed that the CDU and Erhard had become trapped by their own concept at a time when voters wanted to move forward.

Later, when the Germanys were united, the German negotiators trying to dispose of East German assets had a *Gesamtkonzept* that West German industry could best revive the East German economy and should be given priority to do that. They did not permit enough investment by non-German companies and entrepreneurs, although those foreign companies would have brought more fresh air and essential innovation to the East German economic landscape. East German states had to pay a high price, taking longer to develop than they would have if more international investment had come into the area (see chapter 5).

❐   ❐   ❐

As a negotiation proceeds, German negotiators continue to advance their views and to speak directly to the issues before them. Directness does not normally mean rudeness, but discussions can turn contentious and difficult, although not personally insulting. One European diplomat observed that German negotiators could at times be arrogant and "pushy," especially if there were no representatives of the United States or major European powers in the conference room. But even U.S. diplomats and other negotiators recall clear and tough talk on both sides in several German-American negotiations over the past several decades.[25] Some German political figures, such as Chancellor Helmut Schmidt, even prided themselves on having a sharp style in dealing with other world leaders.

Germans do not necessarily spare Americans all the time, although they may offer more deference to such principal allies as the United States and France than to others. Americans who had helped to negotiate several agreements with Germany observed that German negotiators could be "infuriating" with their absolute certainty that they knew better than anybody else what should be done. The Americans resented having German negotiators assume that they knew the U.S. interests better than the Americans themselves and then telling the Americans what they should do.[26]

Despite their occasionally contentious style, Germans do not like to bring emotion into a negotiation. They react with almost visible discomfort to emotional speeches. They do not normally make such speeches and do not like to hear them. Given their experiences with nationalism and Nazism, they prefer not to engage in sloganeering or speechifying. They do not welcome it during a negotiation, especially if they think others are trying to use such speeches to seize a moral high ground and leave them below. The only German since 1945 who made emotional statements (concerning, for instance, family reunions) within or outside the context of a negotiation was Willy Brandt. Those speeches reflected his own convictions and may have helped his negotiations succeed because they persuaded others of his sincerity. But other Germans avoid such talk.

Although German negotiators can be tough, they normally speak in a reasoned manner and without bombast. They usually take care not to suggest that they are trying to force their negotiating partners into a corner. Nor do they want to sound like what people might claim to be "the Germans (or Prussians) of old." They listen very carefully and take full notes on all points. They try to maintain a positive spirit, presenting their ideas courteously even if they do not intend to yield quickly. One senior American lawyer who had not previously negotiated with Germans recalled after his first experience that the Germans had not been as "Germanic" as he had expected, although they had at times been totally unyielding.[27]

Several persons who have negotiated either for Germany or with Germany have described the German opening presentations and subsequent negotiations as *"Zielbewusst,"* which can be best translated as "purposeful" or, more literally, "conscious of their goal." German negotiators know what they want and will continue to try to attain that goal if they do not reach it on first presentation.[28]

As negotiations continue, German negotiators normally repeat and explain their positions and the logic of their views at considerable length. They also repeat their basic goals and justify them many times over in different ways. Moreover, different members of the German delegation, especially if they represent other ministries or the *Länder*, may also want to offer their comments. As in any bureaucracy, every member of the German delegation watches every other member. Nobody wants to appear weak before his or her colleagues. And they all want to get their views on the record to show their constituencies that they are fulfilling their assigned tasks thoroughly and professionally. Americans and Europeans who have negotiated with Germans complain that they have often found the process tedious, especially as some of the German negotiators tend to lecture.[29] The process can indeed become tiresome and often does. It can also become exhausting, for it can take weeks or longer for all the presentations and explanations on any point to conclude. But it must be regarded as unavoidable, for it represents the importance that German negotiators attach to their main concepts and also to their bureaucratic obligations.

German negotiators also always remember that Germany sits in the middle of a continent and that many states closely watch every move it makes, whether in diplomacy or strategy. Thus, German opening positions must take account of other obligations that Germany may have assumed or may be assuming. For example, German negotiators in the SOFA talks at first wanted U.S. soldiers to obtain visas or special entry permits if they wanted to visit parts of the former East Germany. Germans proposed such visas to meet Soviet concerns that U.S. NATO forces might move into East Germany.

Twenty years earlier, Brandt had been forced to keep American and other Western views in mind as he presented his opening position about détente to Gromyko. He did not always conduct his talks exactly as the Americans might have wished, but he still had to think about Washington even as he negotiated with Moscow. As the country in the middle, determined to maintain good relations in all directions, Germany could not take steps or enter into agreements that its allies or its close neighbors might find objectionable.

An American negotiator had two very direct experiences with this German attitude. In 1974, when he was negotiating with Germany and others about the Soviet proposal for the Conference on Security and Cooperation in Europe (CSCE), the German delegation suddenly changed its position on an important element of the negotiations. As he studied the new German position, he realized that it accommodated a Soviet view on human rights without at first appearing to do so. Ten years later, as he was negotiating on arms control arrangements for NATO and Warsaw Pact forces in Central Europe, the same thing happened. The German delegation had quietly shifted its position to satisfy a Soviet demand without telling the U.S. delegation. The U.S. negotiator assumed that the German government had in both cases been in contact with the Soviet government without telling its alliance colleagues.[30]

Middle Phase: Revision

When Germans enter negotiations, they want results. They have a definite purpose in mind for any talks and want to reach it if at all possible. They do not seek an agreement only for its own sake but often also want to use the negotiating process itself to establish or deepen a relationship. They will, therefore, try to avoid a breakdown in a negotiation. As part of their wish for a community of good relations, they recognize that they must make some concessions. But they want to make sure that any concessions they may make help them to reach their *Gesamtkonzept* or at the very least do not violate it.

Therefore, some concessions come easier than others. If Germans reach their *Gesamtkonzept*, they can relax on other matters.

One German diplomat explained that cooperation in itself offers Germany a positive good. Germans want to strengthen, not weaken, their links in all directions. They do not want to be isolated outside a community. Therefore, unless they have concluded that they cannot reach agreement at an acceptable cost, they try to find a compromise that will make an

agreement possible. Another German diplomat, confronting a particularly trying diplomatic agenda, observed, "we are doomed to success."[31]

Therefore, Germans will make concessions and compromises. But they
will not make them in a bazaar spirit, simply splitting differences to reach
an accord somewhere in the middle between competing opening positions.
Germans do not haggle, trying to find any compromise for its own sake.
Instead, they measure each concession carefully against their total concept
and their basic objective. They listen to reason and their partners' arguments, but those arguments must have a logical foundation. Progress can
be made. But that progress will come painstakingly and slowly as the Germans evaluate each move and weigh each argument.

Compromises can best be reached by negotiators offering suggestions
in private conversations outside the formal negotiating forum after the
positions have been exhaustively stated and possible areas for compromise
have become apparent. Either a German delegate or a negotiating partner
may say that he or she might be able to propose a change in position on
one or another point if the other side can change its position on another
point. They may agree to refer that back to the capitals for decision. The
delegations may find a framework for potential agreement on several
points out of a number of such discussions.

After some time and after enough potential areas of compromise have
been identified, German negotiators usually need to return to the political
or bureaucratic level that authorized the original position, most probably
to the Foreign Office. They need to explain in Berlin where the problems
lie. They also need to point out possible areas of agreement on a logical
basis. If they yield, they want to make sure that they yield in a way that
makes sense to the Foreign Office and beyond.

The negotiating delegation and the Foreign Office at that point become
agents for change in the German position. They may propose specific
modifications, arguing that those changes may make agreement possible
or at least more likely. They meet with different elements of the German
bureaucracy, sometimes jointly and sometimes separately, to analyze the
deadlock and try to reach solutions. This can take some time, for the German bureaucracy does not change its views easily.

The foreign minister, who may have followed the negotiations in very
broad terms, must then draw some conclusions about the compromises

Germany might need to accept. He will assume that Germany's negotiating partners are also evaluating potential compromises. The minister can decide on changes in the German position if the discussion concerns a matter purely for the Foreign Office. But most negotiations involve the interests of other ministries or *Länder*, and the Foreign Office needs to consult with them before the foreign minister approaches the chancellor with a recommendation. Those ministries and *Länder* probably know of the sticking points already, as their representatives are usually on the German delegation or are at least following the discussions closely. They may agree with the proposals made by the delegation or the Foreign Office or they may take their differences to the chancellor.

If the differences between the ministries warrant a full review of the negotiations, many meetings may follow and various ministries or others may prepare detailed papers. More probably, the matter can be settled with one or two decision papers for various ministers. Because German negotiators expect to have periodic consultations in Berlin, they try to keep the process as speedy and efficient as possible. But a great deal depends on the pace at which Germany or its partners want the negotiations to proceed and on the degree to which the potential compromises fit within the original *Gesamtkonzept*.

If the chancellor is to be consulted, the issue will normally first be raised with the Chancellery foreign policy staff. The foreign minister and perhaps others will address a recommendation to the chancellor on the basis of that consultation. The chancellor will then act on that recommendation, either agreeing or not.

German delegations, like others, usually want to interrupt a negotiation from time to time for consultations, especially if a lot of different German offices have a stake in the negotiations. They then meet again and the process continues. Because of that, the process of negotiating with Germany tends to move in stages rather than continually. But if the delegations are handling multiple issues, as in the SOFA talks, some delegation members may remain in continual negotiation on some topics even while others are at home discussing compromise formulas on other issues. Consultations with a variety of home offices may also proceed continuously. Even then, however, the delegation heads like to take breaks in order to consult at home.

Germans and their partners can normally reach agreement after several breaks if they are in the mood to make progress. When Egon Bahr negotiated the German-Soviet Treaty with Gromyko in 1970, he had to return to Bonn only two or three times for consultations. Later, Foreign Minister Walter Scheel had to go to Moscow to nail down some additional points. But agreement came relatively swiftly, in part because of a secret channel (see chapter 3).

Sometimes, when issues prove more complicated and the *Gesamtkonzept* seems out of reach, German negotiators will want to take more breaks for consultation in Berlin and elsewhere. The talks may continue longer. In the negotiations over slave labor and forced labor compensation, Germans and their partners had to meet in more than a dozen different sessions, alternating in Washington, Bonn, and Berlin, with delegations returning to their respective capitals and major financial centers between sessions. The Germans had to consult with business and political leaders.[32]

In the SOFA negotiations, senior U.S. and other foreign negotiators had to return to Bonn and Berlin every six weeks or so for three years. The German delegation had to consult with *Länder* offices as well, making the process particularly time-consuming. The German delegation also had to consult frequently in the civil aviation negotiations that were proceeding almost simultaneously. Those did not require as much *Länder* consultation, but discussions with Lufthansa and other air carriers.

The decentralization of the German system can prove particularly frustrating in such negotiations. Even with the best will in the world, the Chancellery and the Foreign Office cannot reach compromises without extensive efforts to bring others along. But informal contacts can proceed almost continuously even when the delegations are not in formal session.[33]

No matter how many variations may emerge, the process of negotiations with Germany usually remains the same no matter how often it may repeat itself: a painstakingly thorough and challenging initial presentation based on the *Gesamtkonzept;* prolonged discussion; deadlock on at least some points; proposals for compromise; an agreement on one or several points; long consultations with the various elements of the German government and other institutions; some progress; another deadlock; further movement from there; and finally, perhaps—but not always —agreement. And Germans usually insist that any agreement be based on a carefully negotiated conceptual logic. That element distinguishes negotiations with Germans from negotiations with others.

Unless both sides are in a desperate hurry to reach an agreement, a negotiation can sometimes continue for years. Some arms control negotiations in which Americans, Germans, other NATO members, and Soviets participated even went on for decades. But the Germans did not bear the main responsibility for the delays. They often tried to reach compromise formulas in accordance with their wish to hold their alliances and their friendships together.

A lot may also depend on the intensity of the emotions that a negotiation evokes. In the negotiations on compensation for Nazi slave and forced labor, many Americans involved in the talks believed that Germany had a moral obligation to pay. The Americans would not yield easily. The East European states from which the laborers had come, such as Poland and Ukraine, shared that belief. So did some German firms. But other German firms insisted that they had no responsibility, either because the Nazis, not the firms, actually drafted the slave laborers or because they were not legal successors to the firms that had used slave labor. Some of the German firms complained that American lawyers were using a form of extortion, compelling the German companies to pay if they wanted to continue to do business in the United States without constant fear of being sued. The Americans rejected those assertions. Emotions ran high on all sides, and some of the sessions proved very difficult for all the parties concerned.[34] One American negotiator later wrote that those negotiations had been the "toughest, most painful and most emotional" he had ever attended.[35]

Suspicions also ran high. Americans often regard German lawyers as excessively pedantic, but Germans often regard American lawyers as excessively inventive. The Germans feared that American lawyers would continue finding new avenues for litigation no matter how many had been closed off. They insisted on trying to seal all possibilities for such litigation. Because of such suspicions, as well as because of conflicting views on all sides, including those of the states from which the laborers had been forcibly recruited, the talks ran longer than most other negotiations.[36]

Schröder had another important *Gesamtkonzept* at stake, one he did not reveal in the discussions. He not only wanted to use the slave and forced labor compensation talks to free Germany from the threat of future litigation but also wanted to use them to remove a problem that could poison Germany's relations with Central and East European states. He was thinking not only of rehabilitation but of a place for Germany in a wider European community. He had to solve a legal and a political problem, but he wanted to do it in the context of Germany's desire to be open in all directions.

The same desire for a wider European community framed Schröder's position in the EU constitutional talks. He wanted to help reorganize Europe on a foundation that would resemble what he regarded as the successful German model. But he wanted to do it without alarming other European states that Germany was taking over. So he spoke in public of federalism, a sound and widely accepted principle. But he reassured other European leaders, such as French president Jacques Chirac, that he would not challenge traditional notions of sovereignty provided that the European Union could move toward further levels of community cohesion and action.

❏   ❏   ❏

Thus every German position contains both a *Gesamtkonzept* and the seeds of a compromise needed to reach it. Schröder and Fischer made their speeches knowing that EU negotiations would take a long time and that they would not get the exact federal system they wanted. They still chose to speak because it was the only way to get discussions that would reveal the compromises needed to reach the *Gesamtkonzept*.

There are, however, two exceptions to a lengthy process: when the chancellor or the foreign minister decides that Germany needs an early breakthrough and is prepared to use all his prestige to force the complex German system of divided authority to act; and when no *Gesamtkonzept* is in question. In such cases, German delegates try to settle an issue or to break a deadlock quickly. That happened not only in 1989–90, when Chancellor Helmut Kohl negotiated for German unity, but again in 1990–92, when Kohl wanted to take the German deutsche mark into a common European currency. It also happened when Germany negotiated on NATO enlargement in the mid-1990s. Kohl wanted NATO enlargement and could act quickly because he saw it as the expansion of an alliance that he already knew and valued. He also thought that Germany would thus have a wider radius of influence. He would have moved much more slowly if he had thought that NATO expansion changed the fundamentals of the alliance.[37]

In most negotiations with Germany, therefore, no matter what the form, progress can and normally will come. It does not come as fast as some might wish or hope, but the German wish for diplomatic success will promote it.

German realism and wish for diplomatic success have their roots in the same German experience during the Holy Roman Empire that produces German tenacity. In the turmoil of German history, with foreign invasions and internecine strife all around, the people wanted peace and agreements that would reach peace. That still remains true.

As a result, German negotiators will accept practical solutions for problems if such solutions appear reasonable. They will not cast about for greater glories to be achieved. But they will want to have those practical solutions framed within the *Gesamtkonzept* that they pursue throughout a negotiation. They will negotiate tenaciously, but they will adjust their views over time if it will produce agreement and fits within their concept of where they want to go.

For example, environmental issues loomed large in the SOFA negotiations cited earlier. The German negotiators wanted U.S. forces to pay for the ecological damage they had done around U.S. bases and training areas; the Americans replied that German forces had used the areas before the Americans did and should themselves be responsible. Finally, they reached agreement that each would pay for its own share of the damage. The Americans and others also promised to exercise greater care in the future. In another dispute, many German communities wanted U.S. aircraft to cease flying without giving long advance notice, a demand that the Americans rejected as impracticable. The compromise arrangement required notice—important for German sovereignty—but left considerable flexibility. The German negotiators could have found many justifications for breaking off the talks if they had wanted to do so, but they did not. They wanted to win some important points of principle, which they did win. They and the Americans, who also wanted agreement, then found mutually acceptable terms.[38]

But that does not always happen. President Lyndon Johnson tried for three years, from 1965 through 1968, to press Chancellor Ludwig Erhard to fund the stationing of U.S. forces in Germany by making "offset" payments through the purchase of U.S. weapons and by using other means to strengthen the U.S. dollar. He also wanted Erhard to send German forces to Vietnam. Erhard never agreed to either. During the mid-1970s, President Jimmy Carter tried to do the same, wanting Chancellor Helmut Schmidt to pay "offset." Schmidt, like Erhard before him, refused. Andrei Gromyko tried to force Chancellor Helmut Kohl to forgo the stationing of NATO medium-range missiles in Germany during the 1980s. He also pressed Kohl to distance himself from President Ronald Reagan's plans for the Strategic Defense Initiative. Kohl would not do what Gromyko wanted in either case. Therefore, German governments cannot be counted on to make compromises if they do not believe such compromises fit within their *Gesamtkonzept* or within their traditions.

❏   ❏   ❏

Negotiations with Germany will thus normally lead to a mutually satisfactory conclusion. But that is far from certain. Nor will a successful conclusion come quickly. It may require a very precise review of all the issues at stake as well as a mutual understanding about the very purpose of the talks themselves and the relationship that they are intended to establish or deepen. There is no guarantee against frustration nor any guarantee of success, and there is even less guarantee of swift action. But German diplomats and German political leaders do not like to call off a negotiation once they have started it, and it pays both sides to keep trying.

The German Democratic Republic

A West German diplomat who had conducted many negotiations with the East German government observed that he often felt rather eerily that he was seeing a mirror image when he negotiated with GDR officials. He said that he came to believe that there were major similarities in East and West German negotiating behavior. He commented that he had never gone so far as to wonder whether those similarities reflected a common German cultural heritage but that it might well be possible.[39]

His talks with the East Germans, he added, took place mainly during the late 1970s and the 1980s, after the heavily ideological style of Walter Ulbricht and the early creators of the SED had passed from the scene. The persons with whom he met often seemed more pragmatic than the early Communists had been. They could discuss practical problems, such as West Berlin passes to East Berlin or mutual trading arrangements, in calm and realistic terms without any anticapitalist diatribes or accusations.

U.S. diplomats have reported the same experience. Those who had spent some years in West Germany and had then gone on to negotiate with GDR officials during the 1980s, after Washington had established relations with the GDR, found remarkable similarities. They encountered a serious and sober style, considerable persistence, a readiness to make agreements but only after prolonged and detailed debate, and a generally professional, if occasionally difficult, atmosphere. The East Germans tended to talk longer than their West German counterparts. They also tended to use the Marxist rather than the Hegelian dialectic, a subtle distinction that might be lost on most of their interlocutors. But the Americans otherwise found East and West German negotiating behavior remarkably similar.[40]

Even during Walter Ulbricht's time, and even in negotiations with the Soviet Union, the GDR paralleled some elements of the West German style. Soviet and East German documents show that Ulbricht himself would make the same kind of lengthy and detailed presentations to his Soviet or East European negotiating partners that the West Germans would make to their Western negotiating partners. During the crisis that led to the building of the Berlin Wall in August 1961, Ulbricht spoke for almost four hours during a meeting of the Warsaw Pact leaders in order to explain why he needed to build the wall. Ulbricht staked his regime's existence on that presentation because Soviet leader Nikita Khrushchev had told him that Moscow would let the wall be built only if the East Europeans agreed to it. The written record of Ulbricht's presentation showed that he outlined a *Gesamtkonzept,* the importance of ending the allied "revanchist" misuse of West Berlin, and that all his subsequent points fitted into that *Gesamtkonzept.*[41]

Adenauer and Ulbricht matched each other on another point. During the Berlin Wall crisis from 1958 to 1962, they each made life very difficult for their principal ally. Adenauer challenged U.S. secretary of state John Foster Dulles's readiness to designate East German traffic controllers as "agents" of the Soviet Union in order to reach agreement with Khrushchev on a new control system for the access routes to West Berlin. And Adenauer directly challenged President John Kennedy's policies during the Berlin crisis, not only by leaking a paper he received from Kennedy (see chapter 3), but also by constantly pressing Kennedy to support West Berlin more firmly. On the other side, Ulbricht wanted Khrushchev not only to let him control the access routes to Berlin but even to control the air corridors, a demand that Khrushchev rejected because such a step could have provoked a major crisis and perhaps even a war between the United States and the Soviet Union.[42]

Some early East German political leaders differed from West Germans in their attitude on diplomacy. The first East German leaders, and especially Walter Ulbricht, did not share Adenauer's yearning for German rehabilitation. They wanted a totally new historical departure. Ulbricht wanted recognition for the German Democratic Republic more than any all-German objective. He believed that such recognition would start Germany on a wholly new road, different not only from Hitler's but from the entire German tradition. Because of that, Ulbricht's negotiating positions sought not agreement but deadlock. He would make an opening presentation that resembled the West German's in its thoroughness and toughness, but he would then avoid making the concessions that might be necessary to reach agreement.

On that basis, the initial papers prepared by the SED Politburo for the inner-German negotiations in 1971 show that the SED planned to make not a single concession on any significant point. Ulbricht wanted recognition on his own terms and no other.[43]

Ulbricht's uncompromising negotiating behavior carried him comfortably through the early decades of the GDR and the Cold War because the Soviet Union did not want agreements with the West about Germany. The early Soviet Cold War leaders, Stalin and Khrushchev, preferred to have their own part of Germany rather than to have dealings with the other part of Germany. Soviet attitudes changed, however, when Moscow needed money and when the East German economy began to show signs of strain. Brandt understood what he needed to do at that point. He used West German economic power to tempt Brezhnev into agreements that would force the GDR to change policy. Ulbricht would not accept that and Brezhnev removed him.

East German negotiators always knew that they did not control their own destiny. The Soviet Union decided what would be done and how matters would be settled. Moscow would, when it wished, tell the East Germans what to do. The same West German diplomat who saw parallels between East and West German negotiating behavior recalled how an East German gave an extensive presentation of GDR views during one particular negotiation but then fell silent when the West German told him that a Soviet official had told him something very different.

An American diplomat negotiating with an East German during a conference on European confidence-building measures during the 1980s remembered a similar incident in which an East German representative gave him a long list of conditions that the United States had to meet at the conference. When the American remarked that the Soviet representative he had just met had not given him a similar list, the East German dropped the subject.[44]

Willy Brandt recalled that, during his meeting with East German premier Willi Stoph at Kassel in June 1970, he at one point told Stoph that he could not comment on a point that Stoph had raised because Egon Bahr was in Moscow at that moment discussing the same point with Gromyko. Stoph showed visible annoyance that Moscow negotiated about East Germany with West Germany, but he realized that he had to do what Moscow decided and that Gromyko, not Stoph, would decide the East German position.[45]

Later, when Bahr encountered a total deadlock with his East German counterpart, Michael Kohl, about whether or not the inner-German treaty should make a reference to the German "nation" as Brandt and Bahr wanted, Bahr went to Moscow to discuss the matter with Gromyko. They reached a compromise formula that used the word, although in a different context. Within weeks, Michael Kohl had endorsed the compromise, although he had vetoed it before Bahr had seen Gromyko.[46]

Closing Phase: Cutting the Deal and Implementing It

At some point, often long after it would appear that a deal should have been cut, the German negotiators will accept an agreement. They want it to follow the *Gesamtkonzept* of their position even if it does not conform to all the details. And they are prepared to accept practical compromises to obtain an agreement.

Virtually all agreements that Americans, Russians, French, British, and others have negotiated with Germans over the past fifty years have been made possible by such compromises. West Germany and later Germany accepted those compromises in the interests of stability and multilateralism, but in each case the Germans also advanced their own *Gesamtkonzept* for rehabilitation and the gradual accumulation of greater influence within the Western alliance. In each case, both sides received what was most important to them. And in each case, compromise could be reached only after prolonged negotiations and under some time pressure.

❑   ❑   ❑

On implementation, Germans take pride in being as good as their word. They generally carry out their agreements fully and to the letter, although the exact interpretation of those agreements may be subject to dispute. Some agreements that leave few open political issues but mainly require new rules to be issued to the bureaucracy, such as consular conventions or the like, can be carried out smoothly and advantageously for all. For other agreements, differences of interpretation may well remain. One American diplomat observed that Germans, like others, carry out agreements "as they interpret them."[47] Nonetheless, persons who have negotiated with West Germany and later Germany have commented unanimously that Germans will respect agreements. Unlike Soviet leaders in their day, Germans do not try constantly to reinterpret agreements in ways that appear intended to reopen or invalidate previous negotiations.

Some compromises can present genuine future complications. For example, German and U.S. negotiators in the SOFA knew very well that the compromise they reached on responsibility for environmental damage would pose tricky problems of implementation. It would be almost impossible to decide whether the German or the U.S. military had caused some particular damage around an installation.

But the compromise was reached under great pressure to meet a deadline as delegates on both sides raced around their respective capitals to get approval. So, wanting agreement, they decided to leave it for others to make it work. And despite differences in interpretation, the agreements are generally implemented to good effect.

Several other parts of the SOFA have also left issues that will provide room for debate for years. The compromises satisfied the basic needs of the Germans and their allies, honoring German sovereignty while providing a practical solution for the Americans and others. If each side wanted to accuse the other of bad faith, each could certainly have done so. They could still do so now, but the Germans appear more disposed to settle the issues than to inflame differences.

In other cases, as in the implementation of the slave and forced labor compensation accord, differences of interpretation can be more complex and take longer to resolve. Some issues may linger for years, in part because many different parties with many different interests took part in the negotiations and may have left those negotiations with their own understandings of what should be done.

But agreements with Germany do function. Germans and their partners do the best they can to work out the details of implementation in a practical manner and move on from there. Germans do not cast the fundamentals of an agreement into doubt once it has been signed. They also want to cement a relationship and do not want to jeopardize that relationship. Once the work is done, Germans want to move on to other matters and new relations.

◻   ◻   ◻

Despite the negotiators' mixture of gladness and relief after they have successfully concluded a negotiation, and despite the usually satisfactory implementation, they do not easily forget the hard work involved in reaching agreement. One American diplomat who had negotiated twice with Germany during the 1990s observed: "When you finish a negotiation with Germans, you know you have been through a real negotiation."[48]

3

The German Negotiator
Personality and Tactics

As NEGOTIATIONS PROCEED, the German delegation and German negotiators normally follow a recognizable set of tactics. They exhibit distinct behavior and follow distinct patterns that differ from those of other negotiators. And while certain forms of behavior may vary from individual to individual, their general style can be predicted with considerable certainty.

The German Negotiator: Training and Style

Most German negotiators work under direct instructions from the Foreign Office, although other ministries often play roles in writing the instructions and may also send delegates to the negotiating sessions. As discussed in chapter 2, Defense Ministry officials or officers generally join strategic negotiations and discussions about arms limitation. Finance and Economic Ministry officials generally join negotiations about economic issues, although the European Union may take the lead in such talks (see chapter 5). And *Länder* representatives will take part as well if the negotiations deal with matters that might affect one or another *Land*. But most of the negotiations conducted by Germany are in the hands of the Foreign Office.

Unlike the U.S. Department of State, which fills most senior and many midlevel State

Department positions and most important ambassadorships with political appointees, the German Foreign Office holds to the classical and still current European tradition of a professional diplomatic service. Normally, only three senior Foreign Office officials come from the political world: the foreign minister himself, who has since the late 1960s been the leader of the minority party in the German ruling coalition, and two ministers of state, usually one from each party in the coalition. The foreign minister can assign to those ministers of state whatever areas of authority he and they may choose. Two other senior officials with the rank of state secretary are members of the career diplomatic service and are normally assigned to a major ambassadorship after finishing their duties as state secretary.

The foreign minister usually asks the two professional state secretaries to divide the main responsibilities of the Foreign Office between them, with one or the other handling Europe, the United States, Russia, Africa, Asia, and/or the United Nations or other topics. Both also keep track of negotiations going on within their assigned areas of responsibility. The foreign minister and the state secretaries rely on professional German diplomats for their negotiating teams.

Depending on the importance of any particular negotiation, the foreign minister and on rare occasions the chancellor may chair the German delegation for the opening session and perhaps for the two or three immediately following sessions. Otherwise, the foreign minister may ask one of the ministers of state to initiate the negotiation. After that, professional diplomats usually conduct the talks, although exceptions have been made.

Below the ministers and secretaries of state, the German career diplomatic service holds virtually all the positions at the Foreign Office, at German embassies, and on German delegations. There are such rare exceptions as the coordinator for German-American Relations, who has normally been chosen directly by the chancellor and who may report directly to the foreign minister and the chancellor. Werner Weidenfeld, a leading German intellectual and a friend of Chancellor Kohl, held that position under Kohl. Karsten Voigt, an important figure in SPD politics since the 1960s, has held it under Schröder. They are the exception, not the rule, and they personify the importance that German chancellors generally attach to relations with the United States. The Chancellery also has an advisor for German-French relations. But neither the coordinators nor the advisor would be expected to conduct a negotiation, although they do sometimes take part in consultations.

Germany does not have the same body of available "in-and-outers" as do Great Britain and the United States. There is no German cadre of persons who regard themselves as the guardians of the national interest, as the American "Establishment" did during the early days of the Cold War. Few men or women below the very top political level float between senior positions in government, business, law, or university life. Men and women generally stick within one bureaucracy or one company throughout their careers, rarely jumping from one world to another and even more rarely jumping back and forth every few years. There have been exceptions, as when Willy Brandt brought a number of outsiders into senior Foreign Office positions because he thought that the bureaucracy would not serve him and his SPD government properly after having served the CDU/CSU for almost twenty years. But they are rare.

Brandt also turned to a long-standing friend and confidant, Egon Bahr, when he wanted to negotiate détente with the Soviet Union, Poland, and East Germany in 1969–72 (see chapter 2). He and Bahr thought alike. But Bahr made West Germany's politicians and allies nervous because they did not believe that he told them what he was really doing. Brandt later had to call on Foreign Minister Walter Scheel and some professional diplomats to conclude the talks in Moscow, in part because he wanted to reopen some of the issues on a more favorable basis and also because Scheel's participation, with his reputation as a solid political figure, would improve the chances for Bundestag ratification and Allied support.

By the same token, Chancellor Helmut Kohl used his own long-standing advisor, Horst Teltschik, to conduct the negotiations in 1989–90 with Mikhail Gorbachev and the Western Allies for German unification (see chapter 2). Kohl also wanted a person he trusted, but he had reservations about Foreign Minister Hans-Dietrich Genscher and about Genscher's top Foreign Office appointees. Kohl later chose a close CDU political associate, Interior Minister Wolfgang Schäuble, to conduct the unification talks with the GDR. Kohl wanted his CDU party to get credit for unification. Like earlier chancellors, Kohl had never used the Foreign Office for relations with the GDR because those relations were not an international but an intra-German matter.

More recently, Chancellor Schröder in 1999 asked Count Otto Lambsdorff, a senior FDP figure of high international and national standing, to lead the German delegation for negotiations on compensation for victims of Nazi slave labor and forced labor. Lambsdorff had the experience and sensitivity to understand the complex political and emotional issues at play in Germany, the United States, Poland, and elsewhere. He knew many American political and economic leaders through his years on the Trilateral Commission. He also understood the thinking of the German business leaders who had to pay the compensation and who after the Cold War found themselves dealing with ever broader revelations about the extent to which German business firms had used slave and forced labor during World War II.[1] Most important, Lambsdorff could carry the kind of political responsibility that the German public and the Bundestag demanded for such a difficult negotiation.

In all of these cases, the negotiations might have failed if the respective chancellors had not picked special envoys. Bahr, Teltschik, Schäuble, and Lambsdorff had qualifications that made them better suited than any other possible negotiators for their very specific tasks.

Such special emissaries are the exception, however. For most negotiations, especially after the opening sessions, Germany sends a team from the professional diplomatic service. The diplomats may be supported by specially designated technical or legal experts as well as by delegates from other ministries or from the *Länder* whenever necessary.

An American observer of German politics and diplomacy criticized the German failure to have a cadre of "in-and-outers" available on call. He indicated that at times such outsiders would be necessary. He wrote of "Germany's Underwhelming Political Elites."[2] But German political leaders prefer to use a professional service because they can trust and control it.

Therefore, as various détente talks with Moscow, Warsaw, and East Berlin proceeded to more structured and more detailed discussions during 1971 and 1972, the Foreign Office increasingly managed the day-to-day negotiations, although the Chancellery still felt free to intervene. Later, in the 1989–90 German unification talks, the professionals at the Ministry of the Interior and the Ministry of Justice also had to become involved at a certain point in order to make sure that the terms fully complied with the West German Basic Law and other legislation.

German professional diplomats, who usually do the main body of the work on any German delegation, negotiate precisely and painstakingly. They proceed with deliberation, trying to carry out their instructions exactly and also trying not to arouse controversy either within or outside the government. They do not seek dramatic breakthroughs. They ask for new guidance when necessary. They pay careful attention to the needs and interests of other ministries or interested *Länder* and—as especially appropriate in negotiations about European Union issues—of other European states. And they do not deviate from the *Gesamtkonzept* that the chancellor or foreign minister has set.

Professional German diplomats are dedicated and serious—a quality that Germans particularly prize. They rarely make mistakes. They are sober, punctilious, and formal. Many have legal training and an attachment to legal norms and values, and many members of a German negotiating team may come from the legal side of the Foreign Office instead of the political side. They often reflect that in their presentations.

Observers have different opinions about the abilities of the German diplomatic service. Many German politicians and senior German officials complain that German diplomats are too hidebound, narrowly focused, and unimaginative. They also complain that too many German diplomats have legal training and thus do not sufficiently understand the political aspects of a negotiation.[3]

But one senior German political figure who had followed diplomatic matters for decades and had watched many international negotiations said that he thought the cadre of German professional ambassadors that he had observed during the 1970s and 1980s matched the diplomatic corps, professional or otherwise, presented by any other state during that time. He said that the German professional diplomatic corps had contributed significantly to the atmosphere of responsibility and reconciliation that made unification possible.[4]

The days of dynastic German foreign policy, when every diplomat came from the aristocracy, passed into history a long time ago. German career diplomats do not, as in the days of Prussia or the united German Empire, come from high social station or from any particular class. Perhaps a few have descended from the old aristocracy and from distinguished families, including the old Prussian service nobility, although more of those descendants have gone into business and finance. Some have a *von* before their family name to reflect their lineage, but some German diplomats entitled to it do not even use it. A number may have had parents in the diplomatic service. Name recognition may give some diplomats a slight advantage in their careers and in their foreign contacts, but it does not guarantee the success it once did.

Most German diplomats come from the broad German middle class and a traditional German social and educational background. As German society has become more homogenized than in the days of the kaisers, they are likely to come from almost anywhere. The Foreign Office has made an effort to have its diplomats represent a cross-section of the entire country, although women are not well represented. Many German diplomats complain that their service is understaffed and overburdened, but it still hires only one or two dozen new members every year out of about two thousand applicants.

More German diplomats come from the north and the west of Germany than from the south and especially the east. Foreign Minister Genscher did not take more than a few of the former East German diplomats into the common diplomatic service when East and West Germany were united in 1990, although German missions abroad grew rapidly after the end of the Cold War. He did not like the link of many GDR diplomats to the East German intelligence service, the Staatssicherheitsdienst (often known as the Stasi).

German diplomats have usually attended a *Gymnasium,* roughly the German equivalent of the American high school or the French *lycée,* around home. After that, they have gone on to one of the major German universities in Berlin, Cologne, Freiburg, Heidelberg, or elsewhere. No university dominates the German diplomatic service.

The German university system does not have a single school that virtually guarantees success in a government career, like the French École nationale d'administration. Germany does not want such an institution, because it wants no more elites of any kind. Nor does Germany have universities that appear to confer intellectual advantage or prestige, such as Harvard, Yale, and Stanford in the United States or Oxford and Cambridge in England. And German diplomats do not belong to social clubs that may offer a particular boost to their careers, as some American or English clubs may, for such clubs do not now exist in Germany.

Many German diplomats have studied for a year or two at American or British universities. Some may have established early friendships with American or European diplomats in those schools, making their later negotiations and consultations easier. Others have studied in France or Italy. Many have friends in the American, British, French, Russian, or other diplomatic services, and they often pass into the senior years of their careers with well-established and easy relationships across ten or more different countries or UN specialized agencies. They may be assigned to various postgraduate centers for political and strategic studies in France, the United Kingdom, or the United States (such as Chatham House in London or the Kennedy School at Harvard).

The majority of German professional diplomats speak good—sometimes astonishingly fluent—English, and many speak good French or Russian. Although German and American officials and diplomats conduct formal negotiations mainly in their respective languages with interpreters, German and American diplomats often alternate in German or English when they confer informally. They may not even remember what language they spoke on any particular occasion.

All German professional diplomats pass through the German Foreign Office diplomatic training academy, known officially as Die Aus- und Fortbildungstätte des Auswärtigen Amtes. Each must take a two-year course there at the beginning of his or her career, concentrating on traditional political, economic, and strategic issues but also learning how to conduct consular business and deal with other new problems that diplomats may be required to understand, such as humanitarian or environment issues. Later in their careers, they may return to the academy for further professional training or study in one or another specialty.

The diplomatic academy does not offer any particular instruction in negotiating technique. The Foreign Office assumes that diplomats will learn that as they advance in their careers, for it is regarded as one of the basic skills of the profession. But the academy does conduct diplomatic exercises using standard "game" techniques first developed and practiced in the United States. During such a game, trainees must learn to handle the kinds of negotiating situations that they are expected to encounter in their careers. The academy assumes that such exercises give German diplomats a good understanding of how to conduct themselves in actual negotiating situations. It deliberately wants to avoid creating a German style of diplomacy, hoping instead for a cosmopolitan, perhaps European, model.[5]

German diplomats say that they appreciate not having studied any particular negotiating technique. They believe that they have a more free-flowing style than used in many other countries, including Russia and the United States, where young diplomats may receive special training. They prefer, as some state it, not to go "by the book." One said that he liked to think, whenever he had a new negotiation to handle, whether he should try to emulate Bismarck, Stresemann, or some other renowned German diplomat.[6] The lack of a set training routine for German diplomats thus means that their negotiating techniques may well reflect unconscious cultural phenomena as well as their own perception of how German negotiators have behaved over the years.

The West German Foreign Office kept its diplomatic academy at Ippendorf near Bonn for many years while Bonn was West Germany's capital. When the capital moved to Berlin, the Foreign Office originally expected the school to remain at Ippendorf in order to permit its students to concentrate on their studies in a calmer environment than that of the capital. Within a few years, however, that arrangement became untenable because many German diplomats were moving to Berlin and senior German Foreign Office diplomats found it inconveniently time-consuming to fly to Cologne to lecture at the academy. As of this writing, the academy is expected to move to Berlin in 2004.

The diplomats who emerge from this academy into a career are schooled in the Latin principle *Fortitur in re, soaviter in modo,* which they translate into German as *Hart in der Sache, sanft in der Methode* (tough on substance, gentle in manner). They learn logical and meticulously detailed presentation. Even as German professional diplomats may utter views that appear totally and irreconcilably opposite to those taken by Germany's negotiating partners, they conduct themselves with punctilious courtesy. Other German delegates who are not in the German diplomatic service and who may become involved in a negotiation might sometimes pound the table or speak harshly, but the professional German diplomats try hard to avoid that kind of unseemly behavior.

Although German diplomats may be polite, they are persistent and—as one West European diplomat observed—very "affirmative" in the reiteration of their positions. As observed in the preceding chapter, they can be direct even as they remain courteous. When they have finished and repeated their positions, they leave no doubt about where they and their government stand. And they have not been trained to start their negotiations by offering compromises.[7]

That said, German diplomats do not rank at the top in terms of their reputation for toughness. One American diplomat who had dealt with many European diplomats over the years said that he thought the French, Greeks, Turks, and Soviets could be much more nationalistic and stubborn. German negotiators, he observed, were "not easy," but they were not as difficult as at least some others. He reiterated that German professional diplomats always behaved in a friendly manner even when they did not yield an inch on the substance of a negotiation.[8]

German negotiators, whether diplomats or others, do not encourage informality in negotiating situations and especially during the early phases of such situations. They do not inject humor into their presentations and do not expect or welcome it in a reply. They do not encourage or welcome the early use of first names, although young Germans do so more often than older Germans and are more disposed to accommodate Americans who want to move to a first-name basis after a few meetings. They do not advance to a nickname basis for a long time. And they often retain a certain formality by addressing their American and other colleagues by the formal *Sie* even when they use the first name.

Personal relationships do count for something in this environment. German diplomats and military or financial professionals who have come to know Americans and others in their respective professions can often meet casually to exchange ideas and papers in order to use their personal friendships to solve problems. This can ease consultations significantly. But it does not happen as much in the formal setting of a negotiation, especially when a basic issue or a *Gesamtkonzept* is at stake. In such a negotiation, Germans are all business and want to be treated in the same way no matter how well they may know—or how long they may have known—their negotiating partners.

Americans who have dealt with Germans and others in multiple negotiations rate Germans very high professionally. They regard them as competent negotiators. But one American added that he had never found negotiating with professional German diplomats to be "a piece of cake."[9]

Initiation and Use of Secret Channels

The German Federal Republic does not normally initiate private and secret channels, often called "back channels" in the U.S. bureaucracy. Secret talks can generate political complications between the Chancellery and the Foreign Office as well as with different parties in a governing coalition. Secret channels even have a bad historical reputation, having been used by Bismarck to keep the German parliament and people and sometimes even his emperor in the dark about his diplomacy. The Federal Republic has, therefore, used such channels sparingly and usually only when others have opened or proposed them. At such times, Germans have used those channels effectively and have been able to protect their privacy better than most states.

Secret channels helped German diplomacy with the Soviet Union during the détente period of 1969–72, after Willy Brandt had been elected chancellor and Egon Bahr had become his assistant for foreign policy in the Chancellery.

The special channel that Brandt used in détente opened just before Christmas 1969, when an envoy from Yuri Andropov, the head of the Soviet secret police (the KGB), appeared in Bahr's office, allegedly to deliver a Christmas greeting. After offering a modest Christmas present, the envoy told Bahr that Andropov stood ready to conduct direct talks for Brandt with Soviet leader Leonid Brezhnev behind the back of Soviet foreign minister Andrei Gromyko. Andropov believed that the Soviet Union could not continue a costly and futile confrontation in Europe. He offered the channel, with Brezhnev's support, because they both knew that Gromyko's conservative leanings and confrontational style would not permit the kind of high-speed diplomacy that both Moscow and Bonn needed and wanted.

When Brandt agreed to the channel, Andropov assigned two KGB agents, code-named Leo and Slava, to serve as intermediaries between him and Bahr. After Bahr had gone to Moscow to negotiate the basic treaty between the Soviet Union and the Federal Republic, Leo and Slava called on him in his hotel and told him that they would carry messages about the state of the Bahr-Gromyko talks directly to Andropov. The KGB chief could then inform Brezhnev, and Brezhnev could issue instructions to Gromyko to break any deadlocks that might develop.

Leo and Slava proved as good as their word. During Bahr's stay in Moscow and afterward they served as vital intermediaries. They prevented Gromyko from obstructing progress and muddying the waters by false reporting. They thus permitted Brezhnev, Andropov, and Brandt to make sure that the negotiations succeeded. More important from Brandt's standpoint, they helped him to get the kind of compromise agreement that the German parliament would ratify.[10]

Bahr said later that he could never have negotiated the Bonn-Moscow treaty if Gromyko had really been in charge of the Soviet position. Only Andropov and Brezhnev himself really wanted to have détente and make it work.[11]

Leo and Slava then played another role in German-Soviet relations just before Christmas 1979, when Andropov sent them to Germany to alert Bahr about plans for the impending Soviet invasion of Afghanistan. Andropov wanted Bahr to inform Helmut Schmidt, then the German chancellor, so that Schmidt would appreciate that he had been notified in advance and would not give up on his own relations with Moscow.

Leo and Slava also kept Moscow informed of the state of talks between East and West Germany from 1970 to 1971, for Andropov did not trust East German leader Walter Ulbricht any more than he trusted Gromyko. They played a lesser role in the simultaneous negotiations for a Berlin agreement, known as the Quadripartite talks, because the four occupation powers of France, the Soviet Union, the United Kingdom, and the United States conducted the talks among themselves. West Germany did not have an official voice in those talks but had a vital interest because the Western powers—and especially the United States—did not want the Bonn-Moscow treaty to be implemented until Berlin had been stabilized. Henry Kissinger, then special assistant for national security to President Richard Nixon, did not want Germany to have détente with Moscow while the Western powers did the hard work of protecting the position in Berlin.

But the Berlin talks also had a secret channel to make sure that the talks succeeded and that West Germany would have a voice in those talks.

Kissinger and Bahr set up a special direct link, bypassing the State Department. Kissinger believed that the State Department professionals would not move quickly enough to get an agreement. Brandt and Bahr for their part feared that the State Department professionals had worked so long with the CDU and had grown so close to the CDU that they would not support the SPD's efforts for détente. To complete the channel, Kissinger selected the U.S. ambassador in Bonn, Kenneth Rush, a personal friend of Nixon, and Brezhnev picked Valentin Falin, the Soviet ambassador to Bonn. Kissinger and Bahr each had their own channels, with each sitting in the middle of a network of contacts. They also talked frequently with each other. One American diplomat found himself profoundly embarrassed when Kissinger instructed him to accept a Soviet position that Kissinger had worked out with Bahr and Gromyko and that the American had rejected only a few days earlier when Moscow had proposed it.[12]

Bahr and Kissinger did not fully trust each other at first. Their channel worked only because they both needed it. But it became extremely complex to handle. The ambassadors and Bahr would discuss all aspects of the Quadripartite negotiations and come to private agreements that Bahr and Rush would later clear with Brandt and Kissinger and that Falin would clear with Moscow. One or the other would then have to introduce that agreement into the formal talks where others had not known of the secret channel. Günther van Well, the German representative in some of the interallied consultations, tried to keep the consultation process on track as best he could by telling everybody what they needed to know at any given moment, although he realized that he himself did not know everything that was going on.[13] Van Well later referred to Bahr as "the Lone Ranger" in all the détente negotiations.[14]

Bahr kept some things even from Kissinger. He did not inform Kissinger or anybody else about his special channel to Andropov through Leo and Slava. He merely told Kissinger in one of their private talks that the Germans dealt with people who could get around Gromyko when they needed to. But Kissinger knew of the channel from other sources. Nor did Bahr or Brandt inform the German foreign minister, Walter Scheel, of the channel, because they did not want the Foreign Office to clog the channel with secondary matters.[15]

The German private talks served an important purpose from the German perspective. Brandt wanted to get right to the top, to Brezhnev. He regarded talks with Gromyko as a waste of time because he knew that the famously stubborn foreign minister would not change his position on anything for years. Brandt did not have the luxury of waiting. He firmly believed, as did Bahr, that they could never have negotiated détente without the private channels.[16]

Almost thirty years later, in the fall of 1999, the German government again became involved in an important private channel to help arrange a peaceful settlement of the war in Kosovo. Berlin then became the site for secret contacts to end the NATO bombing of Serbia and the Kosovo crisis.

As was later revealed, a Swedish financier based in London, Peter Castenfelt, conducted the private talks, having first discussed the prospect with a German foreign affairs consultant, Karl Kaiser, and then with Chancellor Gerhard Schröder's national security advisor, Michael Steiner, and Foreign Office state secretary Wolfgang Ischinger. Ischinger had worked hard to get the channel going because he feared an East-West crisis over Kosovo.[17] Castenfelt joined the Russian government and the Germans in working out a formula that helped the Yugoslav president, Slobodan Milosevic, to accept a peace proposal. Under that formula, Milosevic did not have to agree to two conditions that had made him reject NATO proposals at Rambouillet Castle before the NATO bombing of Serbia and Kosovo had begun: first, Milosevic would not have to accept a NATO presence across Yugoslavia, for the United Nations would be in charge; second, he would not have to agree in advance to accept the results of a referendum on Kosovo independence to be held within three years.

These terms, significantly better than those that the West had offered Milosevic only three months earlier, led him to agree to end the war by withdrawing Serb forces from Kosovo. Castenfelt thus ensured the success of the later front-channel negotiations for an end to the NATO bombing campaign. The terms agreed on with Milosevic permitted the United States to avoid having to conduct a ground invasion of Yugoslavia, which U.S. president Bill Clinton wanted to avoid. More important from the German standpoint, the talks spared Russia from having to oppose a ground war against Serbia, its traditional ally in the Balkans. Germany, always interested in playing the middleman between East and West, did not want to be caught in a confrontation between NATO and Russia.

German government and private intermediaries insisted later that the German government played neither an official nor a substantive role in the talks and that Germans served only as facilitators because they knew all the parties involved and had their confidence. But Schröder wanted to end the Kosovo conflict and was ready to do whatever needed to be done to end it. Schröder believed that he was promoting American, European, and Soviet interests as well as German interests.[18]

German diplomats and Foreign Office officials state that they no longer use private channels as they did in those instances. They point to the highly unusual circumstances of the détente negotiations and of the Kosovo settlement to suggest that they no longer need to get involved in such talks. Certainly, they say, they would not initiate back-channel negotiations. Moreover, they note that many senior people now speak to each other on the telephone and do not need secret intermediaries. But they and others add that secret channels are, by definition, secret, and that there may be things going on that only a privileged few may know. If there were secret channels, they would more probably involve contacts with Russia than with the ever talkative West and particularly with the leak-prone Americans.[19]

The Use of Time

German negotiators usually work slowly. They do not rush a negotiation, for they want to make sure that they have explored every chance to win their points. They do not, however, practice delay for its own sake, as the Chinese and Soviets used to do. Nor do they normally slow down a negotiating process for tactical reasons, such as to gain a psychological advantage over an opponent. They move slowly because they are thorough.

German negotiators will particularly slow down a negotiation when it becomes clear that they cannot reach their *Gesamtkonzept*. They may even break it off. The West Germans did that repeatedly when they were negotiating with the Soviet Union during the Cold War before détente.

Despite this, German negotiators have on occasion moved fast and even very fast. But such a decision must come from the political level. In late 1989 and 1990, for example, as discussed in chapter 2, Chancellor

Kohl wanted almost desperately to hurry the negotiations on German unification. Kohl feared that Gorbachev would fall before a deal could be made and that French president François Mitterrand and British prime minister Margaret Thatcher would use any delays or undue complications to try to block unification. Most of all, Kohl feared that hundreds of thousands of East Germans would lose faith in the diplomacy of unification and would decide to go to West Germany on their own. Fortunately, Kohl had a Moscow partner, Mikhail Gorbachev, who also did not want to dawdle. Henry Kissinger, looking at Kohl's tactics, later wrote that modern Germans had inherited from Bismarck the capacity to act quickly when an opportunity arose.[20]

There have also been some instances when a German negotiator had political reasons to go slow. During the détente talks, Willy Brandt delayed ratification of Bonn's treaties with Moscow and Poland (which had been signed in 1970) because the Western Allies had not been able to arrange the future status of Berlin in their own Quadripartite negotiations with the Soviets until 1971 (see earlier). Brandt did not welcome the delay but accepted it because he knew that Leonid Brezhnev might not make an agreement on Berlin if he could get the Moscow Treaty ratified without it.

Brandt had a personal reason for welcoming delay: he wanted genuine stability in Berlin. But he also had a political reason: he could not afford to have a Berlin crisis erupt during the Bundestag ratification debate on his treaty with Moscow, and he feared that Walter Ulbricht might orchestrate such a crisis to destroy the prospects for détente. Moreover, Brandt felt that he did not have full control of the timing no matter what he did. He suspected that Henry Kissinger sometimes held up progress on Berlin to orchestrate various East-West agreements at his own pace. And it bothered Brandt when Gromyko and other Soviet officials accused him of excess servility to Washington. Although he had to delay the treaty, he would have preferred quick action.[21]

On an earlier occasion, in 1954–55, Chancellor Konrad Adenauer also delayed negotiations for political reasons. He did not want to accept Western demands for a German military force to join NATO until the Allies had accepted his demand to give the Federal Republic of Germany greater sovereignty. He wanted to reduce the powers of the occupiers. Adenauer wanted Germans to be fighting as Germans or as Europeans, not as the mercenaries that Hessian soldiers had been. Because the Allies feared a Soviet attack and wanted German forces quickly, Adenauer's refusal to rush the talks gave him powerful leverage. He received greater sovereign powers, especially over foreign and financial policy, than either Washington, London, or Paris had at first wanted to grant him.[22]

Timing also became a factor in the talks about slave labor and forced labor compensation between 1998 and 2000, although for different reasons. The German objective of "legal peace," under which German companies would be immune from separate prosecution after they had contributed to a compensation fund, required complex consultations between the U.S. negotiators and powerful U.S. lobbies, including the American Jewish Claims Conference and the American Trial Lawyers. The talks also required the "legal peace" accord to be tested and upheld in American courts. These processes delayed the conclusion of the talks. At the same time, all parties to the talks recognized that the potential beneficiaries of an agreement had reached an advanced age, with most being well over seventy and many in ill health, and that many might die without receiving a compensation they richly deserved. This put some pressure on all the delegations, including the Germans, to speed up the negotiations.

Although German negotiators may sometimes wish to hurry, their approach and their tactics more often cause delay. They may not seek that delay or even welcome it, but they do not want to make major concessions merely to gain time. They want to make certain that they achieve their objectives, especially their *Gesamtkonzept,* and that they have thoroughly explored every issue. They will accept delay if it helps them gain their points.

German negotiators also have practical and bureaucratic considerations on their minds when they delay a negotiation. They know that any change requires re-reviewing their position at many levels of the bureaucracy and at whatever senior level approved the German position in the first place. And they do not like to come home with nothing to show for their efforts. So they try to avoid making a concession unless and until they can claim to have gained a counterconcession. They also want to make certain that any compromise will really move the talks forward. Until they can be sure of that, they will keep talking.

Therefore, although German negotiators do not normally delay a negotiating process for tactical reasons, their systematic approach to diplomacy may have that effect.

Use of the Press

The German government, like any modern democratic government, uses the press to influence any negotiations and to push for a successful result. The German Chancellery has a press office with a foreign policy section directed by an official who is often a close associate of the chancellor or a senior diplomat. That office briefs the press periodically on the progress of any particular negotiation.

The Foreign Office also has a press office, usually directed by a professional diplomat. Like the Chancellery press office, it holds briefings about planned or ongoing negotiations, concentrating on the German position and the points that the German delegation and the Foreign Office regard as important. They treat the press with some care. Although German diplomats believe that such major newspapers as the *Frankfurter Allgemeine Zeitung* and *Die Welt* and the weekly *Die Zeit* maintain high standards of professional journalism, German diplomats regard the newsmagazine *Der Spiegel* with deep suspicion because it likes to sniff out and highlight government incompetence and skullduggery. They want to make sure that they get their own reports out as soon and as responsibly as possible. Sensational journalism has a long history in Germany—it was especially voracious during the 1920s—and the Foreign Office prefers not to feed it.

Special German negotiating teams sometimes have their own press offices. The German delegation on compensation for Nazi slave and forced labor victims had a separate press office distinct from the Chancellery and Foreign Office. Count Lambsdorff thought that the sensitivity of the negotiations warranted a special press office. Moreover, neither the Chancellery nor the Foreign Office wanted to have to brief on the highly complex negotiations. The delegation's press officer, Wolfgang Gibowski, had served in Chancellor Kohl's Press and Information Service and knew the German press corps. Count Lambsdorff himself also had many long-standing relations with journalists and used them to set forth the German position on the negotiations, especially as he believed that the U.S. delegation was continually giving its own version.

German negotiators rarely use press leaks for tactical purposes. But they have done it on occasion. Chancellor Adenauer made the most famous leak in postwar German diplomacy in April 1962, when President Kennedy wanted him to accept a "principles paper" that Kennedy wanted to propose to Gromyko and that Adenauer regarded as dangerous to German and Berlin interests. The proposal, which had been given to the chancellor in the greatest confidentiality and under the proviso that he had only forty-eight hours to agree, appeared suddenly in the German press and the *New York Times*. Kennedy accused Adenauer of leaking the paper. Adenauer rejected the accusation. To this date, the source of the leak remains uncertain, but there is no doubt that the leak helped Adenauer because both the German and the American press denounced the "principles paper" for yielding too much on Berlin. Kennedy was forced to withdraw it. Many people suspected that Adenauer or his office leaked it. But German leaks of that kind occur only rarely, much less often than in the United States.

The German government and its negotiating teams use press interviews and background briefings more than leaks. Beginning with Adenauer and Brandt, German chancellors sometimes give interviews to U.S. journalists in order to influence American opinion. During any particular negotiation, either the Foreign Office or the head of the German delegation may cultivate one or more members of the press whom they may have known for years and with whom they feel comfortable. They give background reports to those journalists and perhaps to others. They thus get their story out in the most favorable light. They also conduct the usual deep background briefings in order to provide a framework for journalists once a story about the negotiations may emerge or be announced.

Chancellor Kohl particularly trusted and briefed several journalists whom he had known for a long time. Stories published by those journalists gave Kohl's "spin" without officially carrying his name. Foreign Minister Genscher did the same thing, often giving a different "spin" than Kohl. Chancellor Schröder is also known to favor some particular journalists, as is Foreign Minister Fischer. Those bylines warrant and receive particular attention by those negotiating with Germany.

Other German officials also want to keep the press on their side. The then governing mayor of Berlin, Eberhard Diepgen, used the press in his negotiations with U.S. ambassador John Kornblum about the location of a new U.S. embassy in Berlin. Berlin papers periodically carried stories giving Diepgen's particular version of the state of the negotiations, much to Kornblum's irritation.[23]

The current German press, with the exception of *Der Spiegel,* rarely engages in sensationalism. It usually reports events and briefings rather soberly and does not do Watergate-style investigative reporting. It tends to report events rather than to try to predict them. All that, however, is changing, and German media have become increasingly prone to challenge government releases. That has put some pressure on the government as well as on negotiators to reveal more than they would have done in the past.

Entertainment

Germans are proud of their wine, beer, food, and music. They like to entertain their negotiating partners and they do it well even if not with the same opulence as some others. They present excellent food and make an effort to create a friendly mood.

No matter how formal and how difficult a negotiation may become, the German delegation can normally be counted on to host some lunches and dinners for all delegates. They cannot use such occasions, as the French or the British may, to impress others with the length of their cultural heritage, for most of the buildings that reflect that heritage have been destroyed—especially in Berlin. But they do what they can with what they have.

Thus the German delegates normally invite others to a good German restaurant or *Weinstube* (wine tavern) or to the Foreign Office reception rooms if the talks are being conducted in Germany. The latter are not as luxurious and imposing as those at the Quai d'Orsay in Paris, Whitehall in London, or the Kremlin in Moscow, but they provide a pleasant and relaxed atmosphere.

German diplomats and others often serve a German white wine. Most German wines come from Riesling or Sylvaner grapes and can make excellent and very drinkable light wines. But Germans have learned over time that most Americans and other foreigners do not like the traditionally most precious German whites made from the ripest grapes, the Trockenbeerenauslese or the Spätlese, because they find them too sweet. German vintners originally made those wines to drink apart from a meal and the wines do not go well with food. German delegates now usually offer German whites deliberately selected to be somewhat drier.

Germans may also offer German red wines. Many foreigners find these wines thinner and less robust than the French or California reds because the German wine-growing areas receive less sunshine during the year. But German red wines, like German whites, have over the past ten years been made to appeal more to international style. They are becoming a little more like French and American reds.

Americans who want to drink traditional German wines usually choose the lighter whites of the Moselle or Rhine Valley or the Franconian wines in green circular bottles, the Bocksbeutel wines that are delicately flavored and go well with a meal. They are different from French and California wines, but they are certainly as good in their own way.

Germans face fewer doubts about German beer, which is almost universally welcomed. Americans may find some traditional Bavarian beers too strong for their taste, but German beer comes in many different varieties suitable for virtually any palate. The guests need only to know what they want. Americans should, however, be aware that most German brews have a higher alcohol content than the most popular American beers and may need to be drunk with caution and in moderation.

As for food, German tastes and German restaurants have become very cosmopolitan. They often serve a standard international cuisine. This also pleases some guests and disappoints others. Chancellor Kohl made a point of serving British prime minister Margaret Thatcher some local sausage and pig's stomach when she visited him in the Rhineland. That menu was, reportedly, not a full success. Nowadays, for better or worse, German negotiators are more likely to serve the same style of international cuisine that other professional diplomats serve. But those who like traditional German meats, such as venison, or German specialty sausages, such as the Bavarian *Weisswurst*, or traditional German desserts, such as *Rote Grütze*, can still order them in many German restaurants and the German diplomat who hosts them may appreciate that the guest knows something about German cuisine. However, some foods, such as German white asparagus *(Stangenspargel),* can only be found during the right season.

It is not unusual for German negotiators to invite their partners to an opera or a symphony in Berlin, Düsseldorf, Frankfurt, Munich, or elsewhere in Germany. Many foreigners may be tempted by a Mozart opera, but they may not be so eager to attend a lengthy Wagner opera or an intellectual Richard Strauss opera. But whatever they attend, they will normally find that the performance is excellent and that German theaters make a point of trying to get everybody home early no matter how long the opera. This may mean an earlier start or fewer intermissions than Americans or others expect at home. German symphony orchestras remain among the best in the world, with many tracing their origins back several centuries, and they boast a cosmopolitan repertory along with a phalanx of big-name conductors from everywhere in the world.

German negotiators, especially at the beginning of a negotiation, sharply distinguish entertainment time from official negotiating time. When they are having a pleasant evening with a beer in hand they do not want to talk business. In fact, their break between business and pleasure is so dramatic that some American and other negotiators have found it difficult to adjust to the contrast between the very direct talk that may prevail in a meeting and the very pleasant conversation over drinks immediately afterward.

Germans dislike the American lawyers' habit of continuing to negotiate in the middle of a meal. Germans do not work on the basis of billable hours and they think it is not the time to try to strike a deal or score a point.

However, after a negotiation has gone on for some time and the negotiators have come to know each other well, it can be appropriate to make a casual remark over a drink or a meal, offering an idea or suggestion for settling a sticky point. A German negotiator may pick it up. A great deal depends on the situation and on the relationship that the negotiators have established.

Language

Germans can conduct negotiations in many languages. Because German diplomatic and military officers generally speak very good English, that language is often the language of informal and sometimes even formal negotiation between American and German delegations. Germans sometimes even use English in informal talks or consultations with other nationalities, such as Chinese and Japanese. They almost always use English in such international organizations as NATO or the United Nations. It depends in part, of course, on what language others want to use.

German negotiators sometimes use English for some topics because it has become the accepted international language for those topics. For example, the German-American civil aviation negotiations during the early 1990s were conducted largely in English because that has become the lingua franca of the international air traffic system. The same practice applies in international financial negotiations and some business negotiations, where English terminology dominates (see chapters 4 and 5). This may put Germans at some disadvantage, but many of them command the technical language so well that they appear to be perfectly comfortable. When they are not, they may switch.

At other times, a negotiation may require many languages. The SOFA negotiations included several different states that had troops stationed in Germany. They also included many German ministries and *Länder*. France and Belgium wanted to speak in French, the United States and the United Kingdom in English, and Germany in German. All used simultaneous translation.

The slave labor and forced labor talks had to be negotiated in multiple languages. The U.S. delegation and the German delegation each spoke their respective language with simultaneous interpretation. So many other national delegations took part, including those from Poland, the Czech Republic, Ukraine, and so on, that each delegation had to use its own language. But much of the informal discussion was conducted in English and German because many Central and East European delegates spoke those languages.

In formal negotiations within the European Union, delegates usually speak their own language with simultaneous translation into other EU languages. In less formal EU negotiations or consultations, English has become the increasingly used lingua franca—much to the disgust of France and the French. Germans have no difficulty dealing with either format and will normally switch easily from one into the other. In talks with East European diplomats, Germans often find that their counterparts speak good German. Otherwise, they may all speak English or work through interpreters. Germans generally speak English with diplomats from the developing world, but many of those diplomats have studied in Germany and speak excellent German. Language thus rarely presents a problem in negotiating with Germans.

The final texts of agreements must normally be written in the language of each country. This presented a real problem when the Quadripartite Agreement on Berlin was signed in 1971. The original text of the agreement, which had been negotiated in English, French, and Russian, had to be translated into German. West and East Germans disagreed about a number of terms, for the German words sometimes carried political meanings that only one side accepted. But any such difficulties can normally be overcome, usually by having each delegation proffer its own version and then agreeing to disagree.

The Bureaucratic Factor

German negotiators often have their hands tied by the complexities of the German federal system and especially by the bureaucracy. That bureaucracy, a German tradition since the days of the Holy Roman Empire, slows the process of discussion and especially the process of decision making. Once a German opening position has been reached in Berlin, the very multiplicity of bureaucratic interests in the German interagency process makes it difficult to change the position (see chapter 2).

The same offices that prepare a negotiation and that may be represented on the delegation must join or at least be consulted in any decision to change a position. Layers of professional bureaucrats staff many of those offices. Most are career officials with considerable longevity and influence in their ministries. The German career civil servant (known as a *Beamte*) often exercises more power than a corresponding U.S. or other national official. They do not like to abandon their earlier expressed views and they can marshal excellent arguments. The Finance Ministry and particularly some domestic ministries often show little flexibility in any kind of international negotiation. The *Länder* may remain particularly obdurate. They will usually not change their views until they find it absolutely unavoidable.

Because negotiating positions prepared and decided at senior levels must be brought back to those levels for decision before they can be changed, the German chancellor or at least the foreign minister must often decide what flexibility, if any, German negotiators can show. Although the president or prime minister of any government negotiating with Germany can address the chancellor directly to try to win a point, this does not make for a quick decision except in extremely urgent situations or on topics on which chiefs of government routinely meet, such as on G-8 matters.

The chancellor's advisor on foreign affairs rarely has time to deal with matters not in the chancellor's most immediate areas of interest. Because that office is largely staffed by professional diplomats, military officers, and economists who must rely on the bureaucracy for information and advice, proposals for changes in German views may take time to percolate to the top.

This often means that senior officials have to exert some push to over-rule the bureaucracy, and they may not always prevail. It also means that decisions come slowly and that, when they do come, they may solve only part of a deadlock. They will advance the process of negotiation but not cut through a Gordian knot all at once except in very unusual circumstances when a chancellor or foreign minister decides that a problem must be solved at once. But normally bureaucratic inertia will not permit such dramatic breakthroughs. That is one of the reasons why negotiations involving the German bureaucracy usually move in phases over an extended period of time.

The Commitment to Community: The European Union, NATO, and Beyond

For historical, geographic, and cultural reasons, the Federal Republic of Germany has a powerful commitment to community. West Germany began to attach itself to a number of international organizations even before it had sovereign control over its foreign affairs and before it had an army or a full civil service. Unification has only deepened that commitment because Germans now see a chance to consolidate their position in the center of Europe by developing a circle of friendly organizations around themselves. Those organizations offer the chance to exert influence. They offer Germany the best means to move away from the isolation that Germans often perceived between 1871 and 1945. No German would surrender such associations lightly.

Germany, especially in the years after 1945, needed some kind of recognition. The effects of the war and Hitler's criminality had left the German public traumatized by a sense of loss and shame. Membership in international organizations helped to ease that sense by providing a chance to be accepted and recognized as a civilized state. That tradition has continued to date.

Multilateralism has become a core element of German diplomacy and its negotiating style. Germans seek a place in international organizations and do what they can to make those organizations effective while also trying to make them serve German interests.

The Federal Republic's first chancellor, Konrad Adenauer, began the postwar commitment to community as one of the diplomatic principles that both the Western occupiers and the German people would understand and support. Because the Nazi regime had totally discredited German strategy and diplomacy and because Bismarck's diplomacy still evoked widespread suspicion, Adenauer needed to search in different directions. He took an important specific step, using a new French willingness to cooperate in order to put an end to the centuries of Franco-German hostility. He also took a wider step, making a determined effort to bring the Federal Republic into a host of European and international organizations. He and West Germany helped to establish some of them. These organizations also built a form of federalism throughout Western Europe, which the Germans welcomed.

As Adenauer came from the Rhineland, the core of Charlemagne's empire and the old German lands as well as a key component of the Holy Roman Empire, he saw Western Europe as Germany's main vocation. He established the capital of the new German Federal Republic in Bonn, in the very heart of the Rhineland. He wanted to avoid Frankfurt, which might have been the logical capital for West Germany, in part because it was not in the Rhineland and in part because he did not want West Germany's government to be surrounded by the U.S. Army and Air Force headquarters and bases in the Frankfurt area.[24] He wanted to be surrounded by historical Europe.

Adenauer also wanted to begin to establish structures that would revive Europe and especially Western Europe. Most West Germans agreed with his general purpose even if they may not have agreed on all details. As Adenauer's successors have continued to join other organizations, Germany, once the world's pariah, has become the world's greatest joiner.

The German commitment to community finds its most concrete expression in the following international structures and relationships.

The European Union

This ranks first among Germany's international commitments in both the length and the depth of German association. When French foreign minister Robert Schuman proposed a European Coal and Steel Community (ECSC) in 1950, departing dramatically from Georges Clemenceau's 1919 policy of revenge, occupation, and reparations, Adenauer responded enthusiastically. While he fought hard to win greater German sovereignty from the occupiers, he was ready to yield some elements of German sovereignty to Europe. Since his time, as the ECSC has evolved through the European Economic Community (EEC) and the European Community (EC) into the European Union, West Germany and later all of Germany have continued to be the European Community's and the European Union's most generous financial and political supporter. Germany has paid those sums in order to strengthen the organizations and to keep others committed as well. The vast majority of Germans could not now conceive of trying to function without the European Union, just as the European Union could not function without Germany.

NATO

In 1955, Adenauer brought West Germany into the North Atlantic Treaty Organization, which the United States and some of its European allies had created in 1949 to defend Western Europe against a potential Soviet invasion. Having already decided to put West Germany into the ECSC, Adenauer thus deliberately put the German military as well as the German coal and steel industry—the two main instruments of Prussian and Nazi power—into international structures that would curtail their autonomy. NATO offered the German military a chance to redeem itself, rediscover the roots of its army in the reformist tradition of the early nineteenth century, and show in a very transparent international forum that German officers could function in a democratic society. West German forces also became the second most important element in West European defense, providing half a million soldiers to help protect the main front line across the continent against the Soviet threat. After the end of the Cold War, Chancellor Kohl took the lead in pushing NATO enlargement toward the east. And West Germany has long been the NATO member most committed to strengthening the alliance and to having the alliance use that strength not only for defense but also as a launching pad for negotiations with Russia and other East European states.

The Group of Eight

Finance Minister Helmut Schmidt first brought Germany into the Group of Five (G-5) as a founding member of the "Library Group" of finance ministers launched by U.S. secretary of the treasury George Shultz in the White House Library in 1973. After Schmidt became chancellor, he and French resident Valéry Giscard d'Estaing in 1975 proposed the annual G-5 Summit, which has since become the G-8 with Canada, Italy, and most recently Russia joining the original American, British, French, German, and Japanese members. As the organization has moved from the financial realm increasingly into political and strategic topics, it has given Germany a strong voice in the top councils of the world.

The OSCE

Germany also supported and helped to found organizations that the Soviet Union proposed in the days of détente. When Leonid Brezhnev suggested the Conference on Security and Cooperation in Europe (CSCE), mainly to legitimize the borders of the Soviet satellite states, Schmidt supported the idea strongly. He did so although U.S. presidents Gerald Ford and later Jimmy Carter opposed the CSCE unless it promoted human rights within the Soviet bloc. Schmidt thought that Germany's interests and the interests of East Europeans would ultimately be better served by a pan-European structure and a relaxation of trans-European tensions than by a debate about human rights. West Germany joined the CSCE in 1975 and remained an important member when the CSCE became the Organization for Security and Cooperation in Europe (OSCE) in 1990 with the end of the Cold War. Although German interest in OSCE has declined as NATO has expanded into Eastern Europe, Germany still sees the OSCE as a fundamental element of East-West stability.

The United Nations

The German role in the United Nations has not matched its role in the European organizations, but it has become increasingly important since 1990. West Germany could not join the United Nations until détente, for the Soviet Union consistently vetoed West German membership until East Germany was admitted. They both then joined the United Nations in 1973 and remained there until German unification in 1990. Ever since, united Germany has hoped to join the Big Five as a permanent member of the UN Security Council. Washington has supported this, although only mildly because it does not want to dilute its Security Council veto power. Great Britain and France have shown some support but have been even more reticent than the United States. In any event, German accession to a permanent seat remains improbable for some time because the states of the developing world will not vote for Germany (or Japan) to become permanent members of the council unless at least two or three developing states (perhaps India, Egypt, and Brazil) also receive that status. That could mean the paralysis of the council as ten states would have veto rights. But although Germany will have to wait for permanent Security Council status, it has supported a vast range of United Nations peacekeeping operations all over the world. Germany has participated in well over twenty UN missions, of which half have involved the use of German armed forces for peacekeeping duties. They have ranged from Cambodia to Somalia and the Balkans.[25] Michael Steiner, Chancellor Schröder's former foreign policy aide, became the senior UN official in Kosovo as of January 2002.

The Mix of Global Organizations

Although Germany did not help to found the principal global organizations, many of which were established at the end of World War II and thus predated the existence of the Federal Republic, it has become an important and contributing member in all of them. It has joined the International Monetary Fund, the World Bank, the World Trade Organization, and such UN-affiliated agencies as the United Nations Development Program, the World Food Program, and the United Nations High Commissioner for Refugees. Germany has used its economic strength to make large contributions to those organizations and thus to gain a widely appreciated role. Germany has also begun to hold important positions in those organizations, although most of the positions remain unofficially reserved for the leading Western states such as the United States, Great Britain, and France or for smaller and often developing states that need and deserve greater international recognition.

❏   ❏   ❏

Germany's commitment to international organizations goes beyond membership to an entire way of thinking that deeply affects German negotiating behavior. Germans taking part in negotiations anywhere on any topic always keep their commitments to various organizations in mind, even when those organizations have no role in the negotiations. Germany has in its intra-European consultations often stressed the importance of European links to NATO and the United States. It has sometimes appeared to agree with the Americans, or at least to urge some accommodation with them, during EU-U.S. trade negotiations. Some French officials, usually more ready to confront the United States, have accused Germans of acting as a stalking horse for U.S. interests.[26]

But the Franco-German axis remains a centerpiece of German diplomacy even after unification. Despite their friendship for the United States, Germans have often supported France in European-American arguments. And German diplomats are at pains to point out to Americans that Germany must give priority to its European relationships—or must at least keep them prominently in mind—even as it negotiates with the United States.

Thus Germany defended EU trade barriers, such as those against Chiquita bananas, in its talks with the United States, even as it lobbied within the European Union to change them. It also supported the European Union strongly in the European-American dispute on steel tariffs in early 2002, although still urging reconciliation. German diplomats expect their friends to respect their wish to keep all organizations and all states on good terms with one another. As part of its negotiating behavior in the European Union, Germany has even abandoned some domestic interests, such as lower food prices, to support French demands for farm subsidies under the EU Common Agricultural Program—although it must in fairness be added that many German farmers also benefit from those farm subsidies.

In all their dealings with international organizations, West German and now German leaders have sustained Adenauer's *Gesamtkonzept* of rehabilitation through institutions. Membership in such institutions has helped Germany to reach security and regain legitimacy. In exchange, Germany has supported the organizations financially and politically and has conducted many of its policies through them. Germany has also helped to promote both integration and expansion of those organizations, with Chancellor Kohl playing key roles in changing the European Community into the European Union and also in helping to enlarge NATO. German political leaders as well as negotiators recognize that others accept German power and influence more readily when it is projected through institutions instead of directly.

Germans function with truly remarkable comfort within multilateral organizations such as the European Union, NATO, and OSCE. Of all major European states, Germany has most readily abandoned elements of its sovereignty to European and transatlantic organizations. German officials, whether they are diplomats, military officers, economists, or other professionals, pursue the interests of the international organizations more wholeheartedly than diplomats or officials of other major European powers.

Germany has conducted more of its policies within and through an international organization than any other state. During the United Nations and NATO military interventions in the Balkans from 1996 to the present, whether in Bosnia or Kosovo, German peacekeepers and troops consistently obeyed NATO and UN instructions more readily than did those of other states. U.S., French, Italian, and other forces almost always asked their capitals to confirm military orders from the NATO command. They operated under dual command structures and carried out only those orders that came through national channels. They ignored the orders that came through international organization channels, although they were theoretically serving under international command. German forces, in contrast, generally accepted international instructions without referring them home, although they increased their tendency to check international instructions through their own channels when they realized how much others were doing it.[27]

German negotiating behavior within the organizations themselves tends to be more cooperative than that of the other major powers. They do not insist as often as France or Great Britain on having top commands or special postings, although they do argue strongly for such commands from time to time. They do not insist as often as others that EU or NATO policy follow their own national interests, for they define their interests more broadly than others do and see the success of an organization as an interest in and of itself.

This kind of German attitude has been widely reflected in German negotiating behavior. Chancellor Kohl played a crucial role in the European Council summit at Maastricht in the Netherlands, December 9–10, 1991, the first summit to be prepared and held in the context of a fully united Germany. Kohl had a very simple *Gesamtkonzept* for the summit, to show the other European states that Germany would not begin to throw its weight around indiscriminately because it was united. Equally important, he thought that Europe should become more integrated in order to make sure that it could better contain the larger Germany.

Kohl also had several less important objectives: to introduce more democracy into European decision making, specifically by giving more power to the European Parliament; to begin giving Europe a common policy on some judicial matters, especially migration (on which Germany felt very exposed with the Iron Curtain gone); to give the German *Länder* a more direct role; and to increase the power of Europe in relation to the individual states. France supported some of these objectives but not all. Great Britain had reservations about most of them.

Kohl got much of what he wanted. The former European Community became the European Union to reflect its newer and more important status. The European Parliament received more power, including the power of codecision with the EU Council on some matters. Not coincidentally, the new and larger Germany received ninety-nine seats in the parliament instead of the eighty-seven that it had enjoyed earlier and that other large states kept. And a new Committee of the Regions gave a separate venue to the German *Länder,* as they had wanted.

Kohl worked almost in tandem with French president François Mitterrand, although Mitterrand blocked some of Kohl's efforts to give more power to the EU Commission and the European Parliament. Kohl tried to keep an open line to British prime minister John Major in order to avoid isolating the British leader, whose many reservations about Europe often made him the odd man out at Maastricht. Kohl called on his links with the smaller members of the European Union, who wanted to reduce the grip of the larger members and who shared Kohl's wish for greater integration. Kohl also pledged a larger German contribution to the European Union to help finance the Cohesion Fund that would provide aid to the four poorest members, Greece, Ireland, Portugal, and Spain.

Supported by Hans-Dietrich Genscher, who had many close ties with European leaders, Kohl managed to get his wishes without alienating any of the European states, even when they disagreed with him. He approached issues carefully and systematically but without forcing them, reversing the image of the traditional German bull in the china shop while getting the stronger European Union that he wanted. Genscher, however, did play the villain, insisting that the European Union give full recognition to Slovenia and Croatia as they left the Yugoslav confederation. This proved to be a major mistake for it may have helped to provoke war in Bosnia. There has been some speculation that it may also have accelerated Genscher's resignation shortly thereafter.[28]

As German internationalism continues to develop, an international purpose can become a national purpose to a degree that is inconceivable for any other major state. As indicated in chapter 1, this kind of dialectic logic emerges particularly out of Hegelian philosophy as well as out of German history.

German policy contrasts strongly with the policies of France and Great Britain, perhaps reflecting longer French and British existence as separate national states and governments as well as the difference between Hegelian and linear logic. French officials try to implement EU policies that reflect specific French interests. British political leaders have yet to find a way to reconcile their national vocation with their European interests, as shown by Britain's refusal to join the new European currency, the euro, when most other EU members did so by the beginning of 2002.

German national and EU or NATO interests commingle and interact. In serving either interest, Germans believe that they are serving the other as well. German negotiating behavior often includes negotiating through a community and for a community instead of only on its own account. As part of their commitment to dialectic logic, Germans accept this apparent contradiction without evident difficulty.

German diplomacy wants to go even further. Berlin wants to act as a universal contact point. It wants to hold the Atlantic community, the European Union, and Russia together. Germany has developed what might be termed a "shepherd doctrine" in its diplomatic style and negotiating behavior. Germans like to keep their allies and friends working closely together even as a shepherd tries to keep the sheep together within a herd. And they react swiftly if they perceive that any outsider wants to split the herd or that any sheep wants to go off on its own.

Germans want to build systems. They will sacrifice to make such systems work. An alliance gives them a sense of place. They do not want to run such alliances, but they want to have a respected position. Because of their history and the cultural legacy it has imbued, they feel infinitely more comfortable within such associations than they would feel on their own. Their negotiating behavior reflects that wish.

German negotiators look constantly in all directions. They look backward, to the Holy Roman Empire and to the Reich, for positive and negative reinforcement. They look sideways, either to their EU or NATO partners or to their friends in Eastern Europe and beyond. They look at their transatlantic partners when they negotiate with Russia or within the European Union. They are conscious not only of their own bureaucracy but of a whole world of relationships that they want each negotiation to serve or at least not to jeopardize. A German negotiator sees more images and hears more voices than any negotiator from any other state in the world.

At the end of a negotiation, German negotiators want to see all issues and all relationships settled and definitive. They want everything to be in its proper place and with an agreed-on set of instructions. At that point, all is well.

The best sign of this is in the quintessential German expression of contentment. When Germans are asked how they are feeling or how things are going they do not reply, "All is well," *"Tout va bien,"* or "Okay" as the English, French, or Americans might reply. Instead, they reply, *"Alles in Ordnung,"* or "All is in order."[29] In the structured and logical universe of German thinking, this means that all is as it should be—whether in the complex structures of the Holy Roman Empire or the differently complex structures of today. Or, as an American might say, "a place for everything and everything in its place." That is the objective that a German negotiator wants to reach.

4

German Business Negotiations

GERMAN BUSINESS NEGOTIATING BEHAVIOR resembles German diplomatic negotiating behavior in some ways. Many of the observations about general German negotiating behavior in chapters 2 and 3 apply to German business as well, although to varying degrees, as reflected in this chapter.

But German business negotiations do not fully resemble German diplomatic and political negotiations. German business did not undergo the same traumatic experiences as the German state during World War II and immediately afterward. It does not, therefore, operate under the same inhibitions. German firms act on their own interests with greater determination than does the German state, even if they cannot proceed with total disregard for the attitudes of others.

German business does not have the same kinds of structures as the German government. There is less bureaucracy, although large German firms are often overstaffed. There is no professional diplomatic service; most business negotiations are conducted by managers. Business talks follow less predictable paths than government negotiations.

German business was the first area of German activity to recover after World War II, especially in West Germany. Having seen how their reparations demands had helped bring about the collapse of the German Weimar Republic by stimulating massive inflation and social chaos after World War I, the Western Allies did not repeat the experience after World War II. Joseph Stalin conducted extensive reparations seizures in East Germany for several years after 1945 but then had to stop because he was provoking ever more refugees to flee to the West.

German economic policies and assets, from the stability of the deutsche mark to trade and aid in all directions, became a central element in Germany's return from disgrace and defeat after World War II. The *Wirtschaftswunder,* the "economic miracle" unleashed by the free-market policies of Minister of Economics Ludwig Erhard in the 1950s, did as much to give West Germany genuine influence as any other German activity, including diplomacy.

In the process, the *Wirtschaftswunder* became part of German legend and German culture. It signaled to the German people that they could recover from war and destruction and could again hope to have a future. It helped to bring back German self-confidence. It also gave German business and German economic activity a higher status than business had elsewhere in the postwar years. In other countries, business was under pressure from the socialist movement. In Germany, it became a road to redemption. It became the ultimate form of what Professor Joseph Nye has defined as "soft power."[1] German business and the German economy helped West Germany and later united Germany to gain both influence and prestige. And the German government has repaid the favor handsomely. It generally supports German business firms, whether large or small, in their international dealings.

As indicated in chapter 1, Germans have had an export mentality since the days of the Hanseatic League. They believe firmly in a positive balance of trade. They want to sell abroad and will do all they can to gain a large share of global sales. Germany has a higher percentage of exports as a share of gross domestic product than any other major state. The German government and German business must support an open global trading system if they want to prosper.

Despite political and military upheavals, the German economy has been able to advance along a generally rising line of development dating from the Middle Ages and the Hanseatic League through various waves of German industrial expansion during the peaceful phases of the eighteenth, nineteenth, and twentieth centuries.

But German business faces new problems. With the advent of globalization, many German firms and Germany itself have faced pressures for modernization that they had not faced before. Those pressures emanated largely from the United States and from new competitors around the globe. At the same time, German business has had to adjust to the opportunities and demands of ever-deepening European economic and political integration. Some firms began to react to the combination of those pressures during the 1990s by trying to find a way to combine their traditional management style with the demands of the new economy. Some have succeeded. Some have not.

German business has tried to adapt its negotiating style to deal with the new pressures. This process is far from complete, consistent, or successful. It has registered some triumphs but has also left some dead or wounded bodies lying on the field. A number of German negotiators have overreached themselves and have reacted differently to success and failure.

German Management Style

German management style has its own character, different from American and even from other European styles. It concentrates on three elements of the management process:

❐ First and foremost, a high-quality product. German management wants to deliver something that works and that will work for a long time. German managers insist on superb engineering and on reliable performance. The best-known companies, such as Siemens and Bayerische-Motoren-Werke (BMW), want each product to be as close to perfection as possible. German labor matches German management in this attitude, as German workers take great pride in their ability to deliver top-quality goods.

❐ Second, low production costs. A German plant should be efficiently run and should exhibit what is now called "lean" production methods. Not all German plants are actually lean. Nonetheless, despite high German labor costs, they remain generally competitive. The hundreds of small and midsize companies of the so-called *Mittelstand* (midsize firms) have competitive cost structures as well as top-quality production, although they find it harder than before to meet those double goals because of cheap and increasingly intelligent labor in the developing world.

❒ Third, excellent service. German mechanics travel the world to take care of German-built electric turbines, machine tools, locomotives, trucks, cars, and anything else built by German hands. They pride themselves on their ability to keep their products functioning for a long time after others collapse or decay. They enjoy telling stories about how they kept their trucks going in the middle of the African desert or the South American jungle.

Some of the elements stressed in American management, such as marketing and finance, play a less central role in German management. They are done competently, but they are not as close to the center of a firm's heart as in the United States. For example, German laws prevent German stores from remaining open for more than limited shopping hours, giving the impression that German firms take better care of their products than their customers. And some German firms competing in the United Sates have found that their home offices cannot understand the importance of advertising in the United States because they assume that their products will sell themselves.[2]

Traditional German firms do not put as much weight as many American firms do on hiring persons who have a master's degree in business administration (MBA). Many German firms remain far removed from what they call the American "MBA culture," although an MBA is now considered more favorably than twenty years ago for certain international operations. The annual *Financial Times* listings of global and European MBA programs includes not a single German business school. The top forty-five schools include thirteen from the European Union (with four from France and three from Spain) but not a single one from Germany.[3] Many Germans prefer to go outside Germany to get an MBA, picking up foreign languages and contacts as well as a more up-to-date business education. There are some nascent German business schools trying to compete in the global MBA league with encouragement from the German government, but they have a long way to go before they crack the circle of the best programs.

Most German managers function along traditional principles. They do not look for radical change, although they will try promising new production processes. They do not like to take risks. They watch their costs and value the assets and cash reserves they may have accumulated. They do not look for chances to spend money but can spend a great deal when they want. They hold their top managerial salaries low, much lower than American salaries and lower even than British. Traditional firms have no stock option plans and in many cases do not even have stock on a market.

German business has followed more of a cooperative model than has British or American business. German management and labor do not usually treat each other as mutually hostile forces, and they coordinate closely to get the best deals possible for German workers. German law gives German laborers one-half the seats on the *Aufsichtsrat,* the supervisory board that sits above the *Vorstand,* which corresponds to the American corporate board. German labor has used that eminent position to defend its interests, although German workers rarely engage in strikes. With the highest wages and the highest nonwage benefits in the world, German business has to strive incessantly for cost-cutting efficiencies to remain globally competitive.

Most German managers move slowly and, on the whole, cautiously. They try to expand mainly through their company's own resources. After a German firm accumulates enough capital, it will often invest in a new production line or will purchase some other firm. If it needs outside funds, it usually chooses to get them in long-range low-interest loans from banks, not by floating new issues on the stock exchange or by going to the short-term credit markets. Most German managers like to be debt-free, refusing to leverage their assets as American firms do. Once they have found a good track, they stay in it and in related tracks rather than look for something radically new.[4]

As in German political life, the business environment stresses consensus in the midst of competition. German firms in the same field belong to the same associations and cooperate with one another within those associations. They cooperate in turn with other associations on such common endeavors as government and trade union relations. They are not as

litigious as American firms, with managers and companies preferring not
to sue each other unless it is totally unavoidable. Many German managers
complain that Americans seem to prefer arguments and lawsuits to compromise agreements. The Germans prefer to settle quarrels through medi-
ation or quiet discussion and consultation, sometimes over a beer, instead
of through what they regard as unpredictable court actions. Germany has
only one-fourth as many lawyers per capita as the United States. It forbids
contingency fees. It does not use juries in civil cases, reducing the temptation for huge punitive damage demands.[5]

German firms work closely with their traditional banks, many of
which own shares in German business firms that the bankers first received
or purchased decades and perhaps generations ago when the firms were
founded or when they needed additional financing. German business
and especially German manufacturing are often called "Deutschland
AG," or "Germany, Inc.," to reflect the mutual intertwining of relationships. The cooperation of German banks, companies, labor, and government to some degree reflects the Hegelian dialectic character of German thinking, for similarly close relations do not exist even in other
European countries.

Germany does not have the equity culture that prevails in the United
States and Great Britain. In sharp contrast to American firms that like to
make public stock offerings and reward their managers through hefty
equity price increases, many large German firms remain in private hands.
Twenty-one German world-class engineering firms, many located in what
is known as "engineering alley" in southern Germany and each having
more than a billion euros (about $1 billion) in annual sales, have never
appeared on a public stock exchange. If you ask their owners, they never
will.[6] The owners and managers prefer to keep the companies running in
their traditional style, although they could almost certainly make fortunes
if the companies went public.

Many important German companies are unknown in the United States
or even within Europe except to the professionals in their fields. Thus,
although a third of the largest companies in Europe are German, only two
German corporations sit in the top fifty "most respected" global companies of the *Financial Times* annual survey. Many German companies like
it that way, although others believe they should get more attention and

respect. But German managers must be doing something right. German manufacturing has a larger share of gross domestic product than manufacturing has in any other major economy.[7]

This environment stresses a combination of professional responsibility and careful calculation. The careers of midlevel and even senior managers can be intensely competitive. They must perform consistently well and must particularly avoid mistakes. They execute their tasks conscientiously and look for incremental improvements rather than dramatic new solutions. They often appear unimaginative because they do not stray too far from the beaten path. They try to do a job better than anybody else and to show, through a combination of steady performance and some bureaucratic maneuvering, that they deserve promotion and can carry higher responsibilities.

Americans who work in a German company environment often find it stifling. They find the structures hierarchical and bureaucratic. They find their supervisors tough-minded, often inconsiderate, seeing others more as pegs in certain jobs than as individuals. Relations tend to be formal; office workers address others by their last names and use the formal *Sie* instead of the informal *du* for years and perhaps during their entire careers even if their offices adjoin.

Americans often emerge shocked at the bluntness of some of the remarks that their German colleagues may direct at each other, speaking in much tougher terms than in American firms. Americans miss the kind of casual banter up and down the line that marks many American firms. They find the atmosphere almost Darwinian, with enormous appreciation for success, total disdain for failure, and careers sometimes made or destroyed overnight. Americans believe that this atmosphere to some extent explains the conservative and risk-averse style of German business management, which also influences most German business negotiation.[8]

There is not much chance to move about in this environment. Unlike Americans, Germans are expected to commit to one firm for life. An ounce of loyalty, as the old saying goes, is worth a pound of cleverness. If one wishes to be regarded as responsible, one may be permitted to change companies once but certainly not twice in a career. In exchange, one receives lifetime security and a good pension, although there is always the risk of a career-ending mistake. Senior managers at the very top level shift from one firm to another on occasion, but for the most part promotions come from within.

The German management style has generally worked well for Germany despite its burdens. In combination with a well-trained and diligent labor force, it has given Germany the most powerful economy in Europe and now the third largest in the world.

Traditional Business Negotiating Behavior

As the world has changed, and as global capital markets and management techniques reflect these changes, Germany has now developed two forms of business negotiating behavior. One might be termed the old style and the other might be termed the new.

The old style of business negotiations in some ways reflects the same culture that has shaped the negotiating behavior of the German government. It includes the following four points:

❏ incredibly thorough preparation, on the basis of a *Gesamtkonzept,*

❏ considerable persistence,

❏ a desire to make a deal, if it can possibly be done on the basis of the *Gesamtkonzept,* and

❏ readiness to commit resources as necessary, but within carefully calculated limits.

Americans and others who have negotiated with German firms, or who have consulted with other firms that have so negotiated, unanimously recall those German qualities. They remember the very detailed preparation that their German negotiating partners brought to the table. The array of facts and figures absolutely staggered the Americans because it showed that the Germans knew the American business at least as well as the Americans themselves did.

The Americans also remember the German emphasis on the *Gesamtkonzept.* Sometimes, when the German firm sought a merger or acquisition, that *Gesamtkonzept* might describe how one company was to fit into the broad strategic plans of the other. Or it might describe how the result envisaged by the German firm would be good for all parties. But it always had a definite coherence and was presented in an authoritative tone. A lawyer who served as advisor for an American corporation in negotiations with a Germany company still remembers the vice president of the American firm leaning over to him and asking, in an incredulous voice: "What *is* a *Gesamtkonzept,* anyway?" The vice president was even more baffled when he heard the answer, for he had never before negotiated on that basis.[9]

Another American lawyer who had conducted many negotiations with German firms said that he learned to recognize a very distinct pattern. The German negotiators always made a long opening presentation, often buttressed by considerable data. They then did not deviate very much from that presentation and their original position. They bargained very skillfully within the limits of their position and often won their points. Finally, if nothing else worked, they would raise their bids for a deal, preferring to do that than to change their *Gesamtkonzept.* He was astonished at the financial resources that some small and midsized German companies could muster when they really wanted an agreement and thought that the concept was right.[10]

An American lawyer who had negotiated with German companies as well as with the German government said that he found the German business negotiators even tougher and more persistent than the government negotiators. They tended to take stronger positions at the outset and were harder to shake from those positions. Although they would gradually adjust their positions, and if necessary raise their bids, it took longer than he thought necessary. Also, he felt, some German companies missed possible deals because they did not show enough flexibility in their conceptual thinking at moments when a deal could perhaps have been made.[11]

There, indeed, may lie the real problem for German companies. They may remain trapped within their concept. They may ask for too much or they may ask for it in a way that their negotiating partners cannot address. In that case, no deal can be reached, or at least none can be reached immediately. As in the case of government negotiations, the parties may need to return to their headquarters to refine their positions and come back later. They may take up negotiations with another party. Or it may not be possible for anybody to reach agreement with anybody else. Persons who have negotiated with German firms have experienced all of those results.

Negotiations with German business can thus present a greater challenge than those with the German government. German firms do not need or value agreement for its own sake as much as the government does. Relations may not be as important for a firm as for a government. A firm can walk away from a bargain more readily. A great deal depends on whether a common concept can be shaped.

But most of the time deals can be arranged. And traditional German firms follow a pattern in reaching them. For example, in early 2002 the German engineering company Knorr bought a truck parts subdivision of the American company Henle. The Knorr *Gesamtkonzept* was to produce more cheaply with American instead of German labor and to be closer to the American market. Knorr reportedly paid $200 million, probably without batting an eyelash. It now has almost half of the world's production of truck brakes, a $3 billion industry. And it is privately held.[12]

An even larger privately held company, Bertelsmann Publishing, has expanded by a consistent policy of internal growth and acquisition. With enormous cash reserves, it can buy what it wishes. The longtime chief, Reinhard Mohn, never moved the firm from its rural setting in Gütersloh and worked steadily at his desk until the age of eighty while making Bertelsmann the world's fourth-largest media giant.[13] His *Gesamtkonzept* was global vertical and horizontal integration in every media direction. And money, while a consideration, was no object if a concept made sense.

But Bertelsmann ended its close cooperation with America Online, a firm it had helped to finance as an upstart, when AOL wanted to merge with Time Warner. Bertelsmann did not want to lose its independence, although the AOL–Time Warner merger might have created significant opportunities for synergy and efficiency. Mohn and his management feared that they would not have a sufficiently large voice in the AOL–Time Warner complex.[14] The *Gesamtkonzept* remained expansion, but expansion with control.

Between 1997 and 2000, German real estate investors purchased large holdings in the United States. They raised Germany's rank as foreign investor in American real estate from seventh to fourth (behind only the Dutch, Canadians, and Japanese). An American real estate agent who had negotiated with several German investors and investor groups described the German *Gesamtkonzept* as follows: they know what they want; they negotiate tenaciously and, if necessary, for a long time; they drive a hard and carefully calculated bargain; they prefer long-term leases; they want to buy only the highest-quality properties offering stable and predictable returns over many years; and, finally, they pay top prices.[15] And the resulting agreement represents the essence of the old style of German business negotiating behavior.

As another example of this kind of thinking, Deutsche Bank in early 2002 bought RREEF, one of the ten major American real estate property management firms with a variety of industrial and commercial properties in major American metropolitan centers. It paid $490 million, regarded as a high price by one investment appraiser. In exchange, the bank received an important foothold in the American real estate management business and diversified its portfolio of real estate investment holdings. One observer said that the deal projected Deutsche Bank "into the big league in global asset management," an area long dominated by American, British, and Dutch firms.[16]

But not all German business decisions, even of the old style, are based only on material considerations. During the civil air negotiations at the beginning of the 1990s, Lufthansa wanted to take over the air routes between Berlin and West German cities as all those cities were becoming parts of newly united Germany. Before then, because West Berlin had remained under Allied occupation, the Soviets had permitted only Western Allied lines to fly through the air corridors. Those airlines found it a profitable business because they had a monopoly. Yet although Lufthansa might have had the right to take over those routes, it paid what many regarded as a high price for the PanAmerican rights to fly from West German cities to Berlin.

Heinz Ruhnau, then chairman of Lufthansa, made the decision for moral and political as well as economic reasons. He remembered how PanAmerican and its pilots had flown through the air corridors to Tempelhof and Tegel during the Berlin blockade and later, ignoring periodic Soviet threats and Soviet jets buzzing their planes. He knew that PanAmerican had helped to keep the city alive politically and economically and chose to make a generous gesture. It could not and did not save PanAmerican, which was already on the verge of bankruptcy. But it kept PanAmerican flying until Lufthansa was ready to take over. And it paid what Ruhnau regarded as a debt of honor.[17]

❏   ❏   ❏

Many German firms that try to compete internationally still suffer from the *verspätete Nation* syndrome despite the widening global spread of German business and its massive exports. They believe that the international system runs on the basis of the Anglo-Saxon model originally established by Great Britain and now directed by the United States. Although German firms have accumulated significant capital reserves during the past half century, some German business leaders still fear that Germany will never acquire the kind of resources controlled by the American and British companies. They look back on two lost wars and the enormous destruction those wars caused in Germany while enabling British and American firms to expand across the world and form the international "Establishment." One reason Germans negotiate so hard is that they believe that they must still catch up.

Small German firms reflect that syndrome more than big ones. They are not sure that they can make it internationally on their own. Many of them come to German embassies for advice when they are negotiating in foreign countries, especially in big countries like China and the United States. They seek counsel and, as necessary, support. They receive it from those embassies and also from German business associations. Larger German firms that have long experience with international contacts do not ask for that kind of help. Nor do major German companies with European Union experience contact the German government unless they want support for an EU regulation that will help them.[18]

Even the German government and the *Länder* governments have the *verspätete Nation* element in their thinking. The Schröder government had promised for a long time to try to shake up some of the more encrusted German firms by permitting more foreign takeovers of German firms. But the new regulations that the government published in February 2002 backed away from radical reforms and adopted measures intended to protect German companies from foreign takeover threats. This removed at least one of the incentives for reform and reinforced concerns that the traditional German system will be hard to change no matter what pressures for modernization remain. But it protected German firms from potentially predatory British and American global corporations.[19]

German firms are sometimes suspected and accused of bribing either German or foreign politicians to win contracts or gain favor. Some notorious cases, like an allegedly major French payment to Chancellor Helmut Kohl's CDU in the early 1990s, have created media sensations. So have other scandals involving other parties. According to estimates made by Transparency International, German firms are not the leaders in the bribery leagues—which are the Russians and the Chinese. But neither are they the least likely to bribe, such as the Australians, Swedes, or Swiss. Transparency International estimates that German companies appear to bribe at about the same rate as American or French companies, although nobody can be absolutely sure because neither governments nor companies publish official statistics.[20]

The New Wave and the General Staff

A senior German business leader observed to the author that modern German managers of major corporations now carry the mantle of the extinct Prussian and German General Staff. Those business leaders bring to their work some of the same qualities as the old General Staff: keen intelligence, analytical precision, an enormous capacity for work, single-mindedness, a Spartan dedication, a rigorous code of conduct, and a sense of purpose, as well as a readiness to make major decisions instantaneously once they command the facts.

Young Germans who want meteoric careers now opt for business as they used to opt for the military, he added. And like the former General Staff officers, they amass facts slowly, evaluate them judiciously, decide coolly, and then move with full force and blinding speed. They look for firms where the atmosphere permits those kinds of careers, or they start new firms on their own.

The businessman said that one should not misinterpret this to mean that these leaders are as brutal as were many General Staff officers in World War II. Nor are they wasteful of resources, especially human lives, as armies on all sides were in the twentieth century. He went back in history to the Prussian General Staff as it had been in the early nineteenth century, fundamentally progressive and reformist, not careerist and reactionary as many General Staff officers later became. He added that many of these businessmen want to function on the widest possible scene, the world stage, at least in Europe but preferably beyond.[21]

A German foreign affairs intellectual agreed with this appraisal. He said he had met some of these men and had found them impressive. He had seen their operations, although at a distance, in the case of several German corporate takeovers of other companies. He had been staggered by their capacity to make plans in secret and then carry them out like lightning.[22]

The German move toward more dynamic management resembles the shift in the American style of the 1990s. The Germans whom the business leader cited are very much like those Americans who have founded or grown major corporations, whether Bill Gates of Microsoft, Steve Jobs of Apple Computer, Larry Ellison of Oracle, Jack Welch of General Electric, or Steve Case of America Online. But such a shift was not expected of the Germans, as the previous great wave of German corporate invention and creation came in the latter part of the nineteenth century when Daimler, Siemens, and Krupp founded the companies that made Germany the economic powerhouse of Europe.

During the first half of the twentieth century, as Germany became engulfed in war and depression, many German businesses and managers fought for survival, and many of them still maintain the cautious consensual style that marked that period. The return to a culture of offense and creativity would mark a significant departure, even if only a few German managers of the new type emerge.

Foreigners might applaud the trend toward a new German managerial style, for it means that the most dynamic young Germans are now dedicating themselves to creation in a civilian realm. But they must also react warily, for it means that German business leaders are beginning to move and thrive in an intensely competitive environment that others must respect and enter with full awareness of what awaits them.

The change in German thinking reflects the pressures that have weighed on German management style because of new trends in the global economy during the 1990s. Despite the German record of success, old values do not always carry far beyond the doorstep in a world of new products, new relations, new forms of investment, and new forms of international dealings. German management style has had to respond. Some firms have even become somewhat more conscious of what has been termed "boosting shareholder value," that is, equity appreciation.

Those new types of leaders, like the older, act on the basis of the same four points listed earlier in this chapter: logical preparation, persistence, a readiness to deal, and a willingness to commit massive resources. They put more stress on persistence and on committing resources for they are by nature visionary. And they have an additional point, which is a sense of global and European strategy.

The new leaders have shaken up many old habits in Germany, although not as many as their American colleagues have shaken up in the United States, and they have brought new dynamism and a spirit of expansion. It is not certain how far this will go. Some experts still deride the German economy as old-fashioned, which is certainly true in large part. But others have written about the change, about what they have called "The Metamorphosis of Germany, Inc."[23]

Certain elements of the German economy have followed the roller-coaster ride of the American economy of the 1990s. To match the NASDAQ market, the German stock exchange created the Neuer Markt, where new German and other companies without established long-term credentials could find more risk-tolerant financing than they could find from banks or on the main old German stock market, the Frankfurt Deutsche Börse. And the NEMAX average of the top fifty Neuer Markt companies rose to a dizzying height of almost 10,000 during the late 1990s before plunging down to well below 500 by the fall of 2002—a rise and subsequent decline about three times as vertiginous as the NASDAQ's. In the process, some leaders of the new style have suffered severe setbacks and the Neuer Markt itself is closing at the end of 2003. But not all has been lost. German firms retain significant leadership positions in biotechnology and nanotechnology. And a German software giant, SAP, has made more business backroom software than any American firm. It is ranked as third in the list of global software suppliers, the only European firm in the top ten.[24]

The German government has made some effort at economic reform to bring the traditional German economy more into line with the outside world. It passed a new tax law that permits German banks to sell their long-standing holdings of major German corporations after January 1, 2002, without paying capital gains taxes. Those holdings are immense. Deutsche Bank alone is said to control about $15 billion in industrial assets across the cream of the German corporate world (DaimlerChrysler, Munich Re, Allianz, etc.). Banks control between 30 and 60 percent of voting shares of such giant firms as Bayer and Siemens; they average 45 percent of voting shares of the thirty largest German corporations. Thus any major sales of such assets could change the mentality of corporate management across the board while unleashing gigantic new funds for investment as well as struggles for control.[25]

As of this writing, however, banks are moving cautiously before making major sales. They want to be careful before dumping large blocks on a fragile market. But the very existence of that possibility could put major firms into play for mergers and acquisitions. And it helps to promote a more venturesome German business negotiating style.

Even if German banks sell some of their major holdings very slowly, they still reinforce a current tendency for more German capital than in the past to come from the markets instead of from banks. This could have a wide-ranging impact on German corporate thinking. Banks want safe and steady dividends from their investments. They also want to exercise control. They encourage management to take few chances and mind its assets carefully. Once the bank assets have been sold, the companies will need to rely more on the capital markets than on the banks for investment funds. And the capital markets may demand greater efforts to enhance shareholder value instead of steady dividend payments. They will probably insist on at least some equity appreciation and some effort to reach faster growth.

But German business will almost certainly avoid the accounting manipulation and outright deception that some American firms have used to boost their share prices and stock options, practices that Germans have long derided and still deride. A German "Enron" or "WorldCom" scandal is highly unlikely.

❏   ❏   ❏

Germany has thus begun to join modestly in the "MBA culture." And the negotiating style of the new German business leaders reflects their own brisk style and decisive attitude as well as some change in the culture of management thinking. It also reflects their growing wish to make more money for their shareholders than in the past. They move more quickly than traditional German managers. They study every situation closely, as their predecessors did. But they take bigger risks, although they try to make sure that the risks are calculable. Because of the accumulated capital of fifty years of German prosperity and because they have not paid out all their profits in dividends, they can purchase almost anything they want.

As German business management style has changed for at least some companies, so has German business negotiating style. The new German business negotiators tend to think less in collective terms than their predecessors, although they have generally not gone over to the American style of rampant individualism. If a decision turns out to be wrong, they may reverse it just as quickly as they made it. In the process, careers and fortunes can be and have been made and lost.[26] They will, therefore, do all they can to make a success of their decisions.

The new German business style may appeal more to American and British executives because those German business leaders have often studied in the United States or Great Britain and are much more ready to speak English. They even feel comfortable negotiating in English and may also think in Anglo-Saxon business terms. One well-known business leader, Ron Sommer of Deutsche Telekom (see later), is reputed to have insisted that all decision memoranda on any international topic be prepared in English because that is how he expects to negotiate. The Deutsche Bank managing board now conducts its meetings in English because most of its members are not German.[27]

The new style may also be even more direct than the traditional. The new German managers like to believe that they can speak in the same terms as Americans. A German manager of the new style began a negotiation by asking for his American negotiating partner's strategic plan. He added: "If your plan fits with our strategic plan, we can do business. Even if it does not, we may still be able to do business, but it will not be for the same amount." He obviously wanted to speak in American terms even if he still thought in conceptual terms. And he wanted to know immediately what might be possible.[28]

In terms of personal style, German business negotiators now also fall into two different styles even as their firms do. Managers from the older

firms tend to be as formal as their predecessors or their government counterparts, although they are beginning to adjust to the more casual American
style. They prefer family names with titles for at least the first few meetings.
But the new style of German manager, especially in such modern industries
as computers, media, and telecommunications, is more ready to move
quickly to an informal and first-name basis with Americans (but only
very rarely to a nickname until they have really established a very warm
personal relationship over time).

One American who had conducted many negotiations with a number
of older- and newer-style German managers said that the traditional certainty had gone and an American would have to judge carefully when he
or she might be "pushing things" and when more casual behavior was to
be expected. He said that, even in the modern age, Germans felt "more
comfortable" if relations advanced naturally without being forced.[29] Thus,
the leader of a German delegation would prefer not to be addressed by his
first name during the opening session of a negotiation.

Not everybody is happy with the changes in some elements of the German style. A European businessman who has spent years dealing with
German companies said that he preferred the old style. He knew what
people wanted and what they thought. They could exchange telephone
calls, letters, and handshakes to make solid deals honored on all sides for
years. The new managers, he said, are less reliable. They will not honor
contracts unless they have been signed and sealed and gone over by teams
of lawyers. They challenge existing arrangements. They introduce mis-
trust, which the old managers would never have done.[30]

The new German business negotiating style has not spread very far as of
this writing. The collapse of the Neuer Markt and the damage caused by
the general global economic slowdown have made even the most modern
German managers think twice. But the new style has gone far enough to
warrant a closer look at several examples and especially at the Daimler-
Benz takeover of Chrysler.

The Daimler Takeover of Chrysler

Nothing better reflects the negotiating behavior of the new Germans than
the brash takeover of Chrysler that Daimler-Benz chief Jürgen Schrempp

directed. It converted one of America's storied automobile manufacturers into what is now a subordinate division of a German company.

The Daimler swallow-up of Chrysler reflected most elements of the new style of German business negotiations, although it also reflected some long-standing German habits. The combination determined the outcome. So did Schrempp's negotiation skills.

The disappearance of Chrysler actually began with a bid by Kirk Kerkorian, a billionaire corporate raider, who joined with former Chrysler president Lee Iacocca in a takeover attempt directed against Chrysler in 1995. The Chrysler management, headed by chairman Robert Eaton, fought tooth and nail against Kerkorian and Iacocca, whom they particularly despised. They proved able to block the venture. But Kerkorian had acquired almost 15 percent of Chrysler shares as part of his effort and had left many Chrysler managers nervous about his future intentions.

While the Kerkorian takeover battle raged, Eaton had begun to reflect on the dangers that Chrysler faced as a stand-alone company in a potentially glutted global automobile market. Thus, when Schrempp later approached Eaton and expressed his interest in merging with Chrysler, he found a very ready listener.[31]

Whatever Eaton may have feared, Chrysler had been wildly successful during the mid-1990s. It had sported the highest profit per car of any American automaker. It had reaped great market attention and had attracted many young singles and couples as customers because of its innovative designs and concepts. Schrempp had told his associates as he maneuvered to take over the company that he wanted Chrysler executives to serve as models for Daimler executives by continuing to act with the same kind of imagination in the merged company, for he thought that Daimler itself needed precisely that kind of innovative spirit.

From the beginning of the formal negotiations in early 1998, German negotiating teams showed themselves to be better prepared. Schrempp drew on papers that had been compiled well in advance, when Daimler executives first saw an opportunity at the height of the Kerkorian takeover battle. Schrempp thought that he understood Chrysler's potential at least as well as Eaton did.[32]

Once the actual negotiations began, Schrempp proved to be the perfect model of the dynamic modern manager-negotiator, whether German or American. With a dominating presence, great self-confidence, a passion for power, and a lust for control, he stage-managed all the negotiations from the opening talks to the final seizure. Moreover, Schrempp in the best German tradition consistently made it very clear that he wanted the deal to go through.[33]

But Schrempp talked a different game from the one he played. He had apparently decided early on that Daimler had to have "the leading position." But he realized that an overt takeover battle would drive the price of Chrysler stock to the sky, far beyond the resources that Daimler and even its largest shareholder, Deutsche Bank, could muster. He therefore promised Eaton in their first meeting that it would be a "merger of equals" and he kept talking of that merger of equals throughout the entire negotiation. He did promise Eaton (perhaps to give the Americans a personal incentive) that Daimler would pay a premium on the Chrysler stock, but the premium he did pay was much less than he would have had to pay in a takeover battle.

By February 1998 Schrempp had put together his negotiating *Gesamtkonzept*. It included a German company under his own control with the Daimler name first. But he decided not to push those items forward until the end. Instead, he permitted the Americans to concentrate on their objectives, which were heavily geared to such financial considerations as a large boost in shareholder value and a tax-free transaction. Schrempp wanted a company for himself. The Americans appeared to want a profit for themselves.[34]

As the negotiations proceeded, Schrempp kept winning one point after another, often without making any concessions. As early as March 1998 he had won Eaton's agreement that the future organization should be a German form of corporation, an A.G., or *Aktien-Gesellschaft*. Eaton said that in exchange he would have to have the joint company called ChryslerDaimler-Benz. Schrempp did not reject that directly but said it would be "difficult."[35]

Germans also maintained their own air of formality. When the negotiating teams met for the first time, the German participants were introduced, or introduced themselves, with their full titles ("Herr Doktor," etc.), while the Americans used their first names. In that same session, the German negotiators based their presentations and proposals on enormous loose-leaf binders. They had recorded every possible bit of information about the two companies and their future operations in what an American called "mind-numbing detail." The Americans talked from short memoranda or notes.

The same German attention to detail also showed itself later during the joint management meetings after the merger itself. The Daimler people had a business plan; the Chrysler people did not. It became painfully clear that Daimler was thinking strategically and Chrysler was thinking tactically.[36]

The only point that Eaton appeared to win during the negotiations between him and Schrempp concerned the Chrysler share price at which Daimler would buy. Eaton absolutely insisted that this was a "deal-breaker"; Schrempp had to meet the price Eaton and his colleagues wanted. He finally got a price of $57.50, which was 28 percent above the then current share price on Wall Street. This was more than the 20 percent premium that Schrempp had first said he would pay, but less than the 40 percent that Daimler staff papers had allowed as the upper limit. Schrempp, who was constantly offering the best Bordeaux wines to his negotiating partners, then suggested dinner together to celebrate. He had reason to do so.[37]

Schrempp finally also won his point on the name. As the negotiations drew closer to a conclusion, he made his position increasingly clearer. He no longer said that he found Eaton's proposal of ChryslerDaimler-Benz to be "difficult," now saying that it was "impossible" for him. He insisted on having "Daimler" come first in the company name. Eaton and Chrysler yielded.

Daimler dominance became ever clearer as the negotiations concluded. Schrempp was declared to be the sole long-term chief executive officer (CEO), with Eaton agreeing to step down as joint CEO after three years. Equally important, Germans won a majority of seats on the management board: ten to eight. Chrysler had eight members and Mercedes-Benz had eight, but Daimler received two additional seats representing the conglomerate's space and financial services divisions. Moreover, Manfred Gentz of Daimler became chief financial officer (CFO), a key position.[38] Thus Daimler and Schrempp controlled the company, the board, and the money. Chrysler ceased to function as an independent concern.

After all the details of the merger had been agreed on and the merger announcement had been made on May 7, 1998, the culture clash deepened. Daimler, a massive and top-heavy conglomerate, was taking over a streamlined and relatively nimble automobile producer. Daimler was formal, structured, and hierarchical, given to suits and ties, personal titles, and family names. It moved slowly and massively. Chrysler favored loose ad hoc teamwork, open discussion, and casual wear.

Other differences beyond management style also emerged. All Daimler staff spoke English; only one American, general manager Robert Lutz, spoke German (having been born in Switzerland). Daimler executives had the bigger expense accounts, but Chrysler the bigger salaries and stock option packages. Many Germans reacted in shock when they learned that top Chrysler managers were walking away with tens of millions of dollars in profit from the merger; Eaton himself allegedly received $70 million.[39]

Daimler executives at first rejected Chrysler efforts to improve synergy by sharing some components of Mercedes and Chrysler cars. They apparently feared that such a practice would damage the Mercedes image and weaken its high-quality brand appeal. Only later, after a German executive had taken over the Chrysler operation, would Daimler consent to sharing platforms between its German and its American models.

The new combined firm began hemorrhaging Chrysler executives as it became obvious that their company would cease to exist as an equal partner. Many of them seemed to have been precisely the managers Schrempp allegedly wanted in order to introduce an innovative and imaginative style into Daimler. If Schrempp had hoped to have the dynamic style of Chrysler management shake up the encrusted style of Daimler-Benz, he had dismissed or lost those who might have helped him. But by then he had shown his intent to concentrate all decisions in Stuttgart. Daimler-Chrysler would be run the German way, not the former American way. The best American managers did not want to remain under those conditions, especially as they all had other job offers.

With the merger coming about on November 11, 1998, Lutz, who was later to become president of General Motors and who had a personal reputation as the quintessential "car guy," had already resigned in October. Others followed, including Chrysler's president, its manufacturing and engineering chiefs, and key designers. Eaton, who had first intended to remain for three years as "cochairman" with Schrempp, retired soon after the takeover after breaking down and weeping at a meeting with Chrysler employees.

Daimler paid a total of $36 billion for Chrysler. But the Daimler-Chrysler share price, which had briefly surged close to $100 a share right after the merger, sank to around $40 a share by the end of 2000 and generally remained in the $25–$55 range for some time after that. By then, the entire company had a lower market value than what Schrempp had paid for Chrysler.

Schrempp, one of the new breed of German managers committed to shareholder value, could not regard that as a success. Many of the original German shareholders complained bitterly. It must also have had a severe capital impact on several major German banks, including Deutsche Bank, which held 12 percent of Daimler stock (and which subsequently had its own credit ratings lowered, although not only for that reason).

As a closing comment on the takeover, Schrempp made his original intentions clear in an interview he gave two journalists of the *Financial Times* in October 2000, one year after the merger. He said he had spoken about a "merger of equals" for psychological reasons when he had first approached Chrysler, knowing that Chrysler executives would have said "there's no way we are going to do a deal" if Schrempp had announced in 1997 that he planned to reduce Chrysler to a division of Daimler. But he insisted that he had, from the beginning, planned a takeover. He had presented one *Gesamtkonzept* but actually negotiated on the basis of another (an unusual step for a more traditional German).[40]

Schrempp later apologized to DaimlerChrysler shareholders for this interview, but the damage had been done. He brought down upon his head the wrath of Kirk Kerkorian, who said that he had lost a fortune because his share prices would have risen far more than 28 percent if there had been a takeover battle instead of a friendly merger. Within four weeks of Schrempp's interview, Kerkorian sued DaimlerChrysler for $8 billion, of which $2 billion represented actual damages and $6 billion punitive damages. As of this writing, the case has not been decided.

More seriously for Schrempp, Chrysler lost money even faster than executives. Chrysler profits collapsed in 1999 and even further during 2000, the first full year after Schrempp's takeover. It lost $1.9 billion in 2001. In a market already weakened by a global recession, it could sell its cars only by offering major discounts. Daimler could have wished for a better start. The *Economist* accused Schrempp of having failed to foresee

Chrysler's impending collapse, letting himself and Daimler be taken for
suckers by Bob Eaton and Chrysler negotiators.[41]

With Chrysler in free fall, Schrempp sent Dieter Zetsche, a veteran
Daimler executive and one of the German management team involved in
the Chrysler negotiations, to take over Chrysler and bring it back to prof-
itability. Zetsche, a man of great drive and organizational ability, proceeded to run it as if it were an old-fashioned German company. He cut
costs, closed plants, and moved even further from the innovative Chrysler
management, design, and production style. He did, however, continue to
introduce new models.[42]

At that point, the DaimlerChrysler story ceased to reflect German negotiating behavior but began to reflect German management behavior.[43]
Zetsche announced that the Daimler headquarters in Stuttgart had made
a full commitment to the success of Chrysler and that he expected it to
begin showing a profit by 2002 or 2003. It did, in fact, make a modest
profit in the first quarter of 2002.[44] Chrysler cars would be well made and
economically produced. But they would not race ahead of the market
with high-profit-margin innovative products as they had done before,
and as Schrempp had ostensibly hoped all of Daimler would.[45] And many
American workers resented the German management of Chrysler, complaining that Germans had no understanding of how to run a company
in the United States.[46]

A common riddle ran around Detroit: "How do you pronounce
DaimlerChrysler?" The answer was: "Daimler; the Chrysler is silent."

As a coda to Schrempp's negotiating behavior, he also purchased 34 percent of Japan's Mitsubishi Motors in March 2000. He wanted very much to
have an Asian connection. But Mitsubishi managers proved much tougher
negotiators than Eaton although their company was in deep financial
trouble. Schrempp could not get majority control and did not get the
profitable truck division, which the Japanese saved for themselves. Instead,
he got the loss-leading automobile division and only a minority of seats
on the board. Mitsubishi remained an independent company, at least for
the moment.[47]

Schrempp had proved to be the model of the predatory new German
raider and negotiator. He had taken control of a major American asset
by a combination of careful planning, fast action, and shrewd judgment

of people—especially of Bob Eaton. But he may have negotiated too well, destroying his objective even as he won it. As a case study, it could serve as a model for other German management takeovers if it turns out successfully but could also serve as a warning if it does not.

Beyond the specific management problems at Chrysler, therefore, lay a deeper question for which nobody as yet has an answer: Can the new German style of manager and negotiator control the tensions inherent in the clash between the old German system, the new German system, and the American style? Not only two but actually three cultures might be in conflict with one another.

Other Modern Business Negotiators

Schrempp has not been alone. Germany has had its share of the new dynamic, innovative, and sometimes rapacious managers and investors, although it also still retains its share of those who follow the old style.

Bernd Pischetsrieder of BMW proved another example of the new investor. Having taken over the leadership of BMW in 1993, he concluded that the firm had too limited a market share and needed to branch out into mass manufacturing if it was to survive in a world of consolidating automobile producers. He became attracted by Rover of Great Britain, in part because the company did have a mature name and image and in part because it had been struggling financially and might be easy to buy. Pischetsrieder's *Gesamtkonzept* concentrated on the long-term independence of BMW, which he believed could be guaranteed only by expansion.[48]

Pischetsrieder made no bones about BMW's interest in buying Rover. He put up the full purchase price that Rover wanted and agreed to pick up some of Rover's debt, for a total price of about $2.5 billion. He proved both decisive and flexible, adjusting his position to suit Rover's needs and being prepared to make a full commitment when necessary. Some of this resembled Schrempp's policy toward Chrysler, although BMW was aiming at a much smaller target.

When the British government showed some reluctance to let a foreign company purchase Rover, Pischetsrieder took it upon himself to persuade the appropriate British officials to do so. Showing himself a genial German host, he then invited the two senior Rover executives with their wives to drinks and dinner at an exclusive hotel in the Bavarian hills. After dinner, they signed the deal.

BMW's purchase of Rover proved to be a mistake. The British management that BMW left in place did not properly refurbish the existing models or introduce new ones, although BMW made the resources available. BMW managers had no more experience managing a major foreign company than Daimler had before it bought Chrysler, and they met with the same kind of cultural and management problems.

To make matters worse, the very strong English pound made Rover cars prohibitively expensive in the continental European market on which BMW had set its sights. Sales fell disastrously. Many BMW executives believed that Rover could have been viable if the British government had joined the European monetary zone instead of letting the pound become so strong.

The BMW board decided that the company could not make Rover competitive without years of effort and massive infusions of capital. They also feared that international currency movements might continue to go against them. They then acted, but in a manner very different from Schrempp's. They sold Rover in 1999 for a token amount (reputedly ten British pounds) while offering some continued support to avoid bearing the onus of closing the major Rover factory at Longbridge in England. They did not lose completely, however, for they were later able to sell the Land Rover division for about $4 billion.

The first part of the BMW story with Rover bears some resemblance to the Daimler story with Chrysler. The two German companies showed similar negotiating behavior. In both cases, a German manufacturer led by a highly charismatic and dynamic personality decided to buy an established foreign brand in order to develop a full range of models for different segments of the market. In both cases, the German executive and his team negotiated effectively, with smart tactics and a readiness to commit whatever resources were needed. In both cases, management problems and some culture clashes followed, although Rover faced a different problem as well owing to the strong pound.

Later, the two diverged. In one case, DaimlerChrysler, the board and the principal shareholders decided to continue to support the purchase as well as the executive who had made it. In the other case, BMW, the reverse happened. Pischetsrieder had to leave (he later became chief at Volkswagen), to be succeeded by Joachim Milbert, who was in turn succeeded by BMW's former finance chief, Helmut Panke. But Panke, although he may be expected to follow a more conservative acquisitions policy, is also a manager in the new German style. He studied in the United States and is fully committed to dynamic management.

Selling Rover helped BMW, which began to make record profits by 2001. And although it had lost Rover, it retained the British Mini and in a separate arrangement purchased the Rolls-Royce name. It thus finally had the wide range of models that it had sought from the beginning.

❐   ❐   ❐

Other German merger and acquisitions negotiations illustrate similar points about the clash between the old and the new negotiating styles and cultures, although they each concluded very differently.

Deutsche-Dresdner

The first merger, negotiated in the spring of 2000, was an attempt by Deutsche Bank to merge with Dresdner Bank, an acquisition that would have cost $30 billion and would have created a banking powerhouse worth $1.2 trillion. In an increasingly globalized world, it would have given Germany a major player on the international stage and would virtually have guaranteed that German banking would enter the major leagues, long controlled by British and American firms.

But the negotiations had not been completed when the merger was announced on March 9, 2000. Deutsche's *Gesamtkonzept* included major efficiency gains, including the disposal of Dresdner's investment banking arm. But Dresdner's *Gesamtkonzept* included some autonomy for its own remaining operations, including investment banking. The two had either misunderstood each other or talked past each other, for when they announced the merger they did not hint at any remaining misunderstanding.

The two banks then negotiated furiously over the next four weeks to try to resolve the problem but could not do so. Dresdner chairman Walter Müller sent an angry letter to Rolf Breuer, the chairman of Deutsche

Bank, complaining that Breuer had walked away from the basic under-standing between them.[49] Breuer would not budge. On April 5, they an-nounced that the deal was off. Breuer then told an interviewer that it was better to break up a wedding at the altar than to enter a disastrous mar-riage.[50] But the *Financial Times* observed caustically: "If you are going to act like an American company when your culture remains essentially German, you are likely to end up with a bloody nose."[51]

One year later, the Allianz insurance company made an agreement to buy a somewhat smaller stake in Dresdner, gaining access to Dresdner's wide-ranging branch banking division—which Deutsche Bank had not apparently regarded as highly—while giving Dresdner the freedom to continue its investment banking.[52]

In terms of negotiating behavior, Deutsche Bank had not done its home-work as carefully as German companies would normally have done. But, as Breuer said, they got out when the misunderstanding became clear, as BMW had done when Rover had proved itself a mistake.

Deutsche Telekom

If ever a company fell between the stools of Germany's old and new busi-ness cultures and its old and new negotiating behaviors, it has been Deutsche Telekom.

A model of the most modern German companies, Deutsche Telekom was launched when the German government decided to end the state monopoly of telephone service. It formed Telekom (as it is usually called) as a private company in which the government nonetheless kept a 43 percent stake. The government selected a new style of manager, Ron Sommer, who had been at the Nixdorf computer company and at Sony, because it wanted someone who could revitalize a staid system.

Telekom performed well in modernizing and freeing the German tele-phone system, lowering prices and improving service and flexibility. But it soon became involved in something infinitely more dramatic and ulti-mately costly, bidding for a share of the modern telecommunications market that was to be developed across all of Europe. To finance its bids and services, it made three highly touted and publicized public stock offer-ings between 1996 and 2000, each at a higher price. It also began intro-ducing new technologies.

The technologies had only begun to be developed but were gaining usage and appeared highly promising. They became known by the generic term "third-generation" communications services, or "3G." They included fiber-optic networks and digital subscriber lines that permit use of broadband communications with almost infinite capacity for such applications as the Internet, television, telephones, cable, and countless others. Estimates of annual communications costs for even a small house ran in the vicinity of $8,000, apparently assuring a vast and steady revenue stream for the service providers.[53]

As more and more of these technologies began to appear within range, Telekom and other national telephone companies throughout Europe began bidding to launch and control the services. The *Gesamtkonzept* appeared to boil down to two principles, not only for Telekom but for its British, French, and other competitors: first, to raise profit expectations by offering the most widely diversified services possible; second, not to worry about cost because telecommunications services would expand to repay whatever was invested. Sommer announced that he had a war chest of $100 billion and wanted to build a global communications network.[54]

With this concept, Telekom left the realm of traditional German negotiating behavior far behind. Sommer became a speculative auction bidder, and he succeeded brilliantly in the auctions for government operating licenses, although he did not get all the properties he wanted (the American company Sprint, for example). He became a regular and often high bidder at major telecommunications auctions. He bought licensing rights in Germany and elsewhere in Europe. He also bought an American company, VoiceStream Wireless, as a consolation prize for not getting Sprint. He paid what was regarded at the time—and even more since—as an exorbitant amount of $30 billion, but he was sure that he could recoup it.

The prices at which Sommer purchased his contracts began to burden the company with massive debt and interest payments, in sharp contrast with traditional German management behavior. And investors began to conclude that Telekom would need to invest at least as much to get its services into operation as it had paid for its licenses. They also concluded that the huge initial investments could be recovered only over the very long haul, if at all. They began to pull out.

By the fall of 2001, Telekom debt amounted to $65 billion, more than the national debt of Poland.[55] And the French and British national telecommunications companies, having all competed against one another, faced the same situation, with the *Financial Times* observing that in three years they had accumulated more debt than Great Britain had amassed over two hundred years.[56]

Those who understood the communications industry and its prospects remained calm, insisting that Telekom's steady cash flow from telephone and cable services could repay the debt over the long run. But others questioned that assessment. In a vicious cut that demonstrated dramatically how the old German culture had still not completely coordinated its activity with the new, Deutsche Bank sold a block of forty-four million shares of Telekom in its clients' accounts the day after it recommended the stock for purchase. Sommer denounced the move because it caused a sharp drop in Telekom shares.[57]

Deutsche Telekom's violently gyrating stock price generated its own serious conflict between the new and the old German management culture. At first, as the price rose dramatically, Telekom became the darling of the German investment community and of the German public. It advertised itself as a *Volksaktie,* a stock for the people, just as the old American Telephone and Telegraph (AT&T) stock had been regarded in the United States before deregulation. Many Germans who would not ever have put their faith or their money into anything as volatile as a share of stock took some or perhaps all of their savings out of banks and bought Deutsche Telekom. With three million private, and often small, investors owning 40 percent of Telekom's publicly traded shares, popular magazines began writing that Germany had finally acquired an "equity culture" matching that of the United States.[58]

Unfortunately, the stockholders were to be bitterly disappointed. Having been valued at about $100 per share in late spring of 2000, the stock sank to below a tenth of that value by the fall of 2002, and well below the offering prices at which many Germans had grabbed what they thought was a ticket to a fortune. Other new European communications equities fell about as much or more, as did American companies such as WorldCom and Sprint.

But traditional German culture could not cope as well as British or American. German investors, unaccustomed to dizzying upward or downward lurches, took Telekom's plunge hard. They complained bitterly and vocally, raising some doubts as to whether Germans were truly ready for a new world of globalization and shareholder risk. Sommer himself was forced out in July 2002.

Telekom's negotiating behavior can only be evaluated over time, perhaps only after a decade of operating results if the company is able to survive in its present form. Sommer acted competitively, not sagely, anxious to preserve for a German company its own major share of apparently promising communications assets suddenly available across Europe and the United States. He had done what may prove best over the long run, but the negotiating behavior he had shown had been light-years removed from that of traditional German companies.

◻   ◻   ◻

The culture clash between old and new German business negotiating behavior will continue for some time and may never disappear completely. Traditional German companies have done well and continue to do well in their fields. They may see no need to change. The new ones, striving to keep up in a different world, need to resolve contradictions that would baffle Hegel himself. Neither the old nor the new will leave the field to the other as Germany and Europe try to make their way in an environment that can destroy even those who shaped it.

5

German Official Economic Negotiations

BECAUSE OF THE HISTORIC LINKS between German business and the German political system, the German government also conducts negotiations that have an economic purpose and an economic element. Those negotiations go beyond the activities of German business, sometimes supporting it and sometimes acting in accordance with wider national interests.

Such negotiations reflect a mixture of political and economic interests and deserve separate consideration. As this chapter will show, they can range widely. German diplomats, bankers, and business leaders negotiate on the economic aspects of the European Union and on European monetary policy. German officials may use German economic power to advance political interests and political power to protect economic interests.

German Trade Negotiations through the European Union

Germany no longer officially functions under its own national trading rules. Instead, it acts under the overall direction of the European Union, a trading bloc of fifteen West European states that hopes to expand across Central and Eastern Europe to become a powerful economic bloc of twenty-seven states in the twenty-first century. The European Union has developed and deepened over a period of fifty years from the days when the Frenchmen Jean Monnet and Robert Schuman first proposed the European Coal and Steel Community (ECSC). It became the European Economic Community (EEC) in 1957 with the Treaty of Rome and the European Union in 1992 with the Treaty of Maastricht. It now has a single currency for most of its members and uniform customs regulations and trade rules for all of them. It also aims to become a single market and to have military and judicial functions.

The European Commission, the executive body of the European Union, negotiates commercial agreements, including tariffs, on behalf of all its members. It does so in the context of the World Trade Organization (WTO) and in constant talks with other major trading entities such as the United States, Russia, China, and the developing world.

Every German political and economic leader and every negotiator insists that the German contribution to European integration over the past five decades has yielded immeasurable economic and political benefits. German negotiating behavior within the European Union reflects that attitude. Germans have always stressed European solidarity as one of their most important political and economic objectives.

Among the major EU states, Germany has been the most eager to promote truly free trade. France, which has a more centralized economy that is not as trade-oriented as the German, leans more toward protectionism. But neither Germany nor France alone can make the European Union function. They must work together. They have done so from the days of the ECSC, to the point that the European Union has often been regarded as a Franco-German axis. They have acted as the backbone of the European trading system, although they have long differed in their approach. They form a mutual benefit society, for the European Union has given French agriculture considerable protection and has in exchange offered a market for German industrial products. The United Kingdom sometimes finds itself in the middle but more often finds that Germany cooperates more closely with Paris than with London.

Because of their differing attitudes, the three leading European states often deal directly with the United States outside the framework of the official trade negotiations conducted by the European Union. Although the European Union has the power to negotiate trade and tariff matters on behalf of all its members, many EU members—including Germany—conduct their own consultations alongside the EU negotiations. German officials from the Economics Ministry or the Foreign Office often speak directly to U.S. embassy officials in Berlin even as they are theoretically instructed to negotiate only through the European Union. And the German embassy in Washington maintains a dialogue with the State Department and the Office of the U.S. Trade Representative (USTR).[1]

Germany has wanted to cooperate with the United States despite problems that may be raised by France. Therefore, at crucial stages of the Uruguay Round trade talks in the mid-1990s, as in the 2000–02 preparation for the next round of trade talks, German and American officials consulted frequently and found themselves generally in agreement.

German negotiating behavior about trade matters must take as much account of the German bureaucracy as any political negotiation. Because the most intense trade talks often concern agricultural products, the German Ministry of Agriculture plays a role. And its approach differs from that of the Economics Ministry or the Foreign Office because German farmers also benefit from the agricultural protection arrangements and price subsidies favored by France. Moreover, protection-minded German farmers in Bavaria and Schleswig-Holstein disagree sharply with export-minded German manufacturers in North Rhine–Westphalia.

On such trading issues, the German government must resolve the internal bureaucratic and political debates between ministries and *Länder* before it can even begin to talk to Americans or take positions within the European Union. German negotiating behavior tends to become tentative while the Foreign Office tries to define a course that properly reflects all the competing interests. Trade policy is one of the areas where the Chancellery and often the chancellor himself must step in to define the German position. There has even been talk in Berlin that the State Secretaries Committee on European Matters should be under the Chancellery instead of the Foreign Office, or that Germany should establish a new Ministry for the European Union. The Foreign Office opposes such ideas.[2]

Despite these German bureaucratic problems, U.S. officials have found it well worth their while to speak directly to German officials on agricultural matters rather than to rely only on the EU Commission's agricultural office (from which, Americans believe, all contacts are immediately reported to Paris). Americans believe that they are more likely to have a success with the European Union if they negotiate with Berlin as well as with Brussels. They believe that Germans will weigh the political value of German-American friendship in the balance and will try to adjust the EU and French position to produce an agreement.[3]

But U.S. officials in the State Department and the USTR have not found talks with German officials particularly easy. They have often differed with German officials about agricultural issues, the common European airframe manufacturer Airbus, and chemical and pharmaceutical matters in which German and American interests often conflict. Even in those cases, however, they have found it useful and sometimes necessary to speak with German officials at the same time that they conduct formal negotiations through EU offices in Brussels or the office of the EU representative in Washington.

Americans have found the German style of consensus building on trade matters more to their liking than what they describe as the French penchant for vetoing every possible compromise until the very last moment. They even believe that the Germans benefit from their consensus building more than the French benefit from their veto, because the Germans gain influence over the negotiating process as it advances, whereas the French only have the chance to cut a deal at the very last moment.[4]

Some of this may change with the passing of the U.S. agricultural subsidies law in May 2002. The European Union may well decide that the provisions of that law violate earlier agreements between Washington and the European Union and go against the interests of open trade in agricultural goods. Coming on top of President George W. Bush's earlier decision to offer some tariff protection to U.S. steel companies, the law may help unleash either a trade war or a series of misunderstandings that make further trade cooperation very difficult. If so, Germany may not be able to pursue a policy that protects its European and agricultural interests and also maintains its relations with the United States. But it will continue to try to do both and will negotiate accordingly.

Germany also uses the European Union for international economic cooperation on more than trade matters. That can cost money. Germany has become the "paymaster" of the European Union, helping more than any other state to finance the two most expensive EU programs: first, the

Common Agricultural Program (CAP) and its support for French, German, and other European farmers; second, the Structural and Cohesion funds that offer economic support to the four least-developed EU states, Greece, Ireland, Portugal, and Spain, and to such underdeveloped regions as eastern Germany.

German negotiators have increasingly seen the European Union as a vehicle to increase German economic access and political influence in the East as well as the West. In the negotiations for EU enlargement to include the former Soviet satellite states in Central and Eastern Europe, Germany has indicated that it will be prepared to help the East European states in their development. It has the single largest interest in EU enlargement and will make the largest financial commitment. But German negotiators within the European Union and with the new applicants have made it clear that Berlin will want to have a very precise estimate of any future German contributions and that there will be unprecedentedly tight limits to German generosity. Berlin has, for example, directly and through the European Union, told the applicants that they cannot count on receiving as much agricultural and development aid as the earlier members did.[5]

The Bundesbank, the Deutsche Mark, and Europe

The Bundesbank, the central bank of the Federal Republic of Germany, carried the responsibility for the value of the deutsche mark (DM) for forty-five years, from 1957 to 2002. This represented a highly important task. Germany suffered two disastrous inflations during the twentieth century:

❐ The first inflation occurred after World War I, between 1919 and 1923, radicalizing the German middle class and paving the way for Hitler. The price of a loaf of bread rose into the billions of marks before the inflation ended with currency reform.

❐ The second inflation came after World War II, when cigarettes, nylon stockings, and Parker pens became the only stable standards of value as the German Reichsmark collapsed into a black market that ended only with the introduction of the deutsche mark in 1948.

After those experiences and their grave social and political consequences, the first West German government under Chancellor Konrad

Adenauer and other leaders of the new Federal Republic decided to establish a central bank thoroughly committed to fighting inflation. They wanted stable money and a predictable economic climate, not a roller coaster of growth and recession. They also decided that the bank had to be able to put this mission above any government's short-term political goals. The bank had to be independent in order to be totally credible.

Therefore, the 1957 charter of the new German central bank, the Bundesbank, gave it one principal task: the preservation of the value of the German currency. And it made the bank independent of any political control by the German government, although the bank had the secondary task of supporting the economic policies of the West German government.[6]

The Bundesbank's negotiating culture and its *Gesamtkonzept* consisted of a single word, "value." In all its negotiations with the German government, with other central banks, and with all other institutions, the bank repeated that mantra. It took to its task with singular determination and ferocity, keeping German real interest rates higher than in most other central banks and stabilizing German growth at a low but steady level to prevent inflation and try (with somewhat less success) to avoid cycles of growth and recession. The Bundesbank held to a firm belief that a stable currency offered the best foundation for investment and growth.

During the second half of the twentieth century, the deutsche mark lost less value than any other currency, including the yen and the dollar. It appreciated consistently in international currency markets, driving down other currencies and establishing a standard of value that those others could only envy.

The Bundesbank saw its mission not only in economic but also in societal and political terms. Knowing German history and the terrible price that Germany and the world had paid for inflationary excesses and for currency collapse, the members of the Bundesbank Council felt a heavy burden of responsibility. They would not risk the political and social stability that the deutsche mark had brought except in exchange for something better or at least as good.

The Bundesbank accompanied its monetary policy with virtually unyielding negotiating behavior. It would not alter its policies, no matter who might entreat it to do so. As the deutsche mark rose, it forced even the U.S. dollar into depreciation. In 1971 it helped to provoke the devaluation of the dollar. With that, it put an end to the Bretton Woods financial arrangement for fixed exchange rates that had governed the global financial system after World War II. No other German institution would have presumed to take that responsibility upon itself.

The Bundesbank posed an even more serious problem for European governments and currencies than it posed for the United States. France, Italy, and even Great Britain could only watch in irritation or exasperation as their currencies consistently depreciated against the deutsche mark. Any government or central bank that wanted to preserve the value of its currency had to follow the same policies as the Bundesbank. Thus, over time, the deutsche mark became the standard against which other European currencies found themselves measured. And the Bundesbank became both a model for others to follow and a threat to those that would not or could not do so.

During the decades of its negotiations with other European banks and institutions, the Bundesbank most often found itself in talks with France. That could mean the French central bank or the Ministry of Finance, but sometimes the French presidency itself, for France bitterly resented the Bundesbank's dominance over European currencies, including the franc.

The Bundesbank doggedly pursued its stability goal throughout the entire discussion that began during the 1970s about closer European monetary cooperation and the possibility of European monetary union. Abandoning the central bank tradition of discreet and carefully modulated language, the Bundesbank revealed a blunt and even declamatory negotiating behavior. It made no secret of its views, stating them repeatedly in lead editorials in the monthly reports it published in German and English and also reprinting them—along with speeches by its president and other leading figures—in its publications. Like other German negotiators, it could be very direct.[7]

The Bundesbank's themes acquired an almost religious fervor as it declaimed against those who would risk the stability of the German economy and polity for the sake of an unrealistic and unattainable effort to forge a common currency among countries with radically different monetary and financial philosophies and policies. It scorned the notion that European leaders could devise one unit of exchange and one standard of value among countries that espoused radically different financial and fiscal policies.

But the Bundesbank did not pursue uniformly critical and hostile attitudes toward other central banks and currencies. If a bank or government indicated that it wanted to maintain a solid currency and would emulate Bundesbank philosophy in its policies, the Bundesbank would cut it a lot of slack. For example, if the Austrian, Danish, or Dutch currencies—which had adopted policies like the Bundesbank's—suffered any speculative attack, the Bundesbank would support them with almost dramatic market interventions. It wanted to widen the circle of sound policy and would help those who had joined it.

In 1979 France and other European states wanted to make a definitive try for European monetary union. French president Valéry Giscard d'Estaing and German chancellor Helmut Schmidt, both former finance ministers, persuaded other European leaders to establish a formal European Monetary System (EMS) with a special Exchange Rate Mechanism (ERM) that would lead to fixed exchange rates and ultimately to a common currency. All states within the European Community (EC) would be members of the EMS. Those who wished could also join the ERM and try to link their currencies, recognizing that this would oblige them to try once again to keep up with the deutsche mark.

As in the past, tensions developed between the Bundesbank and various EC members. France asked for a cut in German interest rates. The German government supported France. But the Bundesbank refused. Exchange rates had to be realigned again as the ERM strained to cope with the contrasts in monetary policies of its members. Within a few years, the new EMS looked like yet another failure.

The governing board of the Bundesbank must have felt under tremendous pressure. Helmut Schmidt believed, as he later wrote, that European integration corresponded to Germany's most vital strategic interest "if our country wishes to avoid a third anti-German coalition."[8] The Bundesbank might be looking for an ideally stable European currency, but Schmidt and others warned that it risked jeopardizing something at least equally vital for Germany's future. They weighed the traditional German interest in a friendly surrounding community against its interest in a solid currency.

Finally, to the Bundesbank's relief, the new French president, François Mitterrand, in the mid-1980s reversed French policy. He decided that he no longer wanted to see France repeatedly embarrassed by currency devaluations more worthy of a banana republic than of a great nation. Therefore, he himself began introducing policies to curtail French budget deficits. He also gave more independence to the Banque de France to pursue monetary policies that would preserve the value of the franc. He used his finance minister, Jacques Delors, to consult in March 1983 with the German finance minister, Gerhard Stoltenberg, and with Hans Tietmeyer of the Bundesbank Council. Delors asked Tietmeyer to revalue the deutsche mark to establish a new parity with the franc. Tietmeyer refused, insisting that the Bundesbank would revalue only if France simultaneously devalued. Delors and Mitterrand accepted Tietmeyer's position.

After that, with France committed to a more conservative fiscal and monetary policy, the EMS and the ERM appeared to function. Other states, such as the United Kingdom and Spain, joined the system. Despite some tension, the system held. The European Community began to pursue plans to establish a European monetary union formally linking West European currencies. France and the Bundesbank appeared to act in concert.

German unification and the sudden costs of absorbing East Germany into the Federal Republic destroyed these plans. The Bundesbank, fearing the inflationary effects of the money surge that followed unification, raised interest rates and refused to lower them despite appeals from France, Italy, and other states and central banks. It finally agreed to do so, but only in response to a personal appeal from Chancellor Helmut Kohl.

The Bundesbank reversal came too late. By 1992 the ERM found itself in crisis. Italy devalued the lira. Other Europeans followed suit. Bundesbank president Helmut Schlesinger gave an interview in which he suggested that more currencies needed realignment, a remark widely and correctly interpreted to mean that the pound should devalue. After a day that the British bitterly called "Black Wednesday," the pound fell and Britain pulled it out of the ERM in a rage. Other upheavals followed in subsequent weeks. So did widespread fury at the Bundesbank, with virtually every European state and central bank accusing the bank of suffering from such an anti-inflationary obsession that it risked jeopardizing the future of European economic cooperation and integration.

Once again, France and Germany had to act jointly. When Kohl in 1989 and 1990 asked Mitterrand to support German unification, Mitterrand drove a hard bargain: he would permit German political unity but only if Kohl permitted European monetary unity. Resenting the dominant role that the Bundesbank had exercised over Europe even while Germany was divided, he made clear that he would not tolerate such dominance once Germany was united and, thus, presumably even more able to impose its will.

Mitterrand said that he would allow Germany to unite but that Germany had to give up the deutsche mark and its separate central bank. Europe was to have a common currency and a new European central bank in which all Europeans—and especially France—would have a voice. The rule of the Bundesbank had to end. And the European Community would have to be replaced by a European Union, compensating for German unification by establishing a larger Europe that could contain the newly united Germany's greater power and presence. Germany could unite only if Europe could unite.

Kohl agreed, especially as he himself believed that Europe should be more united. He accepted Mitterrand's bargain. He then informed the Bundesbank and prepared to negotiate a new European treaty that would create a European Central Bank (ECB) and a new currency to be called the euro. All the members of the European Union could join the euro and have a voice in the new central bank.[9]

The Bundesbank did not yield easily. It insisted that the ECB needed a charter that would instruct it to maintain monetary stability and fight inflation. It also insisted that any states that wanted to have a voice in the ECB and over the euro had to fulfill conditions that would reflect a genuine commitment to fiscal and monetary stability. Those conditions required low inflation rates, low long-term interest rates, and low budget deficits.

Like other German negotiators establishing new structures, the Bundesbank negotiated tenaciously to obtain the best possible terms for those structures. The French government generally accepted the Bundesbank's ideas because it wanted a more stable currency for its own reasons. Other governments and central banks also followed the Bundesbank. Finally, perhaps to the Bundesbank's surprise, almost all European Union members met the Bundesbank's conditions to join the ECB and the EMU and to participate in the euro. Only Great Britain, Sweden, and Denmark chose to remain outside the system, although they suggested that they might join later.

The Bundesbank did not stop there, however. In agreement with the German minister of finance, it wanted to institutionalize the new rules governing fiscal responsibility. European Union members, also favoring an anti-inflationary policy, agreed. At the EU Dublin summit of December 1996, the European Union agreed on a "Stability Pact" under which states that exceeded a limit of 3 percent of their gross domestic product in their budget deficit for any single year would have to pay a deposit that they would forfeit if they did not reverse the situation in three years. The Stability Pact guaranteed, at least on paper, that the bank had won its battle to impose anti-inflationary policies on Europe as a whole.

On January 1, 2002, the deutsche mark ended its successful career as Germany's currency and as Europe's dominant standard of exchange and of value. And the Bundesbank became just another member of the European System of Central Banks (ESCB) and the ECB Governing Council, although it certainly had a greater influence than most. In particular, it sent one of its principal economists, Othmar Issing, to be the member of the ECB Governing Board, responsible for overall policy.

Even as it lost its unique power, however, the Bundesbank had achieved at least some goals. It had helped to establish a European currency. It had compelled other European states to pursue policies similar to its own. It could hope that the new currency would, indeed, become as stable as the deutsche mark had been. Like any other German negotiator, it had helped to build a structure shaped to meet its most essential conditions. Like the others, of course, the Bundesbank could not be certain that the structure would hold. But, again like other German negotiators, the Bundesbank presumably reasoned that it could have greater influence through a congenial institution than on its own in isolation.

Bundesbank negotiating behavior had followed the classic German model, at first unbendingly uncompromising but then shifting when a more important objective came within reach. As it turned over its task to the European Central Bank, it could conclude that it had served its *Gesamtkonzept* loyally and well.

Ironically, Germany became the first European state to risk violating the Stability Pact. Because a recession cut into government revenues, the

German budget deficit for 2001 rose to 2.7 percent of its gross domestic product, dangerously close to the 3 percent limit agreed on under the Stability Pact. The European Commission considered issuing a formal "early warning" that Germany would be subjected to fines if it did not remedy the situation. Other European states and their finance ministers in particular could be forgiven a little *Schadenfreude* to see Germany so hoisted on its own petard. In response to Chancellor Schröder's urgent pleas, however, the commission in early 2002 decided not to proceed with such a warning.[10]

The International Monetary Fund Succession

Although Germany had become united in 1990, it had not risen during the following decade to what many Germans regarded as its proper place in the global economic order. Many German political and economic principals believed that the time had come when they could lay claim to a major office within the global institutions that had been established after World War II and that Germans believed they had respected and served responsibly. They did not want a "place in the sun" and did not want to dominate others, but they thought they should get more recognition.

Thus a particular German-American dispute loomed very large during 1999, soon after the government of Gerhard Schröder had come into office. Schröder had been elected in 1998 as the first new German chancellor after unification, Kohl having been reelected in 1994 but having served in divided as well as united Germany. And Schröder thought that the new united Germany should have a wider global weight than the divided Germany.

Schröder thought he saw an ideal chance when Michel Camdessus, the managing director of the International Monetary Fund (IMF), resigned in 1999. Schröder decided that Germany's economic weight and influence justified having a German as Camdessus's successor.

Schröder telephoned U.S. president Bill Clinton to ask his approval and support. Clinton, who had not been briefed but who wanted to be agreeable to the new chancellor, said that seemed like a good idea. He did not think that he had made a definitive commitment. Schröder, however, read Clinton's reaction as an expression of support. He thereupon turned to the German bureaucracy to nominate a suitable candidate. They proposed

Cajo Koch-Weser, who had served many years in senior positions at the World Bank, to succeed Camdessus.

Schröder formally nominated Koch-Weser, confident that Clinton would keep what Schröder thought was a promise and that the United States would support his nominee. Having made his career as a German *Land* politician, Schröder knew little about the ways of international finance and about the existence of an international "Establishment." So he was surprised to find that Washington opposed Koch-Weser, allegedly because he had not functioned at a sufficiently high level to bring the needed senior experience and prestige to the IMF. Schröder heard that U.S. treasury secretary Larry Summers had personally opposed Koch-Weser.[11]

Schröder as well as German political and economic circles reacted in shock. They believed the Americans were trying to create a self-perpetuating privilege for the victors of World War II even in an area where Germany had reached a respected standing. If Germans could not reach high international office in the financial world because they had not previously held such high office, how could they ever hope to get anywhere? Schröder insisted that he had a commitment from President Clinton and he would not be denied.

Despite his irritation, Schröder decided not to challenge Washington over Koch-Weser. Instead, he nominated Horst Köhler, the president of the European Bank for Reconstruction and Development. Schröder believed that nobody could question Köhler's credentials, as he had also been the state secretary in the German Ministry of Finance responsible for international monetary matters.

When Washington then objected to Köhler, Schröder became angry. He thought that the United States was trying to keep Germany subservient. Berlin heard more reports that American opposition came not from Clinton himself but from Summers. According to these reports, Summers wanted to promote his friend Stanley Fischer, the American first deputy managing director of the IMF, to the top spot and also wanted to change the tradition under which an American served as president of the World Bank while a European held the top IMF post.

Washington had wanted the World Bank position for decades as it was at first considered the more important position because of its role in international reconstruction and development after World War II. Germans believed that Summers now wanted the IMF job for his friend because the IMF handled international monetary crises and thus ranked higher in his esteem than the World Bank. And they saw it as a sign that Washington and Summers wanted total dominion over global monetary and financial matters.[12]

German officials heard that France and Great Britain, while ostensibly supporting Köhler as a gesture of European solidarity, had privately told Washington that they would prefer somebody other than a German. Moreover, wanting to keep the World War II victors' privileges intact, they had added that they had names of their own to propose.

Schröder would not be denied. He thought that Clinton and Summers were demeaning the new importance of Germany in the international arena, especially in financial matters, and he went into a full-court press. He insisted that all other EU members, especially France and Great Britain, support Köhler as an EU nominee. He called Clinton again to make clear that this matter could turn into a major crisis in German-American relations.

Clinton told Summers to back off. He agreed to Köhler's nomination and supported the German candidate. Thus, Köhler became the new managing director of the IMF as of May 1, 2000. He also became the first German in the top rank of global financial institution leaders. Germany had broken into the traditional international Establishment.

The IMF nomination illustrated important elements of German negotiating behavior: first, German strategic tenacity on the basis of an important *Gesamtkonzept*—that Germans now belonged in the top rank of international finance; second, German tactical flexibility—a readiness to try a second nomination rather than to insist on the first.

The third element of German negotiating behavior surfaced only at the end, but it ultimately became decisive: Germans do not like to have a bargain altered once they have signed on. Rightly or wrongly, Schröder and others suspected that U.S. opposition to Köhler reflected not only American attitudes about Köhler himself but an American wish to change the arrangement under which a European would direct the IMF. This, they thought, shifted the European-American bargain in fundamental ways and did so at a time when Europe was moving toward a united currency and therefore should have a greater rather than a lesser voice in global monetary matters. If U.S. opposition to Köhler reflected an American power play, then Schröder and the entire German financial world would not accept it.

Germany had worked closely with and within the IMF and had long regarded the IMF as a vital institution because of its powerful role in German and global prosperity. Germany was one of the leading members and contributors. German financial leaders did not want such an organization to become an extension of the U.S. Treasury. They recognized that the United States would always have a leading role in global monetary matters, but they wanted to limit that role to what they regarded as acceptable. And German negotiating behavior reflected that view.

The Use of Economic Incentives

The Federal Republic of Germany has become, by virtually any standard, one of the richest countries in the world. Even though the states of the former East Germany still suffer from major problems, Germany as a whole is prosperous. For the first time since 1914, many Germans expect to be able to leave real assets to their heirs. They still do not have the same vast international capital resources that Great Britain and the United States have accumulated over centuries, but they are much better off than they would have dared to hope in 1945.

As West Germany expanded its wealth after the "economic miracle," its leaders began to realize that they could use their resources for diplomatic purposes. With that realization, German negotiators began to carry a bag full of economic incentives to persuade others to accept their views. Germany's wealth gave first Bonn and then Berlin a significantly larger voice than they would have had without it.

During most of the 1950s and 1960s, the strength of the West German economy helped to give Germany a respected position in the Western alliance. By its export-oriented production mentality, West Germany acquired large trade surpluses and exchange reserves in the tens of billions of dollars. Unlike France's Charles de Gaulle, West German leaders tried to support the U.S. dollar by promising not to convert their dollar reserves into gold. This helped persuade successive U.S. administrations not to reduce U.S. forces defending West Germany.

The Federal Republic also used its funds to protect the Hallstein Doctrine, under which it would break diplomatic relations with any state that recognized the German Democratic Republic. West Germany launched significant aid programs to many postcolonial states in Africa and Asia. Those states then refused to recognize the GDR because they did not want to jeopardize their chances to obtain West German aid. Beyond supporting the Hallstein Doctrine, German aid programs also began to expand Germany's reach abroad. So did the reputation of German products, especially cars and machine tools.

In the 1970s, after U.S. president Richard Nixon had abandoned the gold standard and ended the constant arguments with Bonn about supporting the U.S. dollar, German assets began to carry broader diplomatic weight. After Helmut Schmidt had become finance minister in 1972, he began a collaboration with U.S. treasury secretary George Shultz and French finance minister Valéry Giscard d'Estaing between 1973 and 1975 that led to the creation of the Group of Five (G-5), which has now become the Group of Eight (G-8). Those groups gave the Federal Republic for the first time a real weight in the financial and political deliberations of the major Western nations. Schmidt openly used the strength of the German economy and the deutsche mark to bring Germany back into the ranks of major world players.

Germany also used its economic power to help in its negotiations with the Soviet Union and Eastern Europe. After Brandt had concluded the first détente agreements with Moscow in 1970, he and Brezhnev and their economic and commercial officials reached a series of trade and aid agreements that gave Moscow billions of deutsche marks in credits. Bonn sold high-technology goods, from machine tools to large-diameter pipe, that Moscow could not buy elsewhere. Trade between West Germany and the Soviet Union quadrupled between 1969 and 1975, to a level of $4 billion. Later, despite U.S. reservations, West Germany sold the Soviet Union thousands of high-quality trucks on generous credit terms. The Soviet interest in obtaining this trade and these credits almost certainly helped Brezhnev and his colleagues decide to have détente with West Germany at the expense of the GDR.[13]

Credits for Moscow and trade with the Soviet Union became a hallmark of West German policy during the following decades and of German policy after unification. Kohl granted Gorbachev DM 60 billion in aid and credits in exchange for unification. After Gorbachev's fall and the collapse of the Soviet Union, Kohl helped Boris Yeltsin's Russia and other former states of the Soviet Union. Schröder gave aid and credits to Vladimir Putin and offered generous repayment terms for earlier West German credits to the Soviet Union and Russia. Germany also gave aid and credits to East European and Baltic states, trying to widen the area of European stability. The payoff came in the form of closer relations. Germany essentially bought its way into Eastern Europe and into Russia.

The German *Gesamtkonzept* in any negotiations involving German aid or trade was to use economic incentives to increase German influence. As discussed in chapter 3, the policy remains a hallmark of German negotiating behavior and will almost certainly continue. Aid and trade are the most important assets that Germany can bring to the table, and German negotiators have not hesitated to use them.

The Treuhandanstalt for East German Property

When German unity came in 1990, a German trustee agency called the Treuhandanstalt was given the authority to take over all former East German production and service facilities in order to prepare them for sale. The *Gesamtkonzept* was to sell what could be sold, close down the rest, and make the eastern German states of the newly united Germany economically viable by replacing the old communist structures with companies attuned to the market.

But the Treuhand, as it quickly became known, had a more important but private *Gesamtkonzept:* to preserve as many assets as possible for West German firms by giving those firms preference over foreign bidders. And the Treuhand, under the leadership of Birgit Breuel, followed that specific concept even at some cost to its wider mandate.

Germans, and especially the Treuhand, limited foreign investment in production facilities in the former East Germany and East Berlin. They largely preserved it for West German investment. They thus kept out the modernizing influences that might have come in from other countries, especially the United States.

The Treuhand used a complex negotiating system in which it invited foreign bidders for East German property to submit a bid that included not only a price but a business plan. It could then judge all bids on its interpretation of the business plan. As most German companies knew how to prepare a German business plan better than foreigners, this already gave West German firms an advantage. But even when foreign firms hired German consultants to help prepare plans, the Treuhand almost always decided to the advantage of the West German firms.

Many foreigners, including Americans, complained. Mark Palmer, the president of the Central European Development Corporation, denounced what he termed *"TreuhandSozialismus."* He complained that American firms were being disadvantaged in favor of German firms and that the Treuhand was then spreading the false myth that American firms were not interested in investing in eastern Germany. Frederick Irwin, the president of the American Chamber of Commerce in Germany, made a similar complaint. The French economics minister, Pierre Béregovoy, accused the Treuhand of lacking transparency, with other French officials complaining that the Treuhand secretly forwarded their bids to West German competing firms that could then match or beat them. British and Belgian officials and businessmen also complained.[14] Breuel traveled to the United States and around Western Europe, allegedly to encourage foreign investment, but she did not then make sure that the foreign firms got an equal chance.[15]

In one particular case, an American telecommunications firm offered to install a wireless communications system throughout East Germany and East Berlin, completely modernizing the decaying East German system. Breuel rejected the offer, preferring to have a German system. It took longer to install than the system proposed by the American firm and cost more.[16]

After some time, many American companies decided they would not bother to make the effort any more. Two Washington lawyers with considerable experience in Germany, who had become consultants to a number of large American firms trying to make successful bids for a variety of companies, said that they found the entire experience very frustrating. They traveled to Germany several times to negotiate with the Treuhand. They received many papers to fill out and many promises, but their clients won few contracts, and those were too small to justify the efforts they had been forced to make. Because of their contacts in Germany, they knew the companies that did win the contracts as well as the approximate bids and the conditions those companies had offered. They thought the comparisons showed that the system had not been truly open and that the Treuhand's negotiating behavior had been misleading.[17]

There were some exceptions, such as a General Motors plant at Eisenach, an enormous investment that no German company wished to make. General Motors also had the advantage of working through its German subsidiary, Opel, which would actually manage the plant and make it appear to be a German investment. Another exception was Dow Chemical, permitted to purchase a former East German firm but only after considerable U.S. official intervention because the Treuhand had originally wanted to sell it to a German.[18] Otherwise, Americans won only a few dozen contracts out of thousands, and many of the investments they were permitted to make were in new retail facilities or restaurants, such as McDonald's. And other foreigners, while they may in some instances have won major contracts (the French at the Leuna chemical plant and the Norwegians at the Rostock shipyards), also found few chances.

The German decision to curtail foreign investment proved a mistake for Germany itself. Many West German firms did not carry out the elaborate business plans that they had presented to win Treuhand approval. It later became clear that many had wanted to take over the facilities in East Germany not to produce there but to block potential competitors or to count the East German assets as a loss against their profits in West Germany. And many abandoned their plans altogether during the 1991–92 recession, letting the facilities lie fallow and letting the workers go. The chance to revitalize German business practices by introducing new techniques and different ways of thinking was lost in East Germany.[19]

Only later, after the Treuhand had closed its doors and as the unemployment rate in eastern Germany climbed above 20 percent, could the eastern German states themselves begin to attract foreign investment.

Kurt Biedenkopf, the minister-president of Saxony, made a particular effort to interest foreign and especially American firms. He came several times to the United States and succeeded in attracting a number of facilities, including a major chip-making plant built by Advanced Micro Devices near Dresden. He has kept the unemployment rate in Saxony lower than in other parts of eastern Germany and has developed what he proudly calls a "Saxon Silicon Valley."[20]

Treuhand negotiating behavior did indeed serve its two concepts: to privatize East German productive properties and to keep them largely in German hands. Breuel had no mandate to modernize the German economy, although the Treuhand had the theoretical authority to favor those companies submitting a modernizing business plan. Her negotiating behavior achieved its objectives but at a short-term cost to its credibility and at a longer-term cost to the future of the German economy.

German Economic Negotiating Behavior in Retrospect

German business and official economic negotiations demonstrate, perhaps better than anything else, the lasting effects of culture and the dilemmas that culturally derived behavior faces under new conditions.

On the whole, older German business negotiating behavior has remained almost consistently successful, whereas the new has suffered some reverses along with its successes. German traditional business leaders, with their stress on gradual growth, have continued to negotiate successfully to achieve steady progress and to make some acquisitions (see chapter 4). But they have also had their share of failures, most specifically in the former German Democratic Republic. And traditional German business as well as the German government may not find the formula to bring the German economy into a new age of growth and prosperity.

German government and private economic management and negotiating cultures also need to decide how best to face a world dominated by a different culture, the American. The "MBA culture" is, for better or worse, expanding throughout the world. It challenges traditional German government and business attitudes. And Germans need to find ways to adjust.

Traditional German government negotiating culture on economic matters, like business negotiating culture, may not meet the needs of the hour. It may not produce as much growth as Germany now needs. The Treuhand succeeded in the short term but is failing in the long term. And the new and more dynamic style used by Schrempp at Daimler and by Sommer at Telekom raises problems of its own.

The "MBA culture" faces problems as well, in Germany as in the United States. But the contrast between the old and the new has hit Germany particularly hard and has left some uncertainty about where to turn next.

6

The Future of German Negotiating Behavior

ANY STUDY OF GERMAN negotiating behavior must ask how that behavior will evolve now that Germany has been united again. Will Germans continue the generally successful style of the decades between World War II and the beginning of the new millennium, or will they return to the disastrous style of the empire? Will they become more demanding and more ready to go it alone now that they no longer need NATO, the United States, and the West as a whole to defend them against the Soviet threat?

Some observers have suggested that the Germans may now want to be "*Ja,* a little proud" of what they have accomplished at home and abroad.[1] Does that imply that the world might have to expect a return to the arrogant, swaggering, and aggressive Germany of the first unification? Often, people have that period in mind when they speak darkly of "the German past."[2]

But the simple question about a return to "the German past" misses the point, which is that "the German past" is many things. And the first unification, from 1871 to 1945, actually represented a detour from the long line of German history, culture, and diplomacy. The immense costs that the first unification imposed on Germans and on all the nations with whom Germany wants to have good relations suggest that one cannot answer any question about the future of Germany in such simplistic terms.

That said, the new Germany will clearly need to change its international policies and perhaps its negotiating behavior to account for the effects of German unification and also to reflect the demands of European unity and the new world in which Germany and others now negotiate.

That change will take several forms, including a wider range of topics for negotiation.

Topics for German Policy and for Negotiation

German negotiators already need to deal with topics very different from those that dominated the world from the 1940s to the 1990s. Then, German diplomats negotiated mainly about Germany itself: their own existence as a people; foreign forces on German soil; German sovereignty; family passes for Germans across the Berlin Wall; a German role in the European Union and in NATO; compensation for Hitler's victims; and, finally, a topic they only half expected to arise and whose name they did not dare to utter, unification.

Although West Germany played some important roles in the world even before 1990, especially in economic matters, those roles always appeared linked to its need to accommodate those it relied on for support and for security.

Now, Germany will need to negotiate more about what Germany is to do, not so much about what Germany is to be.

New topics arise almost every month, and most of them will engage German diplomats over the next several years and perhaps decades:

❒ German forces, once strictly confined within Germany's borders and within the limits of the NATO area, now patrol in the Balkans, in Afghanistan, and on the waters of the Indian Ocean. Germans have even held command over international forces in the Balkans and could have had other commands if they had accepted them. German ministries, led by the Foreign Office, the Defense Ministry, the Development Ministry, and the Finance Ministry, must negotiate and consult continually on what Germany is to do and where. This can mean negotiations about a German presence not only in the Balkans but also in such Central Asian areas as Afghanistan or beyond.

❐ The German international role grows almost daily. Germans are not only asked to send more forces but also asked to spend more money and be more active politically in ever more places than before. Sometimes the requests come from allies, such as the United States, France, or Great Britain. Sometimes they come from organizations, such as the United Nations, NATO, or the European Union and its members. Meeting all those requests will require almost endless negotiation and consultation. And Germany will have to judge carefully what it can do to help others and yet not appear too dominant. Germans will no longer need to show loyalty to please their allies, but they will need to decide where their interests lie and where they do not.

❐ Not one of the organizations of which Germany is a leading member can remain as it is in the new world. Those organizations are only beginning the process of adjustment. Germany will want to take a lead role in making those changes. The European Union must integrate further if it really wants to become a single market and a powerful force in the world, and the debate has now begun between those who want the least and those who want the most integration. Chancellor Gerhard Schröder in the spring of 2000 urged the European Union to become a real federation. But France and Great Britain remain opposed. Germany also wants real enlargement of the European Union, bringing in perhaps ten new members over the next decade or two, but Germans do not want to pay the lion's share of the bills as they have done in the past. And NATO clearly cannot continue as it is now if it wants to accommodate a growing Russian role and if it faces greater prospects for its forces to deploy in areas outside its original mandate. It must be restructured, and German leaders must help negotiate how to restructure it.

❐ The German role in the world grows, especially in economic matters. German business leaders have been appearing with ever greater frequency in Russia, the states of the former Soviet Union around the Baltic Sea and in Central Asia, China, and Korea. Almost every state in the world wants to improve its relations with Germany, in part to get German money but also to gain German support in its many organizations. After September 11, 2001, Germans will almost certainly be asked to do even more to help to guide the world in new directions.[3]

It is a far cry from the days of German isolation, and most Germans welcome it despite its costs.

❏ German business will increase its international role and will continue—and perhaps expand—the campaign of acquisitions that it has been conducting. German capital wants to go abroad to cheaper production sites. And German companies have cash reserves that they could invest quite profitably. All these realities will lead to many more rounds of German business negotiations. Some of the expansion will come from the old style of German companies, some from the new.

Even a superficial listing of these topics shows that the German agenda has grown much larger and will expand even further over time. It includes the management of Europe, the management of transatlantic relations, and the management of the world economy. It will resemble nothing that recent German diplomacy has attempted, although the diplomacy of the Holy Roman Empire occasionally veered in that direction under Charles V and the diplomacy practiced by Bismarck sometimes tried it. The new Germany, as well as the German *Länder,* will need to look closely at problems that Germans have not needed to address so consciously in recent decades.

As this review shows, the German national interest in political and diplomatic matters will continue to show itself mainly by international action. It will find expression in international organizations. Germany will not seek greater power for itself, but it will seek greater power and authority for the international organizations of which it is a member. It will try to find greater influence for itself within them and will negotiate for that if necessary.

Young Germans are not nationalistic in the traditional sense and cannot get excited about purely national themes. Instead, they look for international purposes to serve. And they will continue to carry that consciousness into their diplomacy.

If German political leaders, diplomats, and negotiators were to utter the common theme that unites their thinking and negotiating behavior, it would be "structures, structures, and structures again." German negotiating objectives will concentrate ever more on trying to establish strong organizations, widening their radius of activity, and having an influential and sometimes central role.

The idea of Germany as *das Land der Mitte* will revive but in a positive sense: not because it will mean threats toward and from all directions, but because it will mean new contacts toward and from all directions. And Germany will ever more want to be surrounded by members of the same clubs to which it belongs, if necessary by expanding the clubs. It will not want to be a leading actor as much as to have a leading influence.

The Europe of Berlin

As these trends emerge, Europe as a whole will gradually evolve in the direction of what might be termed "the Europe of Berlin."

The essence of the concept can already be seen. Germany has the European Union and NATO as its links to the West. It has the OSCE as well as an expanded NATO and an expanding European Union as its link to the totality of Europe. It has begun to establish closer relations with Russia and is now becoming ever more involved everywhere in Europe. From the Atlantic to the Urals, German diplomats and businesspeople are busily forging new ties and engaging in new activities. Of all European and Atlantic states, Germany has the widest range of contacts and activities throughout all of historical and geographic Europe.

Europe has gone through four historical phases since the end of the Thirty Years' War in 1648, and it is now entering the fifth:

- ❐ The first phase, the Europe of Westphalia, emerged from the Peace of Westphalia of 1648. During that phase, Germans lived in the Holy Roman Empire and had little international role. Napoleon shattered that Europe and threw the Germans into a new and indefinite role in the center of Europe.

- ❐ Next came the Europe of Vienna, created by the Congress of Vienna in 1815. The great powers of the day tried to reconstitute the old Europe but could not do it without finding a way to solve the German problem that Napoleon had precipitated. That Europe, having failed to solve the German problem, was shattered by World War I.

- ❐ After that came the Europe of Versailles, created by the Versailles Treaty. It tried to suppress the German problem but could not do it. That Europe was shattered by Hitler's invasion of Poland in 1939.

❑ Fourth came the Europe of Yalta, created by the Yalta agreement of
1945. It tried to solve the German problem by a new division, but that
also failed. The East Berliners shattered that Europe when they broke
through the Berlin Wall on November 9, 1989.

The fifth phase will be the Europe of Berlin. It must be named for
Berlin because it began with the breach of the wall and because the treaties
ending the division of Germany and Europe—and thus putting an end
to the Europe of Yalta—were signed in Berlin. It has solved the German
problem by uniting the German nation but not suppressing it. It may
have found the best solution yet.

Several factors will dictate that the new Europe will witness the slow
but steady rise of Berlin as the center of a wider Europe. Europe will itself
integrate into a wider political whole. With Russian membership, NATO
has changed totally. It has now become a new super OSCE, an organization primarily dedicated to cooperative diplomacy instead of military
security. Although NATO will keep its headquarters in Belgium, it must
change its thinking to Europe as a whole.

In this context, Germany will play the role of European coalition
builder more than any other European state. It has a greater interest than
any other in the establishment of a European-wide consensus. Unlike
France, the United Kingdom, or even Russia, Germany cannot and will
not achieve anything on its own. It must, and will, work through Europe.
Germans must make the coalitions work and will do it because they have
no choice. And the role of Berlin will become ever more important.

Finally, even as the Germans can do nothing without others, others can
do nothing without the Germans. Berlin must be at the center of a growing number of activities, for the Germans will be the least nationalist
major partner as well as the only one that can really make things happen.
Germans will not be able to avoid a wider role.

The Europe of Berlin is hardly evident yet, especially because Germany
has not and will not give up its culture of reticence completely. And Berlin
is not even one of Europe's leading cities any more compared with London
or Paris. But these things will change and are, in fact, already changing.

European organizations will wrap themselves slowly but surely around
Berlin. The city is located in the geographic center of the wider Europe.

It can become a center for communications, conferences, and diplomacy. It will slowly become the place where the most important decisions are discussed and perhaps made. In the process, Berlin will start to serve as a coordination point not only geographically but substantively.

The international bureaucracies can and will remain in Brussels, but the real centers for consultation and decision will move to the east. Berlin will become the logical middle ground.

The Europe of Berlin will have one very important distinction from that of the more recent past. For the first time since the Napoleonic Wars, Europe will have a kind of federation, the European Union, at its center, instead of being a Europe directed only by nation-states. The two ugly centuries of European wars of aggression, wars of revenge, and then wars of re-revenge can come to an end, as Europe returns to a level of sanity it has not experienced in centuries.

The Europe of Berlin will not come into being because any nation or any single national leader wants it. The Germans themselves do not want it and neither do the French, the British, or the Russians. But it will come into being because it lies within the logic of a new and wider Europe and of a Germany ready to assume responsibility without trying to assume power.

German Wishes

As German leaders and officials have begun to talk about the kind of Europe and the kind of world they want, several traditional objectives have become increasingly clear:

- ❐ Stability. Germany wants to help find ways to prevent disruption. It needs a framework for international peace, solidarity, and mutual reassurance.

- ❐ Strategic multilateralism. Germans want a network of cooperating organizations that becomes so wide and so diverse that it acquires strategic significance.

- ❐ Influence. Germans want to have some weight in that network of cooperating organizations, and they want to gain it primarily through diplomacy. Even when they deploy troops, they deploy them not for military purposes but to reinforce their influence and their diplomacy. Those troops represent security by diplomacy, not by force.

❏ "Normalcy." Germans want to live in what some call a "normal" country. They want to forget about having been divided and about the fears
that others may have of German domination. They want to be able to
make their policies without being constantly examined. They may have
achieved a measure of rehabilitation, but they have yet to establish
their place.

❏ Acceptance. Willy Brandt used to say that the time would come when
Germans would not automatically bend their knee as penitents when
they entered a room.[4] That time has indeed come, but the Nazi stain
still lingers. The Germans would like to see it removed, not in order to
forget—which they themselves say they will not—but in order not to
be reminded.

All these objectives will keep German diplomats very busy, either in
negotiations for new structures or in consultations to reinforce and
expand the old.

❏   ❏   ❏

Yet even as these objectives may be clear, there may well be a tentative
quality to German policy and negotiating behavior for some time. For
Germany still has relatively little experience in conducting the foreign
policy and diplomacy of a united democracy.

Germany became united as a democracy for the first time in 1919, in
what became known as the Weimar Republic (see chapter 1). But the
Weimar Republic lasted only fourteen years before Hitler seized absolute
power in 1933. Germany was then again united as a democracy in 1990,
in what is now sometimes known as the "Berlin Republic."

Counting those years together, Germany has barely passed twenty-five
years of diplomatic experience as a united democracy. The West German
experience, while relevant, is not identical because the borders and depen-
dencies were different. Even the United States, often termed a "young"
nation, has experienced almost ten times as many years of democratic
diplomacy as Germany. Therefore, neither Germans nor others now
know exactly how German diplomacy will evolve over the long run. But
this discussion shows the general direction in which it is moving.

Prospective Negotiating Behavior and the Seven Points

A review of prospective German foreign policy shows that German negotiating behavior will remain as it has been over the past several decades.
German foreign policy objectives are almost ideally suited to precisely this
kind of behavior.

Of the seven points discussed at the end of chapter 1, basic German
interests as expressed in the first three points will find expression in future
policies. The first point, rehabilitation, may not be needed as much as in the
past, as Germany is beginning to find an accepted place in the world.

As for the other two points, Germany will definitely continue to use
negotiations to seek security and stability and a wide community of friends.

The four tactical points will also remain in place. Germans will continue to negotiate logically and tenaciously. They will still be realistic
enough to be able to reach agreements, although not quickly. And unless
the German economy collapses, they will still try to use their economic
assets to help influence negotiations and create incentives for agreement.
Some members of the European Union have noted that Germans are more
ready than before unification to let their economic and population weight
be felt but that they still try to avoid becoming obvious about it.[5]

Germany's ability to use its economic assets will be limited by the sheer
scope of the demands that those assets will face. States and peoples become
progressively poorer as one moves from Western Europe in an easterly or
southerly direction, and even Germany cannot meet all the needs. But it
will do more than others.

Some topics that Germany and its friends must face will definitely
require long and hard negotiation. One that has already begun will be the
organization of the new Europe. Another, if NATO wishes to expand farther
to the east, will be the purpose and operation of the alliance. Those negotiations will require major efforts for dozens of states, and Germany will
need to be at the center of both.

The seven points will remain as the central strategic and tactical guidelines of German negotiating behavior, but they will become more important
as Germany becomes more engaged in the world. They will warrant close
attention and even closer study, for Germany will continue to evolve and
will most likely find an ever more important European and global role.

Business and Economic Negotiating Prospects

German business will continue to have two different styles of negotiating behavior, although both will continue to be based on logic, tenacity, and a sense of purpose. Both styles are needed for any kind of modern economy.

The new style of German negotiating behavior, reflecting the so-called MBA culture, will remain, but in more muted form. It has made many mistakes and has at times overreached dangerously. The mistakes may destroy a number of German firms and banks and may also destroy some German business careers. The new style has shown, unintentionally but clearly, how logic can lead to error.

Yet the new style is necessary for Germany. It is perfectly suited to some industries that will carry the world economy into a wider future. Owners and managers in those new industries think differently than traditional Germans. Therefore, Germans need to act differently if they want to function internationally. One cannot manage modern telecommunications on the same basis as traditional machine tool production. And one must be ready to deal with American and other managers who will expect Germans to share their thinking or at least to understand it.

The future of the new German business style will, of course, depend to some extent on the evolution of the world economy over the next several years. If prosperity and growth return, the new style will return to help shape it and perhaps to lead it. The new style may, however, be less dramatic than it was over the past few years. German banks and German investors may not let another Jürgen Schrempp or another Ron Sommer act as freely as those men did. But the new style will have to return if Germany wants to keep up with the world economy. Of course, if prosperity and growth do not return, the new form of German business negotiating behavior will be severely muted. But so will other forms.

The more traditional style of German business negotiating behavior will remain no matter what may happen to the German and the global economy. It is too deeply embedded in the culture of German business to disappear. Germany has many traditional firms that like to operate in the old ways and they will undoubtedly want to continue to do so. If prosperity returns, the traditional style may itself evolve toward a more dynamic form, but it will never become like the American style. Even if traditional

German business negotiating behavior makes few mistakes, it can probably not carry the German economy fast enough and far enough into the modern world. If prosperity does not return, the traditional style will be reinforced, but it cannot alone lead the German economy into the future.

The two styles will coexist uneasily. As shown in chapter 4, the major German banks and other German economic institutions and business associations have not yet found a way to manage the combination of the two styles in order to get the best of each. All too often the cultures have clashed. One of the main tasks of German banking and business will be to resolve that clash.

❐   ❐   ❐

This analysis shows that German foreign policy will shift in a variety of ways over the next several years and decades. It also indicates, however, that German negotiating behavior will not change. The German negotiating style, with its strong emphasis on stability and on a wide range of associations, suits the essentials of the new German situation and its evolving policies better than any other. The negotiating style can be expected to remain in place.

The thrust of Germany's foreign policy will change more than its negotiating technique. And, as in the past, Germany's negotiating partners may have trouble dealing with the combination of German logic and tenacity. But they have adjusted to date and can be expected to continue to do so.

7

How to Negotiate with Germans

THE PATTERNS OF GERMAN NEGOTIATING behavior can present some very real dilemmas for Americans and others. Germany may be a close ally and German diplomats and managers may be like Americans in many ways, but they are not Americans and do not think like Americans. Nor do they think like other Europeans or like Asians. They have their own history, their own philosophy, and their own way of looking at the world.

Because the differences between German and other European or American thought patterns lie concealed under a surface of mutual compatibility and mutual cooperation, many Americans and others tend to underestimate the importance of careful intellectual and substantive preparation for any negotiations with Germans. Yet that kind of preparation must be seen as the key to a successful negotiation. Without it, one can at best lose a lot of time. At worst, one can make serious mistakes and emerge significantly weakened. One can also miss a possible deal.

Any American or other negotiator may be sure that any team of German negotiators will prepare very carefully indeed, and any group of diplomats or business executives who plan to negotiate with Germans should know what they are doing if they are not to be outclassed.

To help people or delegations organize their negotiations with Germans, the advice given here is divided into three categories, all of which are important:

❐ essential preparation,

❐ basic strategic points, and

❐ tactical pointers.

Essential preparation is, as it says, essential. Only by following these guidelines before or at the beginning of a negotiation can one have any hope of succeeding in any talks, consultations, or negotiations with Germans.

The basic strategic points cover the behavior patterns that must be constantly kept in mind.

The tactical pointers are intended to help in the specifics of a negotiation.

Essential Preparation

Make absolutely sure that you are ready and then make absolutely sure again. Every person who has conducted any kind of negotiation with Germans gives one piece of advice above all: Be prepared; be very prepared. The German negotiators will know their brief and will know it inside out. They may know their negotiating partner's position better than the partner does, and the partner must not show surprise that they do. If Germans are in business negotiations, they will know the other firm and its business as well as the firm's executives know it and perhaps better. They will certainly know what it is worth to them.

By the same token, anybody who prepares for a negotiation with Germans must also know the details of the German situation and the reasons behind a German interest. They must have their own facts and interests firmly in order but also have whatever facts they need on the German position and attitude.

Daimler's takeover success and Chrysler's failure to hold its own on some important points represents an important example. It cannot be entirely attributed to Jürgen Schrempp. He knew everything there was to know about Chrysler—although he may not have understood all its implications—and the Chrysler managers did not know or understand what hit them. If they wanted to sell out, and to sell out reasonably high, they may have done the right thing, but they could probably have done better on at least three counts: (1) the balance on the board, (2) the sale price of their stock, and (3) control over operations. Mitsubishi, in a weaker position, did much better in its negotiations.

A less specific point but an important one is to learn something about German history since 1949. This is of particular importance for the many Americans whose knowledge of German history begins and ends with Hitler or perhaps includes some passing acquaintance with Bismarck. Germans are proud of what they have achieved since the *Stunde Null* and will be surprised and perhaps disappointed if the other negotiators show that they have never heard of either Adenauer or Brandt but expect them to know of Kennedy, de Gaulle, or Thatcher.

None of this is difficult. Any diplomatic service and any business consulting service can get all the necessary information quickly. There is no excuse for not having it.

Being prepared also saves time. In the negotiations for German sovereignty after 1990, where the German objectives should have been obvious from the beginning, the other negotiators all too often thought that things could remain as they had been. They did not realize that they could not deal with Germany as before. Neither the Western Allies nor some of the Soviet negotiators understood that from the beginning. Therefore, the negotiators lost a lot of time before they got down to serious talks. Better preparation would have saved at least six months and perhaps more.

Germans will know their briefs. Americans and others must know their own.

If possible, make a structural connection.
American or other negotiators should also understand the German attachment to organizations. If at all possible, they should try to look for a way to make a structural connection, to hang the discussion on the peg of an organization. Preferably, they should hang it on the peg of an organization that Germans know and appreciate, whether NATO, the European Union, the G-8, the OSCE, or the United Nations. In business talks, it is good to try to find any kind of earlier economic or business relationship. As Germans do not like to be alone, it will increase the chances for success.

If one can make a connection between the outcome of a negotiation and an established organization that the Germans value, one can usually do better. If one wants German support for any operation or German cooperation in any negotiation, it is best to fit the negotiation into the context of an organization that interests them. If no organization can be found, it is best to make clear that the negotiation will lead to a long-term relationship. Germans value such relationships.

This proved invaluable in the various efforts that Washington and the West Europeans made to persuade Germany to play a role in the Balkans. Without a NATO or UN cover, Germany would not have joined.

In business, know the kind of German you are dealing with.

As chapter 4 showed, German business negotiators of the new kind behave differently than the old kind. They are more predatory. They are also less conservative in the kind of business performance they want.

If Americans or others will be meeting the old kind of German business executive, it is best to prepare for a sober negotiation that stresses value, steady income, conservative practices, and good long-term prospects. If they expect to be meeting with the new kind, it is best to prepare to negotiate very toughly and to recognize that new rather than old standards of fast performance will apply. Talk of steady income and long-term prospects may go out the window.

In any kind of business negotiation with Germans, Americans and others should be prepared to face serious and demanding types of discussion. But, as chapter 4 has illustrated, the new German business negotiator seized with the "MBA culture" can be light-years away from the traditional German, and any American or any non-German European should be ready for that new business negotiator. The American or other European should be able to see within minutes the kind of person that he or she is facing.

Look for win-win outcomes.

Germans negotiate insistently and tenaciously. They know what they want. They will try hard to get it. But they usually do not enter a negotiation without wanting some kind of positive result. They want a deal and of course the best possible deal. They also want a relationship.

Negotiating with Germans should not be seen as a gladiatorial context where one wins and the other dies. It need not be a zero-sum game because there is a good chance that everybody can benefit.

Germans look realistically for the prospect of an agreement. It may take a long time to reach one, but they will take the time if the subject matters enough. And those who are negotiating with Germans should approach the result in the same spirit unless they do not want an agreement.

A negotiation with Germans should concentrate on the terms of an agreement, not on whether a deal can be made. Perhaps it cannot be. But German realism will compel German negotiators to look for one, and it is best to approach the talks in that spirit. One should not assume from the beginning that no agreement can be reached, although it may not be quick or easy to find one.

A diplomat or a business executive negotiating with a German individual or a German team should be on the lookout for success. It may not come, of course, but one should not exclude it out of hand. And one should search for it if one can do so without compromising a basic interest.

Therefore, a negotiating team should constantly ask itself where the outline of an agreement may appear and when one should try very consciously to move toward it. There may be many deadlocks. The American or European negotiator may sometimes need to propose solutions, but German negotiators will not necessarily veto them.

One can be easily discouraged when one meets what one negotiator called "a moving wall," an incomprehensible *Gesamtkonzept,* or a constant reiteration of seemingly unacceptable proposals, but one should not be intimidated. It is the first step in a negotiation, not the last.

Basic Strategic Points

Be prepared to argue in logical terms.
As indicated, Germans believe in logic and a *Gesamtkonzept.* They will present their arguments as a coherent whole, based upon a firm logical foundation that will make sense to them. They will not bargain, at least at first, in traditional terms of trying to divide the difference and so on. Instead, they will insist upon the correctness of their logic and analysis,

and they will further insist that any sensible analysis can lead nowhere except to the conclusion that they are offering.

Therefore, it is essential to be ready to argue in logical terms. One cannot argue particulars without arguing the logical basis for them. A negotiator must show how his or her own proposal also serves a logical purpose, preferably the same as that behind the German proposal. For example, during the Status of Forces negotiations during the early 1990s, Americans had to accept the basic premise that Germany had finally achieved its sovereignty and had the right to set certain conditions for the stationing of foreign troops. But the Americans could still argue that some of the German proposals defeated important German and NATO purposes. They had to argue the logic of their proposals instead of only presenting their position.

An alternative is to offer a superior logical position, making the case on the basis of a radically different logical argument. This may compel the Germans to reexamine their attitude but only if the opposite argument holds water.

The logical foundation for an agreement may constitute an important issue in the European negotiations for a new EU constitution. The Germans have advanced a federal concept. If another European state does not wish to accept the details of their position, it will be necessary not only to differ with the specifics but to propose a completely different concept for the future of Europe.

Whatever a negotiator may decide about presenting an argument, it is essential to understand the importance of ideas when negotiating with Germans. One need not accept their ideas, although they will try hard to make their case. But anybody who wishes to persuade a German negotiator of anything must be prepared to argue on those terms and present a logical argument in support of a position. If not, it is not worthwhile to take the position. And one must also be prepared to argue the logic of any change in position, not merely try to find some quick compromise. Even when they appear most unyielding, Germans will usually listen to a rational argument.

Be serious and be respected.
Germans generally do not joke during negotiations, although they may enjoy a good joke over a beer or at the dinner table. A negotiator who

evades points by telling jokes or attempting humor will not get their full attention or respect. A negotiator must be serious and must deal seriously with the material. And he or she must deal with it in the same painstaking detail that the Germans show. In particular, Germans dislike frivolity at the beginning of a negotiation. They regard it as a sign of incompetence or evasiveness.

A negotiator must win the respect of the Germans. Some, like a secretary of state, a minister, an ambassador, or a senior executive, can expect it from the beginning. But he or she must work to keep it. Germans do not suffer fools gladly. They expect detailed and careful analysis and a tough but fair interlocutor. If their interlocutor does not know his or her brief and is not able to defend it, the interlocutor is better off not appearing. Negotiators who are not serious are not taken seriously.

When the Chrysler team of negotiators accepted the German proposal for a German majority in the combined DaimlerChrysler board, they doomed their cause. Jürgen Schrempp and his associates almost certainly expected a tougher fight on that, and the American failure to insist on their views hurt on other fronts. They did not convey the impression of being truly serious about their position and about their interests.

Make sure to gain attention at senior levels.
Whenever negotiating with Germans, Americans or others should start at the highest possible level on both sides to obtain the kind of mandate that is necessary for a breakthrough.

It is useful to begin a negotiation by selecting a senior American or other figure to initiate the dialogue. On a NATO matter, this figure should be the U.S. secretary of state or defense. In the European Union, the figures should be the minister of foreign affairs or, in the context of the continuing Franco-German dialogue, the chancellor of Germany and the president of France who initiate a dialogue. That engages the German government at senior levels and compels the bureaucracy to come up with workable solutions.

It may also be necessary to go back to senior levels from time to time. Chancellor Kohl did this during the German unity negotiations by returning to Gorbachev when necessary. And Gorbachev did it later when he wanted Germany to offer additional financial support to the Soviet

Union. EU leaders do it constantly, maintaining a dialogue in their regular meetings and also calling one another on the telephone. U.S. negotiators did it during the negotiations on compensation for the victims of Nazi slave labor and forced labor practices, returning to the chancellor and the Chancellery whenever a serious deadlock arose.

A negotiator must not go back to the well too often. No foreign leader can call the chancellor or the foreign minister repeatedly and continue to engage the attention of either. It is therefore important to judge the moment carefully. But it is equally important not to hesitate to move when necessary, for German bureaucrats will try to control a negotiation if they believe no senior political figure is engaged.

Be prepared to argue forcefully if necessary.

A German negotiator will present a forceful and logical argument with the intention of making it persuasive. It is important to be ready to argue back.

There is no reason to hesitate. The case for a different position should be made, forcefully and compellingly. German negotiators do not respect a person who fails to state a case. They will assume that their negotiating partner does not believe in his or her own cause, and they will expect to win every argument.

A case must be stated, directly, logically, and firmly, if a German negotiator is to hear it and take it seriously. Without a readiness to state a case that way, it makes no sense to meet with Germans in the first place because they will not respect either the argument or those who fail to make it.

It is important that German negotiators not be left with the notion that they can win every argument and every point. Logic, as stated earlier, can lead to error. For example, firmer Chrysler statements of its own interests might have helped to produce results that would have actually been better not only for Chrysler but even for Daimler-Benz.

Germans may go too far in their negotiations if not met with serious and convincing arguments. It is to everybody's advantage for Germany's negotiating partners to present such arguments.

Avoid emotion.

Germans see negotiation as a logical, not an emotional, process. This does not mean that German negotiators did not recognize the profound emotions at play in some of the negotiations after World War II, as during their negotiations during détente with Poland, when Chancellor Willy Brandt sank to his knees before the memorial to the victims in the Warsaw Ghetto. But Germans do not substitute emotion for reality.

A negotiator who shows emotion loses respect. When Chrysler chairman Robert Eaton wept during a speech discussing the merger, the Germans not only must have felt uncomfortable but also probably felt scornful. Chrysler emerged damaged, although most of the negotiating process had finished.

When President Jimmy Carter made emotional presentations to Chancellor Helmut Schmidt, he did not help his own cause. It is best to remain logical and reasoned.

Listen carefully.

Like all negotiators, German negotiators sometimes send signals that may not be openly stated and that may not even be consciously communicated but that can be helpful in reaching agreement. They may indicate what matters to them by repeating it more frequently or more forcefully than other points. Careful listening can help uncover such clues. Even if the German recital of logical underpinning for their positions seems dull, it may show possible paths to a solution. Or the level of logical support that Germans give different topics may show where compromise is possible and where it is not.

Americans and others must remain alert, looking for openings, possible arguments, and points where agreement can be reached.

Try to understand what matters most to German negotiators.

This relates to the previous comment. Not only do Germans pursue negotiations seriously and tenaciously, but in their minds they often have a list of the points that matter most to them. Some may well prove to be non-negotiable, at least in that forum and at that time. German negotiators may change their tone when they come to those points.

An American or other negotiator must try to understand early on, mainly by careful listening, where the most important German interests lie. If they are totally opposed to U.S. or other interests, the negotiator must know it and know it early.

Germans do not usually negotiate on the basis of a bazaar mentality, although they have been known to haggle over certain issues by making a series of rising offers. More probably, they have in the back of their minds the point that is most important to them. The negotiating partner must try to understand that early and focus on it, deciding whether his or her instructions can accommodate the German interest or somehow reconcile it with the U.S. or other foreign interest. If that can be done, one can then make an offer reflecting that analysis. A negotiator must judge carefully if there is that kind of opportunity. If so, he or she can proceed. If not, it may be best to suspend the talks.

Be prepared to judge and seize the moment for a breakthrough.
Once it appears to a German negotiating partner that a deal is in the works or that progress can be made, that partner could—after enough negotiation to explore all points—make a suggestion along the following lines: "As you can see, what matters most for us is point one, and we are prepared to be more flexible about points two and three as parts of an entire package if we could make a solid deal on point one. Could you think of going ahead on that basis?"

This would invite a counteroffer showing some flexibility, if it is not made too early and if it has some logic behind it. Normally, the German negotiator will make a counteroffer. After several potential compromises have been outlined, it may be useful for the teams to return to their capitals to explore those compromises and pave the way for others.

If the German delegation makes no counteroffer, either then or within a reasonable time thereafter, there may be no deal to be made. At that point, the negotiating partner may well have to show that he or she is ready to break off the discussions. That may be better than continuing to make offer after offer. It may also provoke a German offer.

Timing can be crucial. At a certain point, a quiet personal talk may be helpful. But it should not come too early and in a way that confuses the issues. If any offer is made too early, the Germans may conclude that the negotiating partner lacks conviction. But one does not want to be too late, either, for otherwise the bureaucracy will feel no reason to move. Most important, one should stay within the framework of the logical foundation for the negotiations. German negotiators do not like to go back to their ministry too early or too often. And they do not like to lose the main logical track of the negotiations. But they will look for agreement.

It is, however, also important to be prepared for failure. Germans will sometimes ask for too much, taking positions that are too demanding to allow accommodation. Then it is best to let the talks fail, perhaps to be resumed at some later time. Others may also ask for more than the Germans are ready to yield.

Be aware of bureaucratic, political, and international pressures.
German negotiators operate within a complex organizational mix. They must serve their bureaucracy, their ministers, and the international organizations of which Germany is a part.

Americans in particular need to keep this in mind. With the ever-deepening links in the European Union, more of the German-American economic and perhaps political dialogue will gradually go through the European Union rather than—or as well as—through direct German-American consultations and negotiations. Trade negotiations already go mainly through the European Union. The formation of a European security identity and a European Rapid Reaction Force may mean that even security consultations may at some future point go through EU as well as NATO channels, although this seems unlikely to happen soon because European military coordination and integration are moving very slowly.

American and other non-European negotiators need to be constantly sensitive to this. They need to know when to negotiate with Germany through the European channel, talking to whoever may be in charge of the European Union during that particular period and not even meeting officially with a German. They also need to judge when they must talk directly to Berlin to make their views known even if they are negotiating their business officially in Brussels.

Americans and others also need to understand that any German delegate represents the front of a very large bureaucratic organization and that this may complicate negotiations and impair flexibility. And they need to know precisely when to apply pressure and when to make concessions in either Berlin or Brussels, or in both. The Germans with whom they meet have to report to a great many ministers and bureaucracies at home, in Brussels, and elsewhere, and their negotiating partners may need to help guide the talks through those minefields if they want success. But even if talks do not go through the European Union, German negotiators will keep the European Union constantly in mind.

An American or other diplomat planning to negotiate with the German government will need to learn the views of ministries other than the Foreign Office. He or she may also need to know how German views are shaped by the *Länder*, other states, or organizational obligations. This would apply particularly if the German *Land* with a major interest was one of the biggest *Länder*, such as North Rhine–Westphalia or Bavaria. Any negotiator must be constantly aware of the many factors that weigh on the minds of a German delegation. At the same time, it would be a mistake to try to go behind the back of the German negotiating team directly to the ministry that may be blocking progress. It would be better to start by speaking privately to the representatives of that ministry on the German delegation, or to use an embassy or other office to learn what is happening behind the scenes.

Keep in mind the many things that the Germans see.
Equally important, any person or group negotiating with Germans must understand that German negotiators do not look only at their negotiating partners. They also look backward and sideways. They look at history, some of which they want to repeat and some of which they do not want to repeat. They look at their neighbors and wonder how those neighbors will react to any negotiation. Anybody dealing with them must remain sensitive to the complexity of these perceptions and the differing signals that they may send at any time.

Be patient.
The Germans enter a negotiation to get the best possible agreement. Unless they have some reason to hurry, they will be prepared to spend some time to look for that. Their negotiating partners must be equally patient.

German negotiators do not match the North Koreans or the former Soviet negotiators in deliberately slowing talks for tactical purposes. But the very attention that they give to their material and presentations means that any negotiation is likely to advance only slowly and in stages. German negotiators do not like to get stuck in pointless deadlocks, but they are ready to tread water for some time. And the German bureaucrats who write some of the instructions may also want to take their time before they shift their views.

This does not mean that German negotiators may not be in a hurry. They sometimes are. If they are, it will quickly become obvious because they will make it clear. But if they are not, it is best not to be the party that wants to rush things. They can too easily take advantage of that, in government or business negotiations.

Tactical Pointers

Do not ask for too much or for too little.
Because German negotiators prepare so carefully for any kind of serious negotiation, they normally know fairly well what is possible and what is not possible. They will have some understanding of what they can get and what they must yield. It will do no good to ask them for the moon if they do not need to yield it. But it will do even less good to ask for too little, for they will then underestimate their negotiating partners.

Part of careful preparation for any talks with German negotiators should be to develop realistic expectations for what can be gained and what should be surrendered. And one should ask for more than one expects to get, provided one can develop a logical argument for it, but not for so much or for so little that one does not seem serious. It does not pay to bluff.

Be prepared for formality and be careful about informality.
Germans are formal even when they are informal. They do not unwind as quickly as Americans do. They are more like other continental Europeans. They do not go to a first-name basis as quickly as Americans do, although those who have studied in the United States or England may do so more readily than their elders would have.

An American should let the drift of the relationship determine what is best. If a senior German chairs the delegation for the first negotiating session, it would be highly inappropriate and embarrassing to be too casual toward him or her in that opening session in front of the entire negotiating team.

But Germans can be good friends without being casual, and they can be informal without engaging in the kind of banter and backslapping that Americans often favor as part of the bonding process.

There is a difference between being informal and being casual. Germans will at a certain point be prepared to be informal, but it is rare for them to become casual until they know a person well. Foreign negotiators must recognize and respect these gradations.

A foreign negotiator must learn how to develop personal contacts with German negotiators, but without getting too personal. And one should never assume too early that one has established a relationship.

Know how and when to use social occasions.

Germans, like most others, enjoy a respite from serious conversation. They also like to entertain and to be entertained. They will almost certainly invite an American negotiating team to join them for a beer, a meal, or some other occasion. If in Germany, they might invite their negotiating partners to take a trip along the Rhine Valley, the Berlin canals, or the like.

It is fully appropriate and desirable to join in such tours. They permit relaxed talk and offer some chance for negotiators to get to know one another. They do not, however, offer a chance to negotiate, and they should not be used for that. Perhaps, after two or more negotiating teams or negotiators have worked together for some time and have come to know one another, an American or other negotiator might say something in a social environment that might offer some clue for a possible solution, or that might offer some particular insight that he or she would not want to offer in a formal and recorded session. But the negotiator should not do so lightly and should certainly not do so early in the process.

In particular, in social situations, the American should never make light of his or her German hosts, German culture, or the painful aspects of German history. Jokes or any talk about Hitler or German aggression during World War II will not be welcome in the negotiations, just as Americans would not welcome a German comment about slavery. If a German initiates a talk about German history, an American can certainly respond but must do so carefully and in measured terms until a solid relationship has been established.

The important point is to tread lightly, not clumsily, to be informal and friendly but not too casual. Germans can take longer to relax than almost any other Europeans, and there is little to be gained by pushing informality if it endangers a negotiation. U.S. delegates should not deny their own habits by becoming too formal themselves, but they need to exercise some judgment on how to proceed. It is best to let relations evolve, as they probably will over time.

Look carefully at the age of the German negotiators.
The young often have a sense that Germany should play a more important role than before through its international contacts, but they do not quite know how and at what level. They are still looking for a place where Germany can belong. Not "a place in the sun," but not "a place in the shadows" either.

One American negotiator said that he found the younger Germans to be more tenacious negotiators than the older. He thought they did not feel as inhibited as older Germans did and that they were more prepared to take stands and hold them. American negotiators may need to take account of that.

For an American or any other negotiator with Germany, negotiating with young Germans means talking more about the future than about the past, about the new structures and the future of the new structures—especially the new European Union—than about the old structures like NATO. It means talking about German opportunities to help the rest of the world and not only about what Germans have done for their own recovery during the past fifty years. Young Germans are often very idealistic about helping other countries.

As indicated in chapter 4, young Germans are not nationalistic in the nineteenth-century sense of the word. But they are patriotic and will represent their interests. They are also internationalist, usually wanting Germany to play a more important international role through the organizations to which it belongs. Foreign negotiators, whether American or European, need to take account of that. They need to recognize that Germans, and especially young Germans, continually think in terms of organizations as much as of issues.

A young German diplomat once observed that Americans are not accustomed to dealing with somebody who is both strong and friendly, like the European Union and such European states as France or the new Germany. Americans need to reflect on that and show, accordingly, that they can deal with equals or near equals.

Young Germans can be more personable than older Germans, more relaxed, and often easier for Americans and others to know. Many speak excellent English and have studied in the United States, England, or France. They are much more like Americans or other Europeans than Germans used to be. And they thus present a different kind of challenge in a negotiation.

In business, young Germans will probably pursue the new German business style more than the old. But they know their numbers just as well as the old. They may make mistakes, like the old, but more likely by overreaching than by underreaching.

Watch for press reports on the negotiations.
As indicated earlier, Germans do not usually leak information in the classic sense, but they often use backgrounders to get their version of events into the press. The backgrounders may originate with the delegation, the Foreign Office, or the Chancellery if the negotiation has a high political profile.

The best reaction to any press report, especially if it is not helpful, is to ask the head of the German delegation about it. If it presents a problem, the German negotiator should be told why. Then the American or other foreign delegation needs to decide whether to counter on or off the record or, if the German delegate expresses regret, perhaps to let it go. A great deal depends on the relationship that has been established between the delegates, the tone of the story, and whether it does any damage. If it appears that the German delegation is consistently putting out unhelpful material on a deep-background or background basis, an American delegate should be prepared to react. The German delegates will be surprised if the American does not.

At the same time, an American delegation may want to be careful about getting into exchanges through the press with any foreign delegation. If the negotiation can stir up any political interest, Washington will almost certainly leak more than Berlin. Unless the American negotiators are sure that they can control what the American media will print, it may be best to decide that press stories should not become a contentious topic in the negotiations.

Summary

Negotiating with Germans can be difficult, but it need not be. It demands constant alertness and a readiness to pursue U.S. or other interests with some sense of purpose. Above all, a negotiator must be well prepared and logical, never weak but unfailingly polite. The negotiator must expect to be formal for some time. He or she must be patient and ready to wait for opportunities that will normally come in due course. And the payoff can be an agreement that benefits all parties and that can open new relationships.

Notes

Introduction

1. See Raymond Cohen, *Negotiating across Cultures: International Communication in an Interdependent World,* rev. ed. (Washington, D.C.: United States Institute of Peace Press, 1997), 12.

2. Richard E. Porter and Larry A. Samovar, "Approaching Intercultural Communication," in their edited volume *Intercultural Communication: A Reader* (Belmont, Calif.: Wadsworth, 1988), 19.

3. See, for example, Kevin Avruch, *Culture and Conflict Resolution* (Washington, D.C.: United States Institute of Peace Press, 1998); Hans Binnendijk, ed., *National Negotiating Styles* (Washington, D.C.: Foreign Service Institute, U.S. Department of State, 1987); J. Brett, *Negotiating Globally: How to Negotiate Deals, Resolve Disputes, and Make Decisions across Cultural Boundaries* (San Francisco: Jossey-Bass, 2001); Jeswald Salacuse, *Making Global Deals* (New York: Times Books, 1991); and Salacuse, "Ten Ways That Culture Affects Negotiating Style: Some Survey Results," *Negotiation Journal* 14, no. 3 (1998): 221–240.

4. Jerrold L. Schecter, *Russian Negotiating Behavior: Continuity and Transition* (Washington, D.C.: United States Institute of Peace Press, 1998); Scott Snyder, *Negotiating on the Edge: North Korean Negotiating Behavior* (Washington, D.C.: United States Institute of Peace Press, 1999); and Richard H. Solomon, *Chinese Negotiating Behavior: Pursuing Interests through "Old Friends"* (Washington, D.C.: United States Institute of Peace Press, 1999).

5. Patrick L. Schmidt, *Understanding American and German Business Cultures* (New York: German-American Chamber of Commerce, 1999); and Craig S. Smith, "Beware of Green Hats in China and Other Cross-Cultural Faux Pas," *New York Times,* April 30, 2002, C11.

1. The Foundation

1. Robert Ergang, *Emergence of the National State* (New York: Van Nostrand, 1971), 31.

2. Marshall Dill, Jr., *Germany: A Modern History* (Ann Arbor: University of Michigan Press, 1970), 3–85. Dill offers a good overview of the Holy Roman Empire as a basic part of German history.

3. Thomas A. Brady, Jr., *The Protestant Reformation in German History* (Washington, D.C.: German Historical Institute, 1998); Uwe Siemon-Netto, *The Fabricated Luther* (St. Louis: Concordia Publishing House, 1998).

4. Peter H. Wilson, *The Holy Roman Empire* (New York: Palgrave, 1999), 18, 23.

5. Ibid.

6. For an extended discussion of this particularly German approach toward freedom, see Leonard Krieger, *The German Idea of Freedom* (Chicago: University of Chicago Press, 1957).

7. Ibid., 50–51.

8. Ibid., 87.

9. Hegel has a massive bibliography and deserves reading on his own. For this book, the most relevant source has been Herbert Marcuse, *Reason and Revolution* (Boston: Beacon Press, 1966), 3–250.

10. Friedrich Meinecke, *The German Catastrophe*, trans. Sidney B. Fay (Boston: Beacon Press, 1963), 118.

11. Samuel P. Huntington, *The Soldier and the State* (New York: Random House, 1957), 30–36.

12. Henry A. Kissinger, *A World Restored* (New York: Grosset and Dunlap, 1964). Kissinger offers the best analysis of the Congress of Vienna and its intent.

13. Wilson, *The Holy Roman Empire*, 70–71.

14. Werner Weidenfeld, *Der deutsche Weg* (Berlin: Siedler, 1999), 38–52. Weidenfeld describes this sentiment in detail.

15. Hans Kohn, *The Mind of Germany* (New York: Charles Scribner's Sons, 1960), 69–98.

16. Heinrich Heine, quoted in Fritz Stern, *Dreams and Delusions* (New York: Alfred A. Knopf, 1987), 3.

17. Sebastian Haffner, *The Rise and Fall of Prussia*, trans. Ewald Osers (London: Weidenfeld and Nicolson, 1980), 116–138.

18. The most generous treatment of Bismarck's diplomacy is presented in Henry Kissinger, *Diplomacy* (New York: Simon and Schuster, 1994), 103–137, esp. 135. For another sympathetic look, see Alan Palmer, *Bismarck* (London: Weidenfeld and Nicolson, 1976). For a more critical survey, reviewing Bismarck's domestic behavior as well as his foreign policy, see Erich Eyck, *Bismarck and the German Empire* (New York: W. W. Norton, 1958).

19. A number of German and other observers, from Ralf Dahrendorf to Friedrich Meinecke, have written on the conservatism of Bismarck's domestic regime, the hardening militarism of the Prussian elite, and the path that brought Prussia and Germany to a parting of the ways from the Western liberal democracies. A good summary analysis is in David Blackbourn and Geoff Eley, *The Peculiarities of German History* (Oxford: Oxford University Press, 1984). For a general and more extensive recent record of the period, see Volker Ulrich, *Die nervöse Grossmacht 1871–1918: Aufstieg und Untergang des deutschen Kaiserreichs* (Frankfurt: Fischer, 1997). In this book, I do not dwell on the domestic politics of Bismarck's Reich because Bismarck conducted diplomacy almost independently of domestic politics except when he could use one to buttress his position in the other.

20. Klaus Hildebrand, *Das Vergangene Reich* (Stuttgart: Deutsche Verlags-Anstalt, 1995), 249–300, 849–898.

21. For a summary of the negotiations at Versailles by a highly critical observer, see Harold Nicolson, *Peacemaking 1919* (New York: Grosset and Dunlap, 1965).

22. Meinecke, *The German Catastrophe*, 95.

23. Klaus Hildebrand, "Der alte und der neue Nationalstaat der Deutschen," *Die Politische Meinung*, no. 356 (July 1999): 16.

24. For a summary record of Hitler's foreign policy before his invasion of the Soviet Union in 1940, see Gordon A. Craig, *Germany, 1866–1945* (Oxford: Oxford University Press, 1978), 673–714; Ian Kershaw, *Hitler, 1936–1945: Nemesis* (London: Allen Lane, 2000), 61–125; and Hildebrand, *Das Vergangene Reich*, 563–703.

25. Huntington, *The Soldier and the State*, 115.

26. Craig, *Germany, 1866–1945*, 696.

27. Garvey Asher, "Hitler's Decision to Declare War on the United States Revisited," *SHAFR Newsletter* 31, no. 3 (September 2000): 12–13.

28. Kershaw, *Hitler, 1936–1945: Nemesis*, 118–125.

29. Craig, *Germany, 1866–1945*, 713.

30. Asher, "Hitler's Decision to Declare War on the United States Revisited," 15–20.

31. Kai Bird, *The Chairman* (New York: Simon and Schuster, 1992), 319.

32. Ibid., 321–322.

33. These points are based on countless talks by the author with friends throughout Germany during the postwar years and since. They are the distillation of the German historical experience and the ways in which Germans articulate that experience. They are also based on the author's impressions of what the Germans with whom he has spoken, and whose work he has read, seem to regard as the sum of their analyses. Thus, they shape behavior, consciously or unconsciously, whether in negotiations or other activities.

34. W. R. Smyser, *From Yalta to Berlin: The Cold War Struggle over Germany* (New York: St. Martin's Press, 1999), passim. This book presents the main elements of German foreign policy throughout the history of West Germany and until 1997. For a more detailed German source, see Christian Hacke, *Die Aussenpolitik der Bundesrepublik Deutschland: Weltmacht wider Willen* (Berlin: Ullstein, 1997). A trilingual (German, French, and English) chronology is in Presse- und Informationsamt der Bundesregierung, *Von der Spaltung zur Einheit, 1945–1990: Eine deutsche Chronik in Texten und Bildern* (Bonn: Klett Druck, 1992), 134–211.

2. The Principal Elements of a Negotiation with Germans

1. German Foreign Office Planning Staff official, German diplomat, and German foreign policy intellectual, interviews by author, July 15, 1999, August 26, 2000, and July 12, 2001, respectively.

2. German Foreign Office Planning Staff official, interview by author, July 15, 1999.

3. U.S. diplomats and business figures, interviews by author, August and October 2001.

4. Former German negotiator, interview by author, January 30, 1999.

5. For the best summary on how Germany prepares for a negotiation, see Judith Siwert-Probst, "Die klassischen aussenpolitischen Institutionen," in *Institutionen und Ressourcen*, vol. 4 of *Deutschlands neue Aussenpolitik*, ed. Wolf-Dieter Eberwein and Karl Kaiser (Munich: R. Oldenbourg Verlag, 1998), 13–28. This volume has been translated into English by Deborah Kaiser and Bryan Ruppert and is published as *Germany's New Foreign Policy: Decision-Making in an Interdependent World* (Houndmills, England: Palgrave, 2001).

6. Siwert-Probst, "Die klassischen aussenpolitischen Institutionen," 19.

7. Michael Mertes, a member of Helmut Kohl's 1989 Chancellery staff (lecture at the German Historical Association, Washington, D.C., October 3, 2001).

8. For a general discussion of the *Länder* role in foreign policy, see Michèle Knodt, "Auswärtiges Handeln der deutschen Länder," in *Deutschlands neue Aussenpolitik*, ed. Eberwein and Kaiser, 153–166.

9. For a discussion of how the West German federal system had been designed, see Arnold J. Heidenheimer, "Federalism and the Party System: The Case of West Germany," *American Political Science Review* 52, no. 3 (September 1958): 800–828.

10. Former U.S. diplomats, interviews by author, Washington, D.C., February 15, 2001, October 29, 2001, and January 11, 2002.

11. Knodt, "Auswärtiges Handeln der deutschen Länder," 161–164.

12. Hans Maier, "Das Grundgesetz nach 50 Jahren," *Die Politische Meinung,* no. 356 (July 1999): 32.

13. Retired German professional diplomat, interview by author, May 12, 2002.

14. U.S. official, interview by author, Washington, D.C., February 15, 2000.

15. U.S. officials, multiple interviews by author, June 15, 2001, and September and November 2001.

16. U.S. diplomat, interview by author, Washington, D.C., October 23, 2001.

17. Ingrid Nemine, "Requests in German-Norwegian Business Discourse: Differences in Directness," in *The Language of Business: An International Perspective,* ed. Francisco Bargiela-Chiappini and Sandra Harris (Edinburgh: Edinburgh University Press, 1997), 76–78. For further discussion of this German tendency, see Emily Gildersleeve, "Conflict Style Paper" (submitted in partial fulfillment of the requirements of a course on peace and conflict, American University, March 27, 2002), 3–4.

18. Former U.S. and Allied diplomats, interviews by author, February 15, 2000, and October 23 and December 19, 2001.

19. Former U.S. official, interview by author, Washington, D.C., December 19, 2001.

20. U.S. and German diplomats, interviews by author, April 12 and December 19, 2001, and January 8 and 9, 2002; Otto Graf Lambsdorff, "The Long Road toward the Foundation 'Remembrance, Responsibility and the Future,'" (speech delivered in Berlin, June 25, 2001); and Gerald D. Feldman, "Holocaust Assets and German Business History: Beginning or End?" *German Studies Review* 25, no. 1 (February 2002): 23–34.

21. For text of the Schröder and Rau proposals, see *Internationale Politik,* transatlantic edition, no. 3 (2000): 128–132, and no. 3 (2001): 122–126. For the Fischer speech, see German Foreign Office publication file, May 12, 2000.

22. Former U.S. diplomat, interview by author, June 15, 2001.

23. U.S. and German diplomats, interviews by author, October 28, 2001, and January 10, 2002.

24. Agreement between the Government of the United States of America and the Government of the Federal Republic of Germany concerning the Foundation "Remembrance, Responsibility and the Future," July 17, 2000.

25. European and U.S. diplomats, interviews by author, June and July 2000 and October and December 2001.

26. Former U.S. diplomats, interviews by author, Washington, D.C., November 20, 2001.

27. Former U.S. negotiator, interview by author, April 12, 2001.

28. U.S., Russian, German, and other European diplomats, interviews by author, January 14, November 12, and December 15, 2001.

29. U.S., German, and other European diplomats, interviews by author, January 24, July 11, and December 17, 2001, and January 10, 2002.

30. Former U.S. diplomat, interview by author, August 29, 2001.

31. German diplomats, interviews by author, June 15, 2001, and January 7, 2002.

32. Former U.S. diplomat, interview by author, April 12, 2001.

33. U.S. diplomat, interview by author, Washington, D.C., January 11, 2002.

34. U.S. negotiator, interview by author, April 12, 2001.

35. Katja Gelinscky, "Envoy Encourages German Business to Pay Quickly," *Frankfurter Allgemeine Zeitung*, English ed., May 30, 2001.

36. U.S. and German negotiators, interviews by author, April 12 and December 19, 2001, and January 8 and 9, 2002.

37. Former U.S. diplomat, interview by author, May 12, 2001.

38. U.S. negotiator of the SOFA, interview by author, Washington, D.C., January 11, 2002.

39. Former West German diplomat, interview by author, June 15, 2001.

40. U.S. diplomats, interviews by author, Berlin and Washington, D.C., June 15 and December 19, 2001, and January 9, 2002, as well as the author's personal contacts and negotiations with East German officials and diplomats.

41. Karl-Heinz Schmidt, *Dialog über Deutschland* (Baden-Baden: Nomos, 1998), 76–86. This book discusses the precise document and the record of Ulbricht's presentation. For a full record of the debate between Ulbricht and his Soviet and East European colleagues in preparing for the building of the Berlin Wall, see Hope Harrison, *Ulbricht and the Concrete "Rose": New Archival Evidence on the Dynamics of Soviet–East German Relations and the Berlin Crisis, 1958–1961* (Washington, D.C.: Cold War International History Project, Woodrow Wilson International Center for Scholars, 1993).

42. W. R. Smyser, *From Yalta to Berlin: The Cold War Struggle over Germany* (New York: St. Martin's Press, 1999), 152–172.

43. M. E. Sarotte, *Dealing with the Devil: East Germany, Détente, and Ostpolitik, 1969–1973* (Chapel Hill: University of North Carolina Press, 2000), 164–165.

44. Former U.S. diplomat, interview by author, August 29, 2001.

45. Willy Brandt, interview by author, Bonn, December 11, 1989.

46. Sarotte, *Dealing with the Devil*, 142–143.

47. U.S. diplomat, interview by author, Washington, D.C., December 15, 2001.

48. U.S. diplomat, interview by author, Washington, D.C., October 28, 2001.

3. The German Negotiator

1. For a review of some of these revelations, see Gerald D. Feldman, "Holocaust Assets and German Business History: Beginning or End?" *German Studies Review* 25, no. 1 (February 2002): 23–34.

2. Robert Gerald Livingston, "Germany's Underwhelming Political Elites," *Wall Street Journal Europe*, Monday, May 15, 2000.

3. German political and intellectual figures, interviews by author, April 12, 1998, June 30, 2000, and June 18 and July 12, 2001.

4. German political leader, interview by author, June 30, 2000.

5. Dr. Jürgen Mertens, director of the German diplomatic training school, and a number of German graduates of the school, interviews by author, Washington, D.C., and Berlin, May 4, 1999, and 1998–2001, respectively.

6. Many German diplomats, interviews by author, Washington, D.C., and Berlin, 2000 and 2001.

7. U.S. and European diplomats, interviews by author, Berlin, Bonn, London, Paris, and Washington, D.C., 1998–2002, as well as the author's personal experience.

8. Former U.S. diplomat, interview by author, January 11, 2002.

9. Former U.S. diplomats, interviews by author, February 15, 2000, December 13, 2001, and January 11, 2002.

10. Wjatscheslaw Keworkow, *Der Geheime Kanal* (Berlin: Rowohlt, 1995), 50–53.

11. Egon Bahr, interviews by author, Bonn, June 7, 1992, and Munich, January 21, 1998.

12. Willy Brandt and Egon Bahr, interviews by author, December 11, 1989; and W. R. Smyser, *From Yalta to Berlin: The Cold War Struggle over Germany* (New York: St. Martin's Press, 1999), 259–260.

13. Former U.S. diplomat, interview by author, January 24, 2001.

14. Günther van Well, interview by author, New York, December, 1991.

15. Bahr, interview by author, January 21, 1998.

16. Brandt and Bahr, interview by author, December 11, 1989.

17. Senior German negotiator, interview by author, May 11, 2002.

18. *Financial Times*, June 14, 1999; *Berliner Morgenpost*, August 9, 1999; and German negotiator, interview by author, June 29, 2000.

19. German diplomats and U.S. negotiator with considerable experience in speaking with Germans, interviews by author, June and July 2001 and April 4, 2002, respectively.

20. Henry Kissinger, *Diplomacy* (New York: Simon and Schuster, 1994), 128.

21. Brandt, interview by author, December 11, 1989.

22. Smyser, *From Yalta to Berlin,* 128–129.

23. U.S. diplomat, interview by author, June 22, 2001.

24. Former U.S. member of the U.S. High Commissioner's Office in Germany, August 22, 1999.

25. For a summary, see Auswärtiges Amt, *Twenty-five Years of German Participation in United Nations Peacekeeping Operations* (Bonn: Auswärtiges Amt, 1998), published in German as *25 Jahre deutsche Beteilung an Friedenserhaltenden Massnahmen der Vereinten Nationen.*

26. French intellectual, interview by author, July 9, 2001.

27. German and U.S. officials and NATO officers, Kosovo, Berlin, and Washington, D.C., June 2000 and September 2001.

28. Colette Mazzucelli, *France and Germany at Maastricht: Politics and Negotiations to Create the European Union* (New York: Garland, 1997), 135–207.

29. Emily Gildersleeve, "Conflict Style Paper" (submitted in partial fulfillment of the requirements of a course on peace and conflict, American University, March 27, 2002), 6.

4. German Business Negotiations

1. Nye has defined soft power as "the ability to achieve desired outcomes through attraction rather than coercion, because others want what you want." Joseph S. Nye, Jr., "Soft Power and Conflict Management in the Information Age," in *Turbulent Peace: The Challenges of Managing International Conflict,* ed. Chester A. Crocker, Fen Osler Hampson, and Pamela Aall (Washington, D.C.: United States Institute of Peace Press, 2001), 354.

2. Former employee of a German firm in the United States, interview by author, April 15, 2002.

3. "Business Education," *Financial Times,* May 28, 2002, III.

4. For a more extensive description of German management style and behavior, see W. R. Smyser, *The German Economy: Colossus at the Crossroads* (New York: St. Martin's Press, 1993), 67–83.

5. Patrick L. Schmidt, *Understanding American and German Business Cultures* (New York: German-American Chamber of Commerce, 1999), 73–75.

6. *Financial Times,* October 17, 2001, 11.

7. German international banker, interview by author, May 12, 2001; Survey, *Financial Times,* December 15, 2000 (the two listed in the 2000 Survey were DaimlerChrysler and SAP Software); and "Starke Nachbarn," *Wirtschaftswoche,* June 22, 2000, 84–92.

8. Americans who have worked in German firms as well as with German consultants, interviews by author, August 15, 16, and 23, 2000, and January 29, 2001.

9. American lawyer, interview by author, December 19, 2001.

10. American lawyer, interview by author, August 16, 2000.

11. American lawyer, interview by author, April 12, 2001.

12. *Financial Times,* January 29, 2002, 20.

13. *Die Zeit,* June 13, 2001, 21.

14. *Welt am Sonntag,* March 19, 2000, 72; and *New York Times,* February 6, 2001, W1.

15. *Barron's,* February 14, 2000, 50.

16. *Financial Times,* March 15, 2002, 17.

17. Former U.S. diplomat and Heinz Ruhnau, former chairman of Lufthansa, interviews by author, October 29, 2001, and May 18, 2002, respectively.

18. German diplomat at the European Union, interview by author, June 7, 2000.

19. *Financial Times,* February 27, 2002, 12; March 22, 2002, 12; and March 25, 2002, 13.

20. "Russia and China Called Top Business Bribers," *New York Times,* May 2, 2002, 12; and "Germany Goes for the Big Clean-Up," *Financial Times,* May 7, 2002, 10.

21. German business leader, interview by author, June 22, 1999.

22. German professor, interview by author, July 12, 2001.

23. Margarita Mathiopoulos, *Die Geschlossene Gesellschaft und ihre Freunde* (Hamburg: Hoffmann und Campe, 1997); and *New York Times,* April 3, 2000, 4–5.

24. *Financial Times,* May 8, 2002, 17.

25. *Financial Times,* May 7, 2002, 20; and Smyser, *The German Economy,* 73–90.

26. German banker and an American who has worked in a German firm, interviews by author, April 26, 2001, and June 15, 2000, respectively.

27. *Financial Times,* May 21, 2002, 23.

28. American businessman, interview by author, May 2, 2002.

29. Ibid.

30. European businessman, interview by author, February 6, 2002.

31. The story of Daimler's takeover of Chrysler and the results have been best told by Bill Vlasic and Bradley A. Stertz in *Taken for a Ride* (New York: William Morrow, 2000). A number of articles have also covered it in part or in whole, including Edmund L. Andrews and Keith Bradsher, "This 1998 Model Is Looking More Like a Lemon," *New York Times,* November 26, 2000, Business Section, 1–4; Tim Burt and Richard Lambert, "The Schrempp Gambit," *Financial Times,* October 30, 2000, 14; Tim Burt, "Steering

Straight with His Foot to the Floor," *Financial Times,* February 26, 2001, 7; and Lutz Spenneberg, "Superman ist Minus-Mann," *Die Woche,* December 1, 2000, Wirtschaft, 12.

32. Vlasic and Stertz, *Taken for a Ride,* 122.

33. Ibid., 201.

34. Ibid., 292.

35. Ibid., 205.

36. Ibid., 213–214.

37. Ibid., 218–223.

38. Ibid., 236.

39. Ibid., 249–256; Peter Schneider, "Scenes from a Marriage," *New York Times Magazine,* August 12, 2001, 47.

40. Burt and Lambert, "The Schrempp Gambit," 12.

41. *Economist,* November 25, 2000, 22.

42. Andrews and Bradsher, "This 1998 Model Is Looking More Like a Lemon," 1–4.

43. Joann Muller and Christine Tierney, "Can This Man Save Chrysler?" *Business Week,* September 17, 2001, 86–94.

44. "Der Front Mann," *Wirtschaftswoche,* October 10, 2001, 58–62; and *New York Times,* May 12, 2002, B4.

45. *Financial Times,* February 7 and April 29, 2002.

46. *Wall Street Journal,* February 9, 2001, A8; *New York Times,* April 6, 2001, C5; April 11, 2001, C4.

47. Emily Thornton, "Did Mitsubishi Get the Best of Daimler?" *Business Week,* April 10, 2000; and Miki Tanikawa, "The Daimler-Mitsubishi Deal Quickly Comes under Stress," *New York Times,* January 20, 2001, B2.

48. For a detailed review of BMW's purchase and later sale of Rover, see Chris Brady and Andrew Lorenz, *End of the Road* (London: Financial Times/Prentice Hall, 2001).

49. *Manager Magazin,* no. 5 (2000): 10.

50. Ibid., 11.

51. "Small Earthquake in Frankfurt," *Financial Times,* April 6, 2000, 12.

52. *Wall Street Journal,* April 7, 2001.

53. *Financial Times,* September 6, 2001, 9.

54. *New York Times,* July 5, 2000, C1.

55. *Financial Times,* September 16, 2001, 14.

56. *Financial Times,* September 7, 2001, 9.

57. *Welt am Sonntag,* August 19, 2001, 3.

58. *Financial Times,* March 30, 2002, 26.

5. German Official Economic Negotiations

1. German diplomat, interview by author, May 15, 2001.

2. *Financial Times,* March 25, 2002, 4.

3. Former U.S. trade official, interview by author, October 9, 2001.

4. Ibid.

5. Member of the German Foreign Office Planning Staff, interview by author, July 15, 1999.

6. For a summary history of the Bundesbank, see W. R. Smyser, *The German Economy: Colossus at the Crossroads* (New York: St. Martin's Press, 1993), 47–52; for a longer and more official history, see Deutsche Bundesbank, ed., *Fifty Years of the Deutsche Mark: Central Bank and the Currency in Germany since 1948* (Oxford: Oxford University Press, 1999).

7. The Bundesbank views on these topics and others are published monthly in the bank's *Monatsbericht,* also available in English as the *Monthly Report* (Frankfurt: Bundesbank), as well as in a compendium of articles from the international financial press that the Bundesbank publishes several times a month in *Auszüge aus Pressartikeln.*

8. Helmut Schmidt, "Deutsches Störfeuer gegen Europa," *Die Zeit,* September 29, 1995, 1.

9. Jeffrey Anderson, *German Unification and the Union of Europe* (Cambridge: Cambridge University Press, 1999), 208–211.

10. *Financial Times,* February 1, 2002, 2.

11. German officials, interviews by author, Washington, D.C., and Berlin, June 7 and August 19, 2000.

12. Ibid.

13. M. E. Sarotte, *Dealing with the Devil: East Germany, Détente, and Ostpolitik, 1969–1973* (Chapel Hill: University of North Carolina Press, 2000), 142–143.

14. Margarita Mathiopoulos, *Die Geschlossene Gesellschaft und ihre Freunde* (Hamburg: Hoffmann and Campe, 1997), 277–281.

15. Former U.S. diplomat in East Germany, interview by author, January 9, 2002.

16. Ibid.

17. U.S. lawyers, interview by author, December 17 and 19, 2001.

18. "Big Mac Diplomacy," *Wall Street Journal,* January 21, 1997, 1.

19. Mathiopoulos, *Die Geschlossene Gesellschaft,* 29–37.

20. Kurt Biedenkopf, interview by author, December 18, 1998.

6. The Future of German Negotiating Behavior

1. *Economist,* November 4, 2000, 54.

2. See, for example, Jan-Werner Müller, *Another Country: German Intellectuals, Unifications, and National Identity* (New Haven, Conn.: Yale University Press, 2000).

3. Robert Gerald Livingston, "Sept. 11 Transformed German Foreign Policy," *Foreign Service Journal,* April 2002, 44–46.

4. Willy Brandt, interview by author, Bonn, December 11, 1989.

5. European foreign ministry official, interview by author, June 20, 2002.

Index

About the Author

W. R. Smyser writes and lectures on German and European politics, diplomacy, and economics. He teaches German and European political economy at Georgetown University and is a consultant to American and European business firms and foundations. His recent books include *From Yalta to Berlin: The Cold War Struggle over Germany* and *The German Economy: Colossus at the Crossroads,* both published by St. Martin's Press. He writes regularly for American and European publications.

Dr. Smyser went to Germany in 1953 with the U.S. Army during the occupation. He was at the U.S. Mission in Berlin from 1960 to 1964 and served as assistant to General Lucius Clay during the Berlin Wall crisis when Clay was the personal representative in Berlin of President John F. Kennedy. From 1975 to 1979, he was counselor for political affairs at the U.S. embassy in Bonn. He continues to travel frequently to Germany and other parts of Europe.

Smyser has also held senior positions in the U.S. government and at the United Nations. He served at the White House at the request of Henry Kissinger, joining Kissinger in several secret negotiations, including the opening to China in 1971. He became assistant secretary of state for refugee programs in 1980. He then joined the United Nations as assistant secretary-general and as deputy UN high commissioner for refugees.

Smyser has a Ph.D. from George Washington University, an M.P.A. from Harvard University, an M.A. from Georgetown University, and a B.S. in Economics from the Wharton School of the University of Pennsylvania.

United States Institute of Peace

The United States Institute of Peace is an independent, nonpartisan federal institution created by Congress to promote research, education, and training on the peaceful management and resolution of international conflicts. Established in 1984, the Institute meets its congressional mandate through an array of programs, including research grants, fellowships, professional training, education programs from high school through graduate school, conferences and workshops, library services, and publications. The Institute's Board of Directors is appointed by the President of the United States and confirmed by the Senate.

How Germans Negotiate

This book is set in American Garamond; the display type is Univers Ultra Condensed. Hasten Design Studio designed the book's cover; Mike Chase designed the interior. Helene Y. Redmond made up the pages. David Sweet copyedited the text, which was proofread by Karen Stough. The index was prepared by Sonsie Conroy. The book's editor was Nigel Quinney.